Popular Complete Smart Series

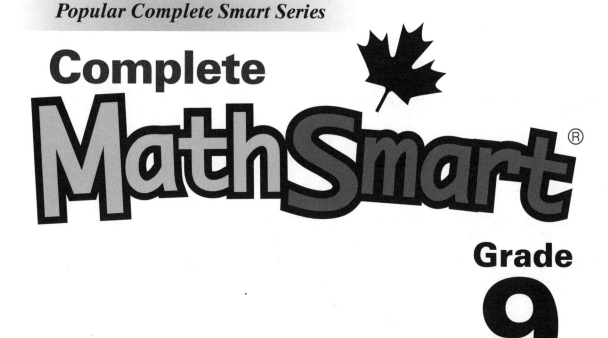

Complete
MathSmart®

Grade 9

 Proud Sponsor of Math Team Canada 2019

Credits

Artwork (Front Cover "3D White Sphere" Senoldo/123RF.com)

Printed in China

ISBN: 978-1-77149-220-1

Contents

Chapter 5: Analytic Geometry

Chapter 6: Properties of Two-dimensional Shapes

Chapter 7: Measurement Relationships in Three-dimensional Figures

ISBN: 978-1-77149-220-1

Overview

Complete MathSmart is our all-time bestselling series. *Complete MathSmart (Revised and Updated)* Grade 9 is designed to strengthen students' math foundation, and allow them to learn the key concepts and demonstrate their understanding by applying their knowledge and skills to solve real-world problems.

This workbook covers the four strands of the Mathematics curriculum:
- Number Sense and Algebra
- Linear Relations
- Analytic Geometry
- Measurement and Geometry

This workbook contains seven chapters, with each chapter covering a math topic. Different concepts in the topic are each introduced by a simple example and a "Try This" section to give students an opportunity to check their understanding of the concept. The basic skill questions that follow lead up to application questions that gradually increase in difficulty to help students consolidate the concept they have learned. Useful hints are provided to guide students along and help them grasp the essential math concepts. In addition, a handy reference containing definitions and formulas is included to provide quick and easy access for students whenever needed.

A cumulative review is provided for students to recapitulate the concepts and skills they have learned in the book. The questions are classified into four categories to help students evaluate their own learning. Below are the four categories:
- Knowledge and Understanding
- Application
- Communication
- Thinking

The review is also an ideal testing practice to prepare students for the Math examination in school.

At the end of this workbook is an answer key that provides thorough solutions with the crucial steps clearly presented to help students develop an understanding of the correct strategies and approaches to arrive at the solutions.

Complete MathSmart will undoubtedly reinforce students' math skills and strengthen their conceptual foundation that is a prerequisite for exploring mathematics further in their secondary programs.

1 Basic Skills Review

1.1 Integers and Real Numbers

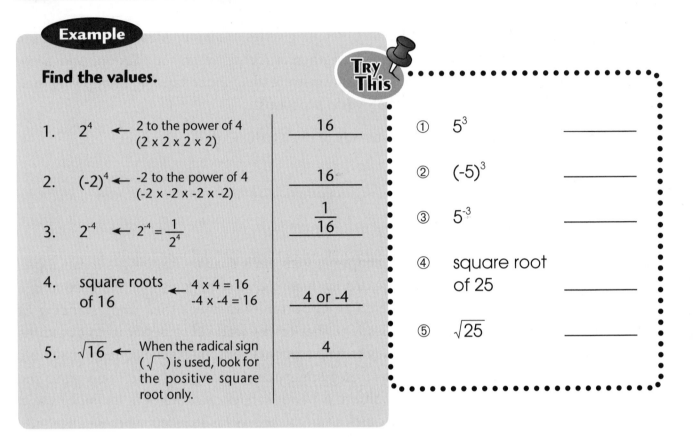

Example

Find the values.

1. 2^4 ← 2 to the power of 4 $(2 \times 2 \times 2 \times 2)$ __16__

2. $(-2)^4$ ← -2 to the power of 4 $(-2 \times -2 \times -2 \times -2)$ __16__

3. 2^{-4} ← $2^{-4} = \dfrac{1}{2^4}$ $\dfrac{1}{16}$

4. square roots of 16 ← $4 \times 4 = 16$ $-4 \times -4 = 16$ __4 or -4__

5. $\sqrt{16}$ ← When the radical sign ($\sqrt{}$) is used, look for the positive square root only.   __4__

Try This

① 5^3 _____

② $(-5)^3$ _____

③ 5^{-3} _____

④ square root of 25   _____

⑤ $\sqrt{25}$ _____

Find the values.

① $6^3 =$ _____

② $10^5 =$ _____

③ $5^{-2} =$ _____

④ $3^{-2} =$ _____

⑤ $8^0 =$ _____

⑥ $7^{-3} =$ _____

⑦ $4^{-2} =$ _____

⑧ $2^{-5} =$ _____

⑨ $9^3 =$ _____

Find the square roots of each number.

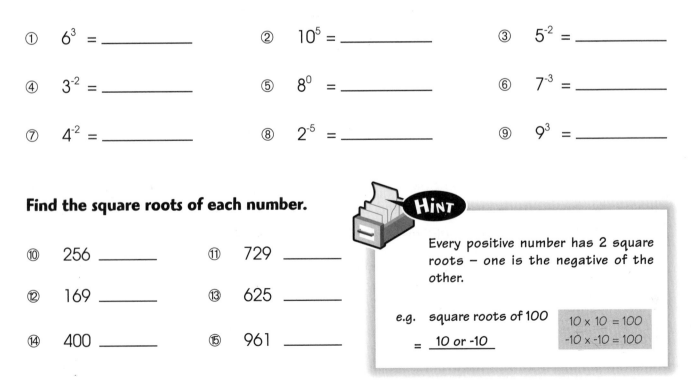

⑩ 256 _____

⑪ 729 _____

⑫ 169 _____

⑬ 625 _____

⑭ 400 _____

⑮ 961 _____

HINT

Every positive number has 2 square roots – one is the negative of the other.

e.g. square roots of 100

= __10 or -10__ $10 \times 10 = 100$ $-10 \times -10 = 100$

ISBN: 978-1-77149-220-1

Tell which two square numbers that each number lies in between. Then estimate and find each square root to 2 decimal places using a calculator.

⑯ 52 is between _____ and _____ .

So, $\sqrt{52}$ is between _____ and _____ .

$\sqrt{52}$ is about _____ .

⑰ 156 is between _____ .

So, $\sqrt{156}$ is between _____ .

$\sqrt{156}$ is about _____ .

⑱ 98 is between _____ .

So, $\sqrt{98}$ is between _____ .

$\sqrt{98}$ is about _____ .

⑲ 395 is between _____ .

So, $\sqrt{395}$ is between _____ .

$\sqrt{395}$ is about _____ .

Find the square root of each fraction and decimal.

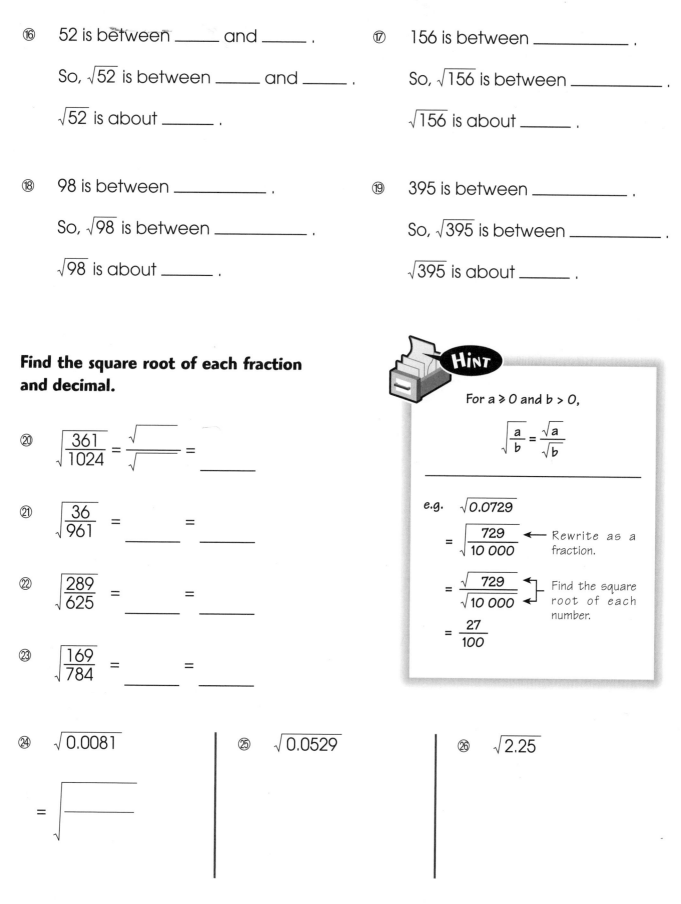

HINT

For $a \geqslant 0$ and $b > 0$,

$$\sqrt{\frac{a}{b}} = \frac{\sqrt{a}}{\sqrt{b}}$$

e.g. $\sqrt{0.0729}$

$= \sqrt{\dfrac{729}{10\,000}}$ ← Rewrite as a fraction.

$= \dfrac{\sqrt{729}}{\sqrt{10\,000}}$ ⤵ Find the square root of each number.

$= \dfrac{27}{100}$

⑳ $\sqrt{\dfrac{361}{1024}} = \dfrac{\sqrt{}}{\sqrt{}} = $ _____

㉑ $\sqrt{\dfrac{36}{961}} = $ _____ $= $ _____

㉒ $\sqrt{\dfrac{289}{625}} = $ _____ $= $ _____

㉓ $\sqrt{\dfrac{169}{784}} = $ _____ $= $ _____

㉔ $\sqrt{0.0081}$

$= \sqrt{\dfrac{}{}}$

㉕ $\sqrt{0.0529}$

㉖ $\sqrt{2.25}$

ISBN: 978-1-77149-220-1

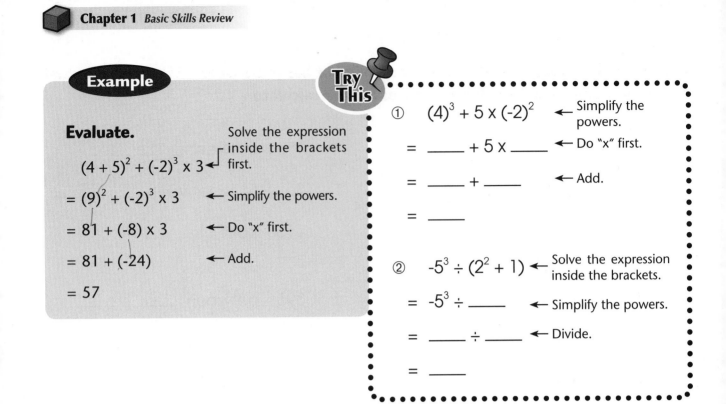

Example

Evaluate.

Solve the expression inside the brackets first.

$(4 + 5)^2 + (-2)^3 \times 3$

$= (9)^2 + (-2)^3 \times 3$ ← Simplify the powers.

$= 81 + (-8) \times 3$ ← Do "x" first.

$= 81 + (-24)$ ← Add.

$= 57$

Try This

① $(4)^3 + 5 \times (-2)^2$ ← Simplify the powers.

$= \underline{\hspace{1cm}} + 5 \times \underline{\hspace{1cm}}$ ← Do "x" first.

$= \underline{\hspace{1cm}} + \underline{\hspace{1cm}}$ ← Add.

$= \underline{\hspace{1cm}}$

② $-5^3 \div (2^2 + 1)$ ← Solve the expression inside the brackets.

$= -5^3 \div \underline{\hspace{1cm}}$ ← Simplify the powers.

$= \underline{\hspace{1cm}} \div \underline{\hspace{1cm}}$ ← Divide.

$= \underline{\hspace{1cm}}$

Evaluate.

㉗ $33 - (-7)^2 \div (2 \times 3 + 1)$

$=$

㉘ $(12 - 5)^2 \times 2^3 \div (-4)^2$

㉙ $7 \times (-3)^2 + (-4)^3 \times (-2)$

㉚ $(-5)^2 \div (-2 \times 2 - 1) + (-2)^3 \times 4$

㉛ $3 \times (-4)^2 - (-8)^2 \div (-2)$

㉜ $3 \times (4^2 - 18)^2$

ISBN: 978-1-77149-220-1

㉝ $\dfrac{6^2 - 5 \times 3^3}{(-4) - (-3) + (-2)}$

$= \dfrac{\boxed{} - 5 \times \boxed{}}{-4 + \boxed{} - \boxed{}}$ ← Simplify the powers.

← Remove the brackets.

$= \dfrac{\boxed{} - \boxed{}}{\boxed{} - \boxed{}}$

$= \dfrac{\boxed{}}{\boxed{}}$

$= \underline{}$

㉞ $\dfrac{(-7) \times (-9) - (-8 \div 2^3)}{5^4 \div 5 - (-3)}$

$= \dfrac{\boxed{} - (\boxed{} \div \boxed{})}{\boxed{} \div 5 + \boxed{}}$

$= \dfrac{\boxed{} - (\boxed{})}{\boxed{} + \boxed{}}$

$= \dfrac{\boxed{}}{\boxed{}}$

$= \underline{}$

㉟ $\dfrac{(4^2 - 5^0) \div (-3)}{(-2) \times 4 - (-12)} = \underline{}$

㊱ $\dfrac{5^2 + 9 \times (-1)^2 + 1}{4^3 - (4 \times 2)^0} = \underline{}$

㊲ $\left(\dfrac{4 \times (-3)^2}{2^4 - 3^0}\right) \times (-2)^3 = \underline{}$

㊳ $\dfrac{(-4)^2 \times \sqrt{36}}{\sqrt{9} + 3 \times 7} = \underline{}$

㊴ $\dfrac{(-2)^4 \times (-1)}{\sqrt{400} + (-2)^3} - \dfrac{4^2 - 3^0}{\sqrt{144}} = \underline{}$

Challenge

It is easier to find the value if you simplify each expression first.

e.g. $a^2 + b^0 + c^0$
$= a^2 + 1 + 1$
$= a^2 + 2$

Evaluate each expression for a = 4, b = -3, and c = -2. Check the one with the greatest value.

Ⓐ $(a^2 + b^0 + c^0) \div (\sqrt{a} - c^2) :$ _____

Ⓑ $(-3)(b^0 + c^0 - a^2) \times (c^2 + b^0 - 1) :$ _____

Ⓒ $a \times b \times c \div (a \times b \times c) \times (a \times b) :$ _____

1.2 Ratios, Rates, Proportions, and Percents

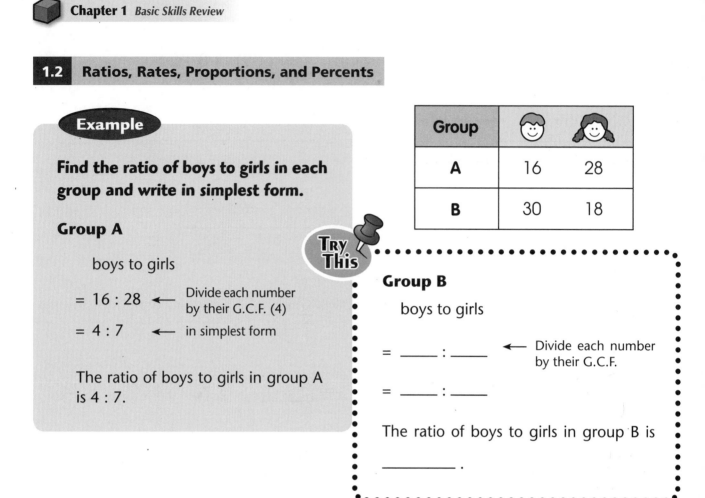

Example

Find the ratio of boys to girls in each group and write in simplest form.

Group	😊	😊
A	16	28
B	30	18

Group A

boys to girls

= 16 : 28 ← Divide each number by their G.C.F. (4)

= 4 : 7 ← in simplest form

The ratio of boys to girls in group A is 4 : 7.

Try This

Group B

boys to girls

= _____ : _____ ← Divide each number by their G.C.F.

= _____ : _____

The ratio of boys to girls in group B is _____ .

Write as a ratio in simplest form. Then answer the questions.

①

Box	A	B	C
apples to oranges			
apples to all			
oranges to all			

②

Boxes	A and C	A and B	B and C
apples to oranges			
apples to all			
oranges to all			

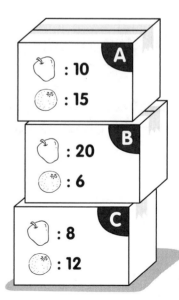

A 🍎 : 10   🍊 : 15

B 🍎 : 20   🍊 : 6

C 🍎 : 8   🍊 : 12

③ If Kevin takes out 5 apples from box A, what will be the new ratio?

    a. apples to oranges: _____

    b. apples to all: _____

    c. oranges to all: _____

④ If Anna puts 4 oranges into box B, what will be the new ratio?

    a. apples to oranges: _____

    b. apples to all: _____

    c. oranges to all: _____

Find the unit rate of each group. Then answer the questions.

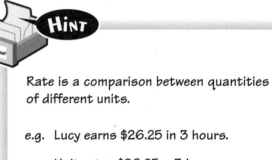

HINT

Rate is a comparison between quantities of different units.

e.g. Lucy earns $26.25 in 3 hours.

    Unit rate: $26.25 ÷ 3 h

        = $8.75/h ◄— money she earns in 1 h

Lucy earns $8.75 in 1 hour.

⑤ 6 boxes for $17.94

    unit rate: $ _____ /box

 4 boxes for $12.72

    unit rate: $ _____ /box

Which group has a lower rate?

_____

⑥   210.4 km in 4 h   unit rate (speed): _____

    716.1 km in 6.2 h   unit rate (speed): _____

    93.2 km in 0.5 h   unit rate (speed): _____

Which means of transport has the highest speed? _____

⑦   Sue can type 204 words in 3 minutes.   unit rate: _____

  Katie can type 468 words in 6.5 minutes.   unit rate: _____

  Michael can type 405 words in 5.4 minutes.   unit rate: _____

Who has the highest typing speed? _____

Solve the proportions using cross multiplication.

⑧ $\dfrac{k}{5} = \dfrac{9}{12}$

     $12k = $ _____

       $k = $ _____

⑨ $\dfrac{m}{12} = \dfrac{6}{8}$

⑩ $\dfrac{2}{y} = \dfrac{182}{637}$

⑪ $\dfrac{57}{114} = \dfrac{u}{19}$

⑫ $\dfrac{8}{15} = \dfrac{68}{a}$

⑬ $\dfrac{72}{171} = \dfrac{k}{38}$

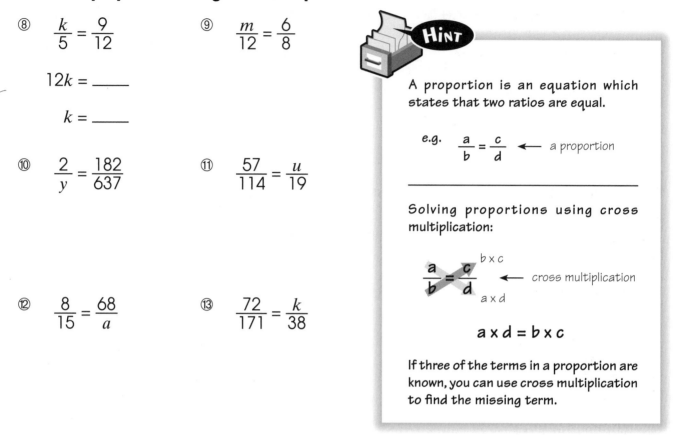

HINT

A proportion is an equation which states that two ratios are equal.

e.g. $\dfrac{a}{b} = \dfrac{c}{d}$ ← a proportion

Solving proportions using cross multiplication:

$\dfrac{a}{b} = \dfrac{c}{d}$ ← cross multiplication

$a \times d = b \times c$

If three of the terms in a proportion are known, you can use cross multiplication to find the missing term.

Solve the problems using proportions.

⑭   Each customer can get 3 free children tickets with every 2 adult tickets purchased. If Mr. Cowan buys 18 adult tickets, how many free children tickets will he get?

     Set up a proportion: $\dfrac{3}{\boxed{}} = \dfrac{y}{18}$ (y = no. of free children tickets)

     He will get _____ free children tickets.

⑮   The cost of 5 combos is $42.50. If Joe pays $153 for some combos, how many combos does he buy in all?

Solve the problems involving percents using proportions.

⑯ 44% of 600 children are boys. How many boys are there?

Write 44% as a fraction. ⟶

⟵ y = no. of boys

Set up a proportion. ⟶ $\dfrac{}{100} = \dfrac{y}{600}$

There are _____ boys.

⑰ 28 out of 35 eggs are brown. What percent of the eggs are brown?

Write m% as a fraction. ⟶

⟵ 28 out of 35 eggs

Set up a proportion. ⟶ $\dfrac{m}{100} = \dfrac{}{35}$

_____ % of the eggs are brown.

⑱ 16% of 800 boxes of juice are delivered to M&C Convenience Store, 23% to St. George Grocery Store, and 42% to General Store. How many boxes of juice are delivered to each of the stores?

⑲ Jason has $1200. If he spends $240 on clothing and $456 on travelling, what percentage does he spend on each?

Challenge

The ratio of red beads, blue beads, and yellow beads is 3:2:4. If there are 270 beads, how many red beads are there?

The ratio 3:2:4 means "for every 3 red beads, there are 2 blue beads and 4 yellow beads".

So, "for every 30 red beads, there are 20 blue beads and 40 yellow beads".

ISBN: 978-1-77149-220-1

1.3 Proportional Reasoning

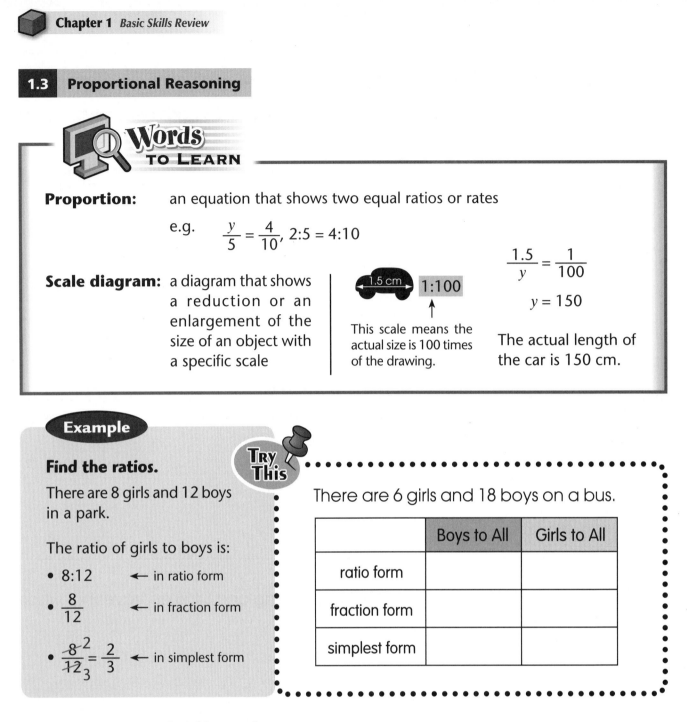

Words TO LEARN

Proportion: an equation that shows two equal ratios or rates

e.g. $\dfrac{y}{5} = \dfrac{4}{10}$, 2:5 = 4:10

Scale diagram: a diagram that shows a reduction or an enlargement of the size of an object with a specific scale

1.5 cm 1:100

This scale means the actual size is 100 times of the drawing.

$\dfrac{1.5}{y} = \dfrac{1}{100}$

$y = 150$

The actual length of the car is 150 cm.

Example

Find the ratios.

There are 8 girls and 12 boys in a park.

The ratio of girls to boys is:

- 8:12   ← in ratio form

- $\dfrac{8}{12}$ ← in fraction form

- $\dfrac{8^{2}}{12_{3}} = \dfrac{2}{3}$ ← in simplest form

Try This

There are 6 girls and 18 boys on a bus.

	Boys to All	Girls to All
ratio form		
fraction form		
simplest form		

Write each ratio in 2 different forms.

①

Birthplace	Boy	Girl
Canada	6	2
U.S.A.	4	1
China	1	3
Germany	2	1
Sweden	2	2

What is the ratio of

a. the children born in Canada to the rest of the class?

_____

b. the girls to the boys born in Sweden?

_____

c. the children born in China to the children born in the U.S.A.?

_____

ISBN: 978-1-77149-220-1

Write an equivalent ratio to make a proportion.

② $\dfrac{10}{25} = $ _____   ③ $\dfrac{3}{10} = $ _____   ④ $\dfrac{5}{9} = $ _____

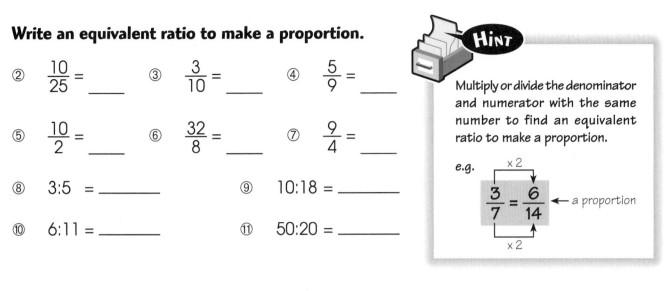

Multiply or divide the denominator and numerator with the same number to find an equivalent ratio to make a proportion.

e.g.

⑤ $\dfrac{10}{2} = $ _____   ⑥ $\dfrac{32}{8} = $ _____   ⑦ $\dfrac{9}{4} = $ _____

⑧ 3:5 = _____   ⑨ 10:18 = _____

⑩ 6:11 = _____   ⑪ 50:20 = _____

Write each ratio in simplest form to make a proportion.

⑫ 6:12 = _____   ⑬ 10:15 = _____   ⑭ 2:4 = _____   ⑮ 9:6 = _____

⑯ $\dfrac{15}{20} = $ _____   ⑰ $\dfrac{40}{16} = $ _____   ⑱ $\dfrac{36}{18} = $ _____   ⑲ $\dfrac{20}{30} = $ _____

Solve the problems. Write the answers in simplest form.

⑳ Sam has 18 cookies. Sue has twice as many cookies as Sam. Laura has 2 more cookies than Sam. What is the ratio of

   a.   Laura's cookies to Sam's cookies? _____

   b.   Laura's cookies to Sue's cookies? _____

㉑ ABCD is a line segment. What is the ratio of

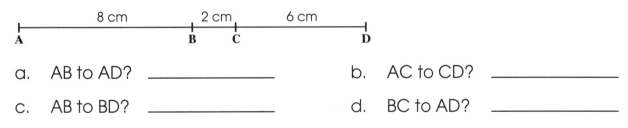

   a.   AB to AD? _____   b.   AC to CD? _____

   c.   AB to BD? _____   d.   BC to AD? _____

㉒ Mr. Cowan spends 8 hours working and 6 hours sleeping every day. What is the ratio of

   a.   his sleeping time to his working time? _____

   b.   his working time to the time of a day? _____

Solve the proportions.

㉓ $\dfrac{3}{12} = \dfrac{4}{x}$

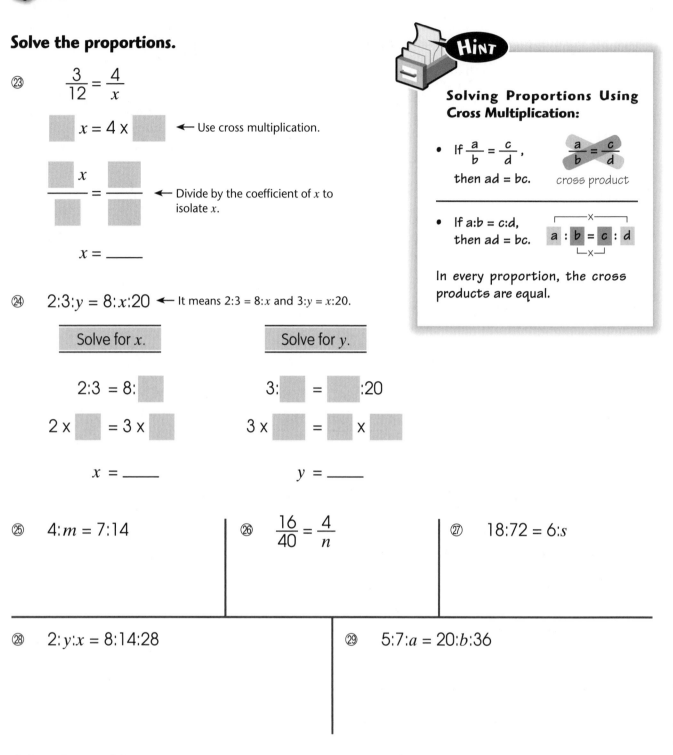

[ ] $x = 4 \times$ [ ] ← Use cross multiplication.

$\dfrac{[\ ]\, x}{[\ ]} = \dfrac{[\ ]}{[\ ]}$ ← Divide by the coefficient of x to isolate x.

$x = \underline{\quad}$

㉔ $2:3:y = 8:x:20$ ← It means $2:3 = 8:x$ and $3:y = x:20$.

Solve for x.	Solve for y.
$2:3 = 8:$ [ ]	$3:$ [ ] $=$ [ ] $:20$
$2 \times$ [ ] $= 3 \times$ [ ]	$3 \times$ [ ] $=$ [ ] $\times$ [ ]
$x = \underline{\quad}$	$y = \underline{\quad}$

Hint

Solving Proportions Using Cross Multiplication:

- If $\dfrac{a}{b} = \dfrac{c}{d}$, then $ad = bc$.   *cross product*

- If $a:b = c:d$, then $ad = bc$. $a : b = c : d$

In every proportion, the cross products are equal.

㉕ $4:m = 7:14$

㉖ $\dfrac{16}{40} = \dfrac{4}{n}$

㉗ $18:72 = 6:s$

㉘ $2:y:x = 8:14:28$

㉙ $5:7:a = 20:b:36$

Solve the problems using proportions.

㉚ The cost of 3 tickets is $50. If Jason wants to buy 12 tickets, how much does he need to pay?

㉛ 3 cups of milk and 4 bananas are needed to make one jar of banana shake. How many cups of milk are needed if there are 28 bananas?

Look at each scale diagram. Then answer the questions.

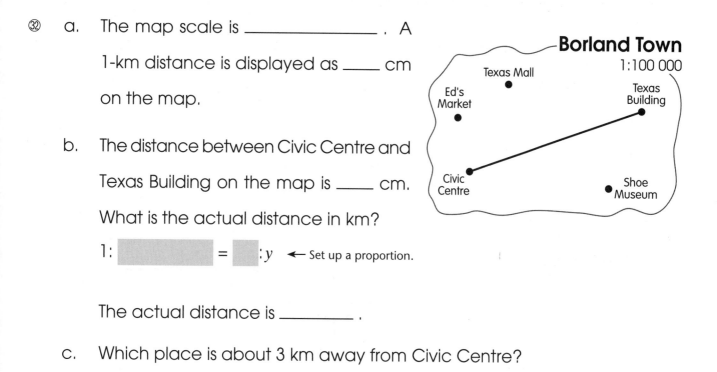

③② a. The map scale is _____ . A

   1-km distance is displayed as ____ cm

   on the map.

b. The distance between Civic Centre and

   Texas Building on the map is ____ cm.

   What is the actual distance in km?

   1 : ▯▯▯ = ▯▯ : y ← Set up a proportion.

   The actual distance is _____ .

c. Which place is about 3 km away from Civic Centre?

   _____

d. General Garden is 2.5 km south of Texas Mall. Locate General Garden
   on the map.

③③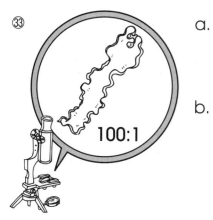

a. The microscope is in a scale of _____ . A 0.1-mm

   length is displayed as ____ mm under the microscope.

b. The bacterium under the microscope is ____ cm long.
   What is its actual length?

   _____

c. If the actual length of a bacterium is 0.09 mm, how long will it be under
   the microscope?

   _____

ISBN: 978-1-77149-220-1

An architect draws the floor plan for an office. Find the actual dimensions. Then complete the table.

1:100

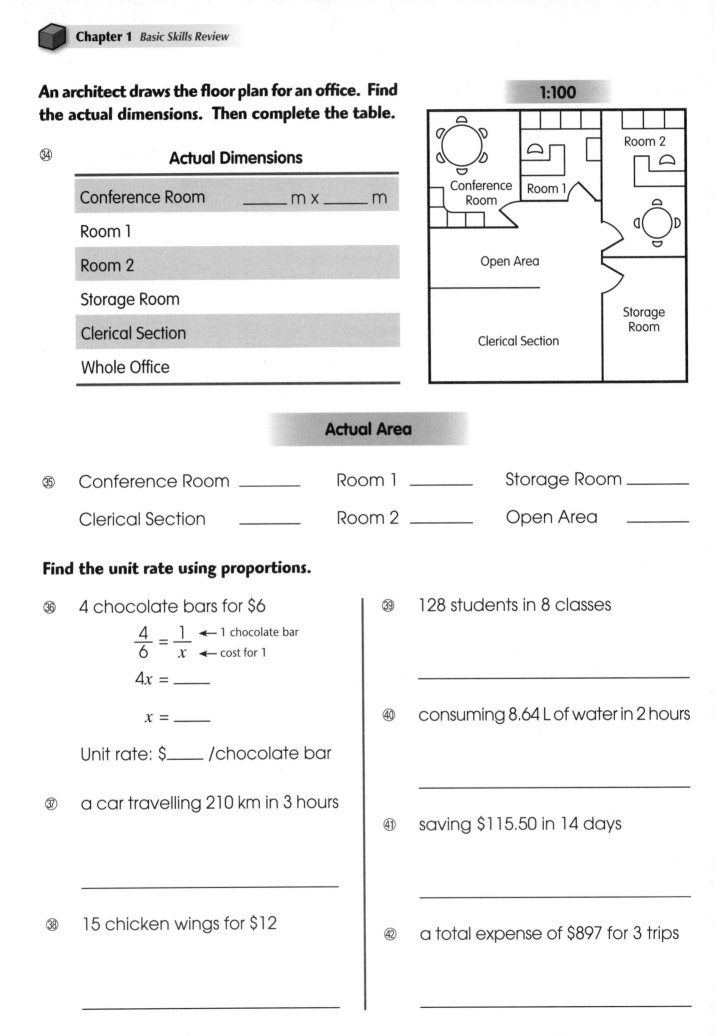

③④ **Actual Dimensions**

Conference Room	_____ m x _____ m
Room 1	
Room 2	
Storage Room	
Clerical Section	
Whole Office	

Actual Area

③⑤ Conference Room _____ Room 1 _____ Storage Room _____

Clerical Section _____ Room 2 _____ Open Area _____

Find the unit rate using proportions.

③⑥ 4 chocolate bars for $6

$$\frac{4}{6} = \frac{1}{x}$$ ← 1 chocolate bar
                              ← cost for 1

$4x =$ _____

$x =$ _____

Unit rate: $_____ /chocolate bar

③⑦ a car travelling 210 km in 3 hours

_____

③⑧ 15 chicken wings for $12

③⑨ 128 students in 8 classes

_____

④⓪ consuming 8.64 L of water in 2 hours

_____

④① saving $115.50 in 14 days

_____

④② a total expense of $897 for 3 trips

_____

  ISBN: 978-1-77149-220-1

Solve the percent problems using proportions.

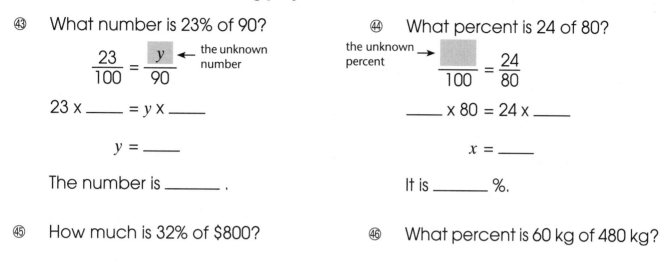

43   What number is 23% of 90?

$$\frac{23}{100} = \frac{y}{90} \leftarrow \text{the unknown number}$$

23 x _____ = y x _____

y = _____

The number is _____ .

44   What percent is 24 of 80?

the unknown percent → $\frac{}{100} = \frac{24}{80}$

_____ x 80 = 24 x _____

x = _____

It is _____ %.

45   How much is 32% of $800?

46   What percent is 60 kg of 480 kg?

_____

_____

47   Julie has saved $225.80. If she spends 25% of her savings to buy a gift for her mom, how much is the gift?

_____

48   The regular price of a sweater is $39.99. The store is having a 20%-off sale. What is the sale price?

_____

49   A bottle of shampoo is priced at $2.96 in Store A and $2.22 in Store B. What percent is the cost of the bottle of shampoo at Store B of that at Store A?

_____

1.4   Solving Problems with Proportional Reasoning

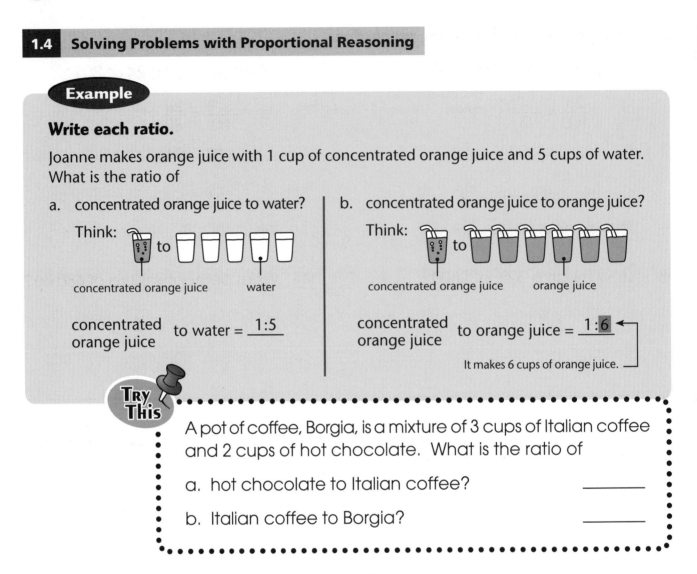

Example

Write each ratio.

Joanne makes orange juice with 1 cup of concentrated orange juice and 5 cups of water. What is the ratio of

a. concentrated orange juice to water?

Think: to

concentrated orange juice   water

concentrated
orange juice   to water = __1:5__

b. concentrated orange juice to orange juice?

Think: to

concentrated orange juice   orange juice

concentrated
orange juice   to orange juice = __1:6__

It makes 6 cups of orange juice.

Try This

A pot of coffee, Borgia, is a mixture of 3 cups of Italian coffee and 2 cups of hot chocolate. What is the ratio of

a. hot chocolate to Italian coffee?   _____

b. Italian coffee to Borgia?   _____

Solve the problems. Write the answers in simplest form.

① A box of multigrain cereal consists of 4 portions of cornflakes, 8 portions of rice, and 2 portions of oat flakes. What is the ratio of

a. cornflakes to oat flakes? _____

cornflakes to rice?   _____

rice to oat flakes?   _____

b. cornflakes to the cereal? _____

rice to the cereal?   _____

oat flakes to the cereal? _____

②

Grade 9 Students	🙂	👧
Milk	4	1
Juice	3	6
Pop	3	1

What is the ratio of

a. the boys who prefer milk to all the boys?   _____

b. the girls who prefer juice to all the girls?   _____

c. the students who prefer pop to all the students?   _____

   ISBN: 978-1-77149-220-1

Set up a proportion for each question. Then solve the proportion.

③ Eric earns $185 in 20 h. If he earns $157.25, how many hours does he work?

$$\frac{185}{\boxed{}} = \frac{157.25}{y}$$ ← y: no. of hours

$185 \times y = \boxed{} \times \boxed{}$ ← Cross multiply.

$y =$ _____

He works _____ .

④ A bakery makes a cake with 3 eggs and 4 cups of flour. If they have 2 dozen eggs to make cakes, how many cups of flour are needed?

_____

⑤ The scale of a floor plan is 1:500. If the dimensions of a rectangular garden are 12.5 cm by 8.4 cm, what are the actual dimensions of the rectangular garden? If the fencing costs $18.50 per metre, how much does the fencing of the garden cost?

_____

⑥ a. Find the fuel efficiency of each car.

Car	Amount of Gasoline Consumed (L)	Distance Travelled (km)	Fuel Efficiency (L/100 km)
A	65	450	
B	46	295	
C	72	518	
D	55	382	

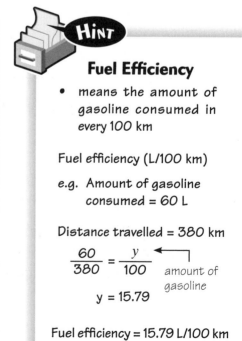

Fuel Efficiency

• means the amount of gasoline consumed in every 100 km

Fuel efficiency (L/100 km)

e.g. Amount of gasoline consumed = 60 L

Distance travelled = 380 km

$$\frac{60}{380} = \frac{y}{100}$$ ← amount of gasoline

$y = 15.79$

Fuel efficiency = 15.79 L/100 km

b. Which car has the highest fuel efficiency? _____

c. Which car will be your choice? Explain.

_____

_____

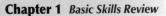

Solve the problems using proportions.

⑦ The regular price of a jacket is $209.99. If Joe buys a jacket at a discount of 25%, what is the sale price?

_____

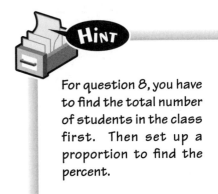

⑧ The ratio of girls to boys in Mr. Neal's class is 15 : 19. What percent of the students are girls?

For question 8, you have to find the total number of students in the class first. Then set up a proportion to find the percent.

_____

⑨ Judy saves $240. If she spends 60% of her savings on computers, how much will she have left?

_____

⑩ 36% of the students voted in an election for the next president of the student association. If there are 450 students in the school, how many students voted in the election?

_____

⑪ A plant was 160 cm tall. If it is 20% taller now, how tall is it?

_____

⑫ Last year, 40% of 80 members in a movie club were interested in action movies. This year the club has 120 members and 35% of them are in favour of action movies. How many more members prefer action movies this year?

_____

Solve the problems.

⑬ Our skin is the largest organ in our body. It is about 12% – 15% of our body weight. Determine the range of skin weight of a 60-kg person.

_____

⑭ The life span of a possum is 5 years, which is 9.5% of the life span of an elephant. What is the life span of an elephant?

_____

⑮ Babak ran 250 m in 35 s, Mark ran 300 m in 40 s, and Diane ran 350 m in 45 s. Who was the fastest?

_____

⑯ The area of Jason's room is 16.8 m^2. The area of Mark's room is about 80% of Jason's. What is the area of Mark's room?

_____

⑰ The actual dimensions of a rectangular field are 1.5 km by 2 km. If the drawing scale is 5000:1, what are the dimensions of the field on drawing?

_____

⑱ Aunt Katie makes a jar of fruit punch with 32% of 4.5 L of pineapple juice and 75% of 7.2 L of orange juice. How much fruit punch does Aunt Katie have in the jar?

_____

⑲ Find the side lengths of this isosceles triangle with the given scale. Then draw it in the box.

Scale 1:1.5

2 Algebraic Expressions

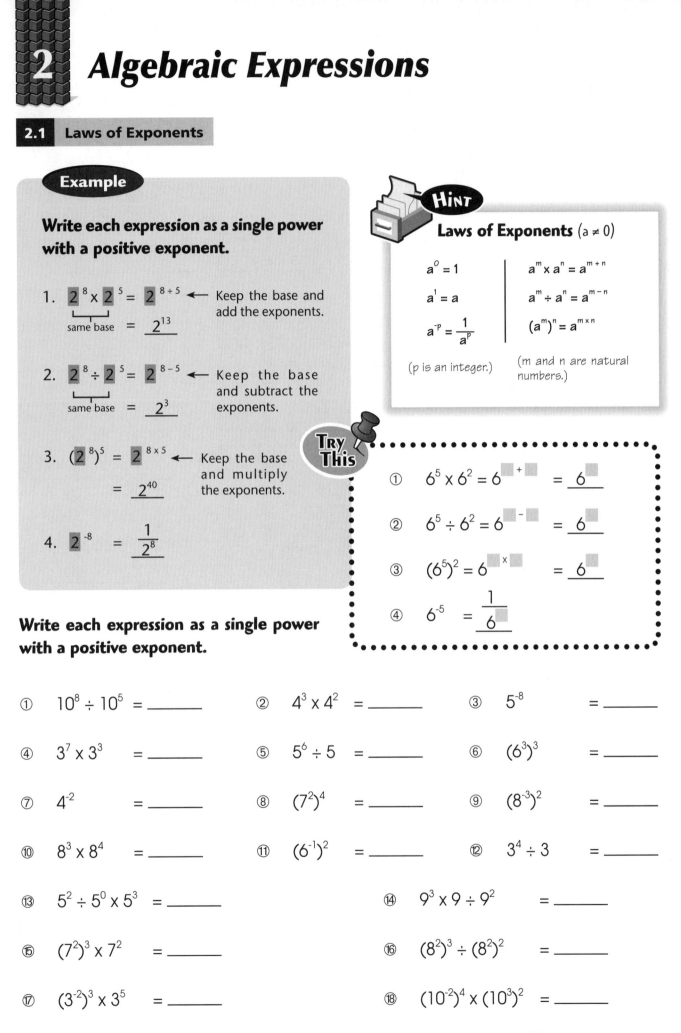

Example

Write each expression as a single power with a positive exponent.

1. $2^8 \times 2^5 = 2^{8+5}$ ← Keep the base and add the exponents.

   same base $= \underline{2^{13}}$

2. $2^8 \div 2^5 = 2^{8-5}$ ← Keep the base and subtract the exponents.

   same base $= \underline{2^3}$

3. $(2^8)^5 = 2^{8 \times 5}$ ← Keep the base and multiply the exponents.

   $= \underline{2^{40}}$

4. $2^{-8} = \dfrac{1}{2^8}$

HINT

Laws of Exponents $(a \neq 0)$

$a^0 = 1$ $a^m \times a^n = a^{m+n}$

$a^1 = a$ $a^m \div a^n = a^{m-n}$

$a^{-p} = \dfrac{1}{a^p}$ $(a^m)^n = a^{m \times n}$

(p is an integer.)   (m and n are natural numbers.)

Try This

① $6^5 \times 6^2 = 6^{\blacksquare + \blacksquare} = \underline{6^{\blacksquare}}$

② $6^5 \div 6^2 = 6^{\blacksquare - \blacksquare} = \underline{6^{\blacksquare}}$

③ $(6^5)^2 = 6^{\blacksquare \times \blacksquare} = \underline{6^{\blacksquare}}$

④ $6^{-5} = \dfrac{1}{6^{\blacksquare}}$

Write each expression as a single power with a positive exponent.

① $10^8 \div 10^5 = \underline{\hspace{1.5cm}}$

② $4^3 \times 4^2 = \underline{\hspace{1.5cm}}$

③ $5^{-8} = \underline{\hspace{1.5cm}}$

④ $3^7 \times 3^3 = \underline{\hspace{1.5cm}}$

⑤ $5^6 \div 5 = \underline{\hspace{1.5cm}}$

⑥ $(6^3)^3 = \underline{\hspace{1.5cm}}$

⑦ $4^{-2} = \underline{\hspace{1.5cm}}$

⑧ $(7^2)^4 = \underline{\hspace{1.5cm}}$

⑨ $(8^{-3})^2 = \underline{\hspace{1.5cm}}$

⑩ $8^3 \times 8^4 = \underline{\hspace{1.5cm}}$

⑪ $(6^{-1})^2 = \underline{\hspace{1.5cm}}$

⑫ $3^4 \div 3 = \underline{\hspace{1.5cm}}$

⑬ $5^2 \div 5^0 \times 5^3 = \underline{\hspace{1.5cm}}$

⑭ $9^3 \times 9 \div 9^2 = \underline{\hspace{1.5cm}}$

⑮ $(7^2)^3 \times 7^2 = \underline{\hspace{1.5cm}}$

⑯ $(8^2)^3 \div (8^2)^2 = \underline{\hspace{1.5cm}}$

⑰ $(3^{-2})^3 \times 3^5 = \underline{\hspace{1.5cm}}$

⑱ $(10^{-2})^4 \times (10^3)^2 = \underline{\hspace{1.5cm}}$

Write each expression as a base of 2 or 3 with a positive exponent.

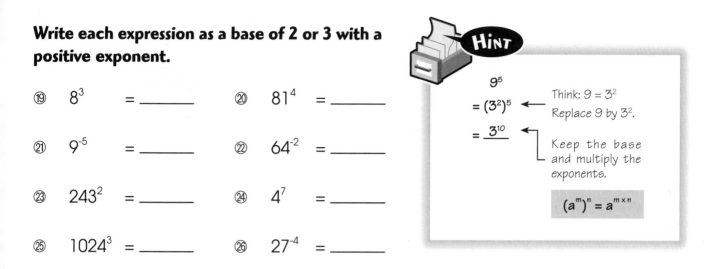

HINT

9^5

$= (3^2)^5$ ← Think: $9 = 3^2$
Replace 9 by 3^2.

$= \underline{3^{10}}$ ← Keep the base and multiply the exponents.

$(a^m)^n = a^{m \times n}$

⑲ 8^3 = _____

⑳ 81^4 = _____

㉑ 9^{-5} = _____

㉒ 64^{-2} = _____

㉓ 243^2 = _____

㉔ 4^7 = _____

㉕ 1024^3 = _____

㉖ 27^{-4} = _____

Write each expression as a single power. Then evaluate each power.

㉗ $\dfrac{4^3 \div 2^2}{2^0 \times (2^3)^3}$

㉘ $\dfrac{5^2 \times 5^4 \div 5^3}{5^0 + 2^2}$

㉙ $\dfrac{(7^2)^3 \times 7^4 \div 7}{(49)^3 \div 7^0}$

㉚ $5^{-3} \times \dfrac{(5^2)^2}{25^3}$

㉛ $9^8 \div 3^2 \times \dfrac{3^{-6}}{2^3 + 2^0}$

㉜ $\dfrac{512^3 \times 2^{-9} \div 2^8}{9^2 \div 9 - 5^0}$

㉝ $\dfrac{64^4 \div (2^7 \times 2^6)}{5^2 - 3^2}$ = _____

㉞ $216^{-4} \times \dfrac{(6^{13} \div 6)}{5^2 - 5^0 + 2^3}$ = _____

㉟ $\dfrac{(5^6)^2 \div (5^3 \times 5^2)}{5^3 \div 125}$ = _____

㊱ $\dfrac{243 \times 3^6}{5^4 \div 5^2 + 2^6 \div 2^5}$ = _____

㊲ $\dfrac{8^3 \times (4^3 \div 2^7)}{64 \div 2^3 \div 2}$ = _____

㊳ $\dfrac{54 - 3^3}{9^6 \div 3^9 \times 81}$ = _____

Write each expression as powers with positive exponents.

㊴ $5^3 \times (\frac{2}{5})^2$

$= 5^3 \times \dfrac{2^{\blacksquare}}{5^{\blacksquare}}$

$= 5^{\blacksquare - \blacksquare} \times 2^{\blacksquare}$

$= \underline{\hspace{2cm}}$

㊵ $20^2 \times \dfrac{1}{4^2}$

$= (4 \times \blacksquare)^2 \times \dfrac{1}{4^2}$

$= 4^{\blacksquare} \times \blacksquare^{\blacksquare} \times \dfrac{1}{4^2}$

$= \underline{\hspace{2cm}}$

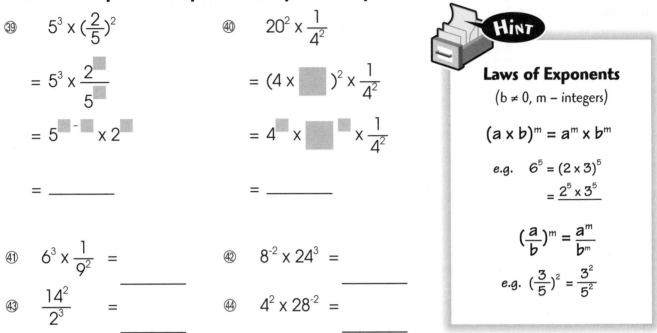

Laws of Exponents
($b \neq 0$, m – integers)

$$(a \times b)^m = a^m \times b^m$$

e.g. $6^5 = (2 \times 3)^5$
$= 2^5 \times 3^5$

$$\left(\frac{a}{b}\right)^m = \frac{a^m}{b^m}$$

e.g. $\left(\dfrac{3}{5}\right)^2 = \dfrac{3^2}{5^2}$

㊶ $6^3 \times \dfrac{1}{9^2} = \underline{\hspace{2cm}}$

㊸ $\dfrac{14^2}{2^3} = \underline{\hspace{2cm}}$

㊷ $8^{-2} \times 24^3 = \underline{\hspace{2cm}}$

㊹ $4^2 \times 28^{-2} = \underline{\hspace{2cm}}$

Write each number in scientific notation.

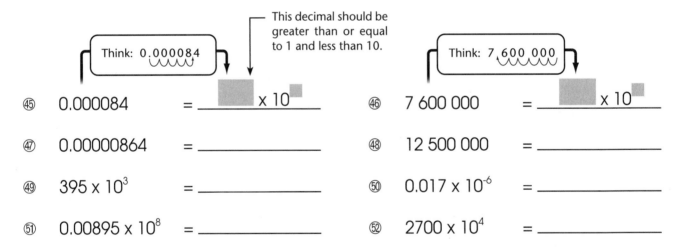

Think: 0.000084

This decimal should be greater than or equal to 1 and less than 10.

㊺ $0.000084 = \underline{\hspace{1cm}\blacksquare} \times 10^{\blacksquare}$

Think: $7\,600\,000$

㊻ $7\,600\,000 = \underline{\hspace{1cm}\blacksquare} \times 10^{\blacksquare}$

㊼ $0.00000864 = \underline{\hspace{2cm}}$

㊽ $12\,500\,000 = \underline{\hspace{2cm}}$

㊾ $395 \times 10^3 = \underline{\hspace{2cm}}$

㊿ $0.017 \times 10^{-6} = \underline{\hspace{2cm}}$

� $0.00895 \times 10^8 = \underline{\hspace{2cm}}$

52 $2700 \times 10^4 = \underline{\hspace{2cm}}$

Evaluate each expression without a calculator. Then write the answer in scientific notation.

53 $9 \times 10^{-5} \times 8 \times 10^2 = \underline{\hspace{2cm}}$

54 $6 \times 10^8 \times 50 \times 10^{-2} = \underline{\hspace{2cm}}$

55 $70 \times 10^8 \times 200 \times 10^{-5} = \underline{\hspace{2cm}}$

56 $4 \times 10^{-3} \times 5 \times 10^{-6} = \underline{\hspace{2cm}}$

57 $\dfrac{3 \times 10^{-5} \times 10^2}{6 \times 10^3 \times 10} = \underline{\hspace{2cm}}$

58 $\dfrac{2 \times 10^7 \times 10^2}{8 \times 10^3} = \underline{\hspace{2cm}}$

ISBN: 978-1-77149-220-1

Solve the problems. Write the answers in scientific notation.

⑤⑨ The surface area of the Earth is about 510 000 000 km². About 71% of the surface is covered by oceans and the rest is covered by land.

    a. What is the surface area of the Earth's oceans? _____

    b. What is the surface area of the Earth's land? _____

⑥⓪ The volume of water flowing over Horseshoe Falls is about 343 200 000 L/min in peak flow season.

    a. What is the volume of water in a second? _____

    b. What is the volume of water in an hour? _____

⑥① The distance between the sun and the Earth is about 1.5×10^8 km. The speed of light is 3×10^8 m/s.

    a. What is the distance between the sun and the Earth in m? _____

    b. How long does it take for light to travel from the sun to the Earth? _____

⑥② The population of Canada in 2005 was about 3.2×10^7. There were about 77% of Canadians living in cities and towns.

    a. How many Canadians lived in cities and towns in 2005? _____

    b. The population of Canada in 2007 was about 4% more than that in 2005. What was the population in 2007? _____

The radius of the Earth is about 6.3×10^3 km. Find its volume in terms of π.

> **Volume of a Sphere**
>
> $= \dfrac{4}{3}\pi r^3$, where r = radius

_____

ISBN: 978-1-77149-220-1

2.2 Algebraic Expressions with Exponents

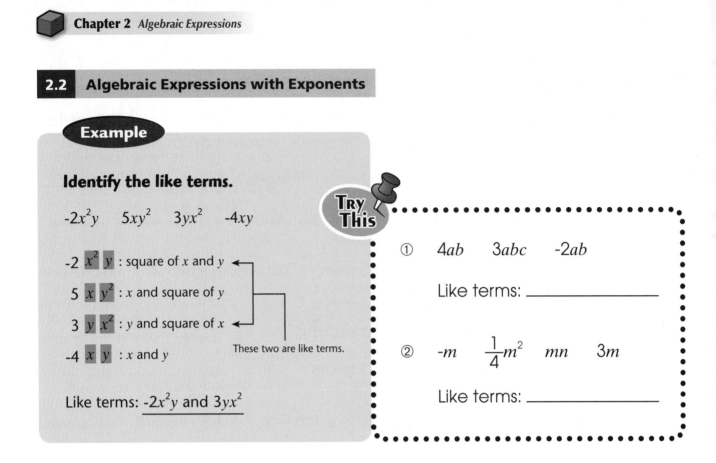

Example

Identify the like terms.

$-2x^2y$ $5xy^2$ $3yx^2$ $-4xy$

-2 x^2 y : square of x and y

5 x y^2 : x and square of y

3 y x^2 : y and square of x

-4 x y : x and y

These two are like terms.

Like terms: $-2x^2y$ and $3yx^2$

Try This

① $4ab$ $3abc$ $-2ab$

Like terms: _____

② $-m$ $\dfrac{1}{4}m^2$ mn $3m$

Like terms: _____

Identify like terms. Then give an example to go with each pair of like terms.

① $3m$ $-2n$ $4m$ $6m^2$

_____ ; _____

② $-0.5y$ $3xy$ $-2yx$ $2x$

_____ ; _____

③ $2p^2$ $-q^2$ $-pq$ $4p^2$

_____ ; _____

④ $-3a^3$ $2a^2$ $4a$ $\dfrac{1}{2}a^3$

_____ ; _____

⑤ mn^2 $-mn^2$ $4mn$ $2nm^2$

_____ ; _____

⑥ abc $-3ab$ $8cba$ $-2a^2bc$

_____ ; _____

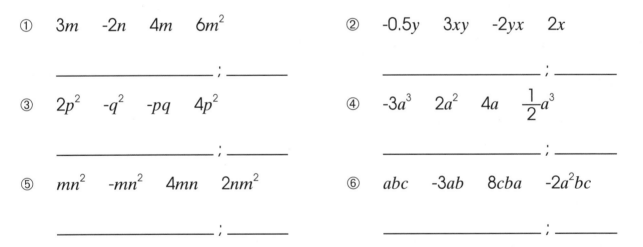

Simplify by adding or subtracting the coefficients of the like terms.

⑦ $4m + 2m$ = _____

⑧ $3y - 8y$ = _____

⑨ $-k + 7k$ = _____

⑩ $4j - 2j$ = _____

⑪ $-5x^2 - 2x^2$ = _____

⑫ $w^2 + 4w^2$ = _____

⑬ $-2k + 6k - 3k$ = _____

⑭ $3y^3 - 2y^3 + 5y^3$ = _____

⑮ $\dfrac{3}{5}x^3 - \dfrac{2}{5}x^3 + \dfrac{4}{5}x^3$ = _____

⑯ $0.6a^2 + 2.7a^2 - 4.2a^2$ = _____

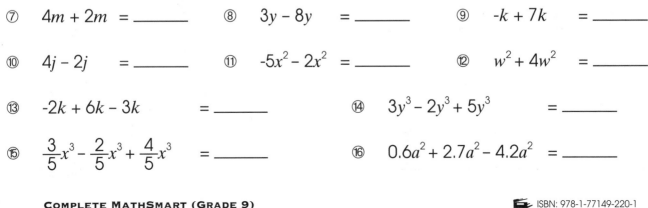

ISBN: 978-1-77149-220-1

Simplify each expression.

⑰ $8n - 4 + 2n + 7$

$= 8n + \boxed{}\, n - 4 + \boxed{}$ ← Group the like terms.

$= \boxed{}\, n + \boxed{}$ ← Combine the like terms.

⑱ $3 - \dfrac{4}{5}y - \dfrac{1}{2} + y$

$= \boxed{}\, y + y + 3 - \boxed{}$

$= \boxed{}\, y + \boxed{}$

⑲ $12a + 3 + 6a$ = _____

⑳ $5b - 2b - 1$ = _____

㉑ $9 - k + 5$ = _____

㉒ $-3x - 6 - 4x$ = _____

㉓ $\dfrac{4}{9}p + q + \dfrac{2}{9}p$ = _____

㉔ $\dfrac{3}{8}c + \dfrac{1}{8}c + d$ = _____

㉕ $8k - 4 - 2.5k$ = _____

㉖ $-0.8m + 2.4m - n$ = _____

㉗ $3x - 2y + 4x + 6y + 5 - 7$ = _____

㉘ $8 + 6m + n - 4m + 3m - 2n$ = _____

㉙ $p - 2q - 3 + p + q - 4q$ = _____

Find the value of each expression for n = -1.

㉚ $6 - 4n$

$= 6 - 4(\boxed{})$ ← Replace n with -1.

$= 6 + \boxed{}$ ← Multiply to remove brackets.

$= \underline{}$ ← Add to find the answer.

㉛ $n^2 - 8n$

$=$

㉜ $4n - 18$

$=$

㉝ $3n - 9$ = _____

㉞ $\dfrac{1}{5} - n$ = _____

㉟ $n^2 - \dfrac{1}{4}$ = _____

㊱ $0.4n + 2$ = _____

㊲ $-3 + 6n$ = _____

㊳ $-\dfrac{4}{5} + n^2$ = _____

㊴ $-n^2 - 4 + n =$ _____

㊵ $n^2 - n$ = _____

㊶ $n^2 + 2n - 1 =$ _____

ISBN: 978-1-77149-220-1

Simplify each expression. Then find its value for *m* = -3 and 3.

Value

| $m = -3$ | $m = 3$ |

㊷ $4m - 6 + 3m$ = _____   _____   _____

㊸ $8 - 2m + 4 - 3m$ = _____   _____   _____

㊹ $6m - 2 - 4m + 5$ = _____   _____   _____

㊺ $-3 - 2m + 1 + 8m$ = _____   _____   _____

㊻ $7m - 5 - 6 - 9m$ = _____   _____   _____

Simplify each expression. Then find its value when the variables have the given values.

㊼ $3k + 5 - 6k + 9$

= _____

k	Value
-2	
0	
1	
3	

㊽ $2m - 9 + 3m$

= _____

m	Value
-4	
-2	
0	
2	

㊾ $3a - a - 4$

= _____

a	Value
-1	
0	
1	
3	

㊿ $-x + y - 5 - 6x$

= _____

x	y	Value
-1	1	
0	3	
2	0	
5	2	

51 $2c - 2d - c + 4d$

= _____

c	d	Value
1	2	
3	1	
0	0	
-2	6	

52 $p^2 - q + 7p^2 + 2q$

= _____

p	q	Value
0	3	
-1	0	
2	1	
1	4	

ISBN: 978-1-77149-220-1

Solve the problems.

53 a.   Write an expression for the perimeter of the rectangle.

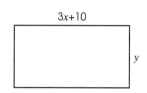

b.   Find the perimeter when $x = 2$ and $y = 5$.

54 a.   Julie has two options to earn her allowance. Her allowance contains two parts – one is the basic and the other is from doing the chores. Write an expression for each option.

Option **A** : The basic is $12.50 and the rate of each chore is $0.50.

Allowance: _____

Option **B** : The basic is $8.25 and the rate of each chore is $0.75.

Allowance: _____

b.   If Julie does 5 chores, which option should she take? Explain.

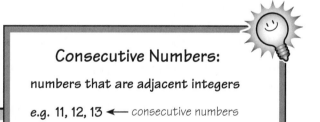

The sum of 3 consecutive numbers is 111.
What are the numbers?

2.3 Extending Algebraic Skills

Words TO LEARN

Power: a simple way to write repeated multiplication, e.g. $3 \times 3 \times 3 \times 3 = 3^4$

Exponent: the use of a superscript in mathematics to denote repeated multiplication, e.g. The exponent of 3^4 is 4.

Like terms: terms that have the same variables and exponents, e.g. $3x^2y$ and $-8x^2y$

Unlike terms: terms that have different variables or exponents, e.g. $-2xy$ and $4x^2y$

Example

Translate each sentence to an algebraic expression.

1. twice the product of two different numbers
   - $x \times y$ ⟵ product of two different numbers
   - $(xy) \times 2$ ⟵ twice

   $\underline{\quad 2(xy) \quad}$

2. three times a number minus two
   - $3 \times y$ ⟵ 3 times a number
   - $3y - 2$ ⟵ minus two

   $\underline{\quad 3y - 2 \quad}$

Try This

① 10 less than twice a number

_____

② 5 times a number plus 4

_____

③ half of a number minus the square of the number itself

_____

Translate each sentence to an algebraic expression or vice versa.

① a quarter of a number increased by 4 _____

② the cube of a number plus 8 _____

③ 2 times the square of a number _____

④ $5(100 - x)$ _____

⑤ $xy + 4$ _____

ISBN: 978-1-77149-220-1

Simplify each expression.

⑥ $2 \times 2 \times 2 \times 3 \times 3 = \underline{2^{\blacksquare} \times 3^{\blacksquare}}$

⑦ $4 \times a \times a \times a \times 4 \times a \times a = \underline{4^{\blacksquare} \times a^{\blacksquare}}$

⑧ $(-b) \times (-b) \times k \times k \times k \times (-b) = \underline{\qquad}$

⑨ $(-5) \times (-3) \times (-3) \times (-3) \times (-3) = \underline{\qquad}$

⑩ $\dfrac{1}{5} \times \dfrac{1}{5} \times m \times \dfrac{1}{5} \times m \times \dfrac{1}{5} = \underline{\qquad}$

⑪ $-\dfrac{1}{3} \times -\dfrac{1}{3} \times k \times k \times -\dfrac{1}{3} = \underline{\qquad}$

⑫ $\dfrac{1}{2} \times (-n) \times \dfrac{1}{2} \times (-n) \times \dfrac{1}{2} \times (-n) \times \dfrac{1}{2} = \underline{\qquad}$

Find the base area and volume of each solid. Simplify each expression.

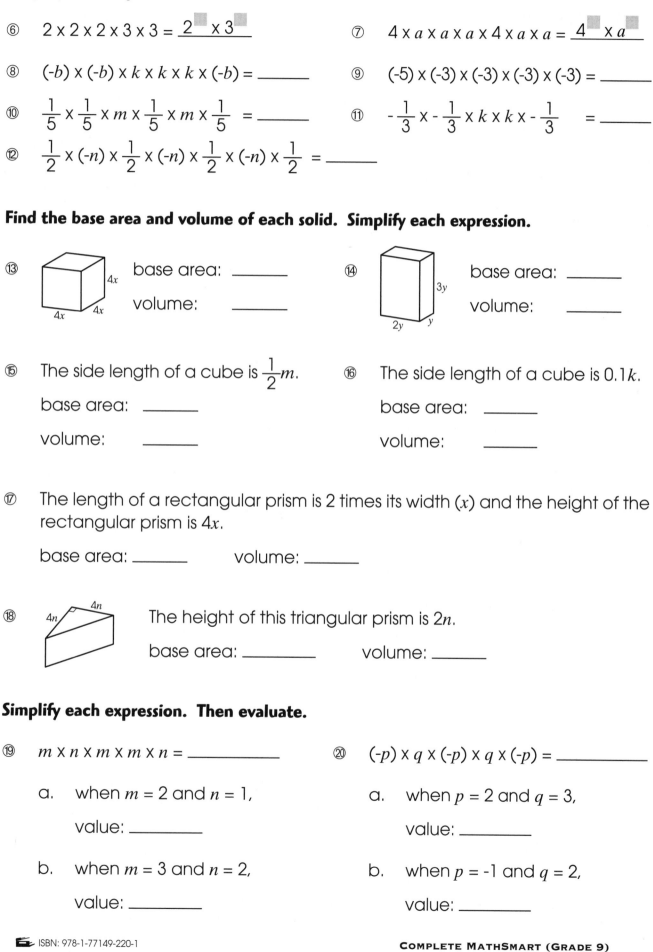

⑬   base area: _____

    volume: _____

⑭   base area: _____

    volume: _____

⑮   The side length of a cube is $\dfrac{1}{2}m$.

    base area: _____

    volume: _____

⑯   The side length of a cube is $0.1k$.

    base area: _____

    volume: _____

⑰   The length of a rectangular prism is 2 times its width (x) and the height of the rectangular prism is $4x$.

    base area: _____   volume: _____

⑱   The height of this triangular prism is $2n$.

    base area: _____   volume: _____

Simplify each expression. Then evaluate.

⑲ $m \times n \times m \times m \times n = \underline{\qquad\qquad}$

    a.   when $m = 2$ and $n = 1$,

       value: _____

    b.   when $m = 3$ and $n = 2$,

       value: _____

⑳ $(-p) \times q \times (-p) \times q \times (-p) = \underline{\qquad\qquad}$

    a.   when $p = 2$ and $q = 3$,

       value: _____

    b.   when $p = -1$ and $q = 2$,

       value: _____

Write each expression as a single power with a positive exponent.

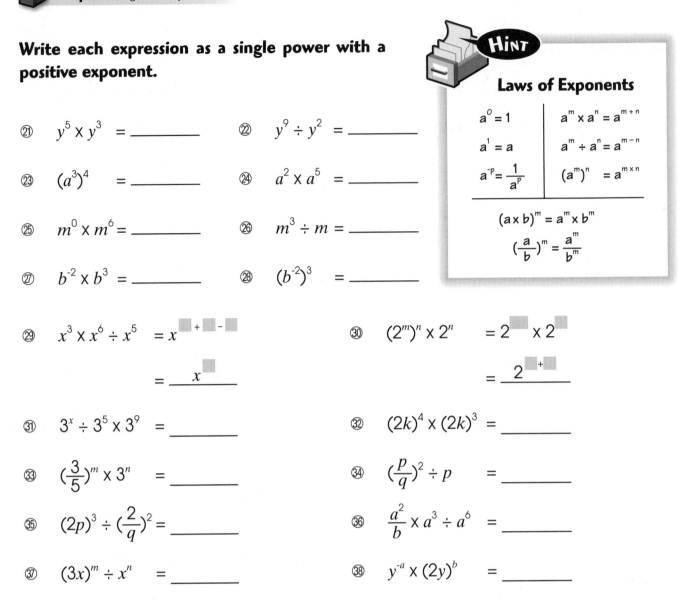

Laws of Exponents

$$a^0 = 1 \qquad a^m \times a^n = a^{m+n}$$
$$a^1 = a \qquad a^m \div a^n = a^{m-n}$$
$$a^{-p} = \frac{1}{a^p} \qquad (a^m)^n = a^{m \times n}$$

$$(a \times b)^m = a^m \times b^m$$
$$\left(\frac{a}{b}\right)^m = \frac{a^m}{b^m}$$

㉑ $y^5 \times y^3 =$ _____

㉒ $y^9 \div y^2 =$ _____

㉓ $(a^3)^4 =$ _____

㉔ $a^2 \times a^5 =$ _____

㉕ $m^0 \times m^6 =$ _____

㉖ $m^3 \div m =$ _____

㉗ $b^{-2} \times b^3 =$ _____

㉘ $(b^{-2})^3 =$ _____

㉙ $x^3 \times x^6 \div x^5 = x^{\blacksquare + \blacksquare - \blacksquare}$

$= \underline{\quad x^{\blacksquare} \quad}$

㉚ $(2^m)^n \times 2^n = 2^{\blacksquare} \times 2^{\blacksquare}$

$= \underline{\quad 2^{\blacksquare + \blacksquare} \quad}$

㉛ $3^x \div 3^5 \times 3^9 =$ _____

㉜ $(2k)^4 \times (2k)^3 =$ _____

㉝ $\left(\frac{3}{5}\right)^m \times 3^n =$ _____

㉞ $\left(\frac{p}{q}\right)^2 \div p =$ _____

㉟ $(2p)^3 \div \left(\frac{2}{q}\right)^2 =$ _____

㊱ $\frac{a^2}{b} \times a^3 \div a^6 =$ _____

㊲ $(3x)^m \div x^n =$ _____

㊳ $y^{-a} \times (2y)^b =$ _____

Find the value of each variable.

㊴ $2^5 \times 2^x = 2^{10}$ $\qquad x =$ _____

㊵ $3^x \div 3^6 = 3^4$ $\qquad x =$ _____

㊶ $6^4 = 2^y \times 3^4$ $\qquad y =$ _____

㊷ $7^y \times 7^6 = 1$ $\qquad y =$ _____

㊸ $5^4 \times k = 5^5$ $\qquad k =$ _____

㊹ $A^k \times A^8 = A^8$ $\qquad k =$ _____

㊺ $(4^2)^x = 4^8$ $\qquad x =$ _____

㊻ $(9^3)^x = 1$ $\qquad x =$ _____

㊼ $(z^p)^5 = z^{15}$ $\qquad p =$ _____

㊽ $(2^a)^p = 2^{2a}$ $\qquad p =$ _____

㊾ $3^b \div 3^4 = 3^2$ $\qquad b =$ _____

㊿ $b^5 \div 4^2 = 4^3$ $\qquad b =$ _____

ISBN: 978-1-77149-220-1

Tell whether each expression is a monomial, binomial, or trinomial. Find the coefficient of each term and the constant term. Then simplify and evaluate.

		Type of Polynomial	Coefficients of y^2	y	xy	Constant Term
(51)	(A) $4y^2 - 9$	________	____	____	____	____
	(B) $3xy - 9y + 7$	________	____	____	____	____
	(C) $-2y + 6y^2$	________	____	____	____	____
	(D) $-yx - 3 + y^2$	________	____	____	____	____
	(E) $9yx$	________	____	____	____	____
	(F) $4y - 3 - 6y^2$	________	____	____	____	____

(52) (B) + (C) + (E)

Evaluate for $x = 1$ and $y = 5$.

(53) (F) + (A) – (E)

Evaluate for $x = 0$ and $y = -1$.

(54) (B) + (A) – (C)

Evaluate for $x = -1$ and $y = 1$.

(55) (E) – (F) – (D)

Evaluate for $x = -3$ and $y = 2$.

ISBN: 978-1-77149-220-1

Find the perimeter or area of each figure. Then evaluate.

(56)

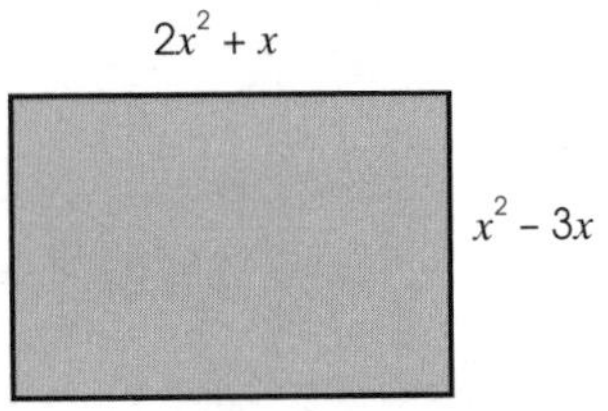
$2x^2 + x$
$x^2 - 3x$

Perimeter: ________ + ________ + ________ + ________

= ________

Evaluate

x	4	5	6	-4	-5	-6
Perimeter						

(57)

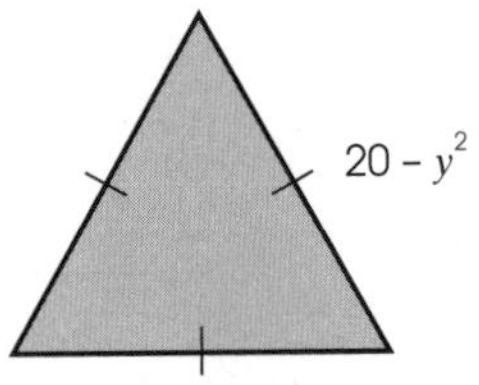
$20 - y^2$

Perimeter:

Evaluate

y	-2	-1	0	1	2	3
Perimeter						

(58)

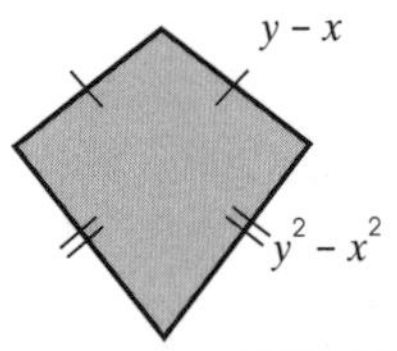
$y - x$
$y^2 - x^2$

Perimeter:

Evaluate

x	-3	-2	-1	0	1	2
y	4	5	6	1	2	3
Perimeter						

(59)

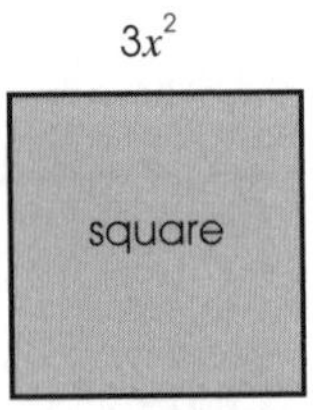
$3x^2$
square

Area:

Evaluate

x	1	3	4
Area			

(60)

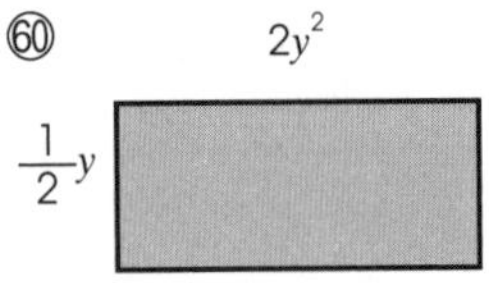
$2y^2$
$\frac{1}{2}y$

Area:

Evaluate

y	2	3	9
Area			

ISBN: 978-1-77149-220-1

Solve the problems.

⑥① The length of a rectangle is y times its width. The width of the rectangle is $4y^2$.

    a.   What is the area of the rectangle?   _____ square units

    b.   If y is 4, what is the area?   _____

⑥② Leo has $\$(x + 6)$ and Sue has $\$(x^2 + 2x - 3)$.

    a.   How much do the children have?   _____

    b.   If x is 5, what is the amount?   _____

⑥③ Mr. White's earnings are $\$(m + 7)$/h and Mrs. White's are $\$(m^2 - 2m)$/h.

    a.   How much do they earn in all in an hour?   _____

    b.   If m is 6, what are their total earnings in an hour?   _____

    c.   If m is 5, who has a higher hourly rate?   _____

⑥④

$(\frac{1}{2}y^2)$ m   **Aunt Tiffany's Garden**

$(2xy)$ m

y^3 m

square

This is Aunt Tiffany's garden.

    a.   What is the area of the garden?

    _____

    b.   If y is 2 and x is 3, what is the area?

    _____

⑥⑤

$\$(0.6n^2)$/kg

$\$1.52$/kg

Mr. Smith buys a watermelon which weighs 4.8 kg and a bunch of bananas which weighs n kg.

    a.   How much does he need to pay?

    _____

    b.   If n is 1.5, what is the amount?

    _____

2.4 Applying Algebraic Skills

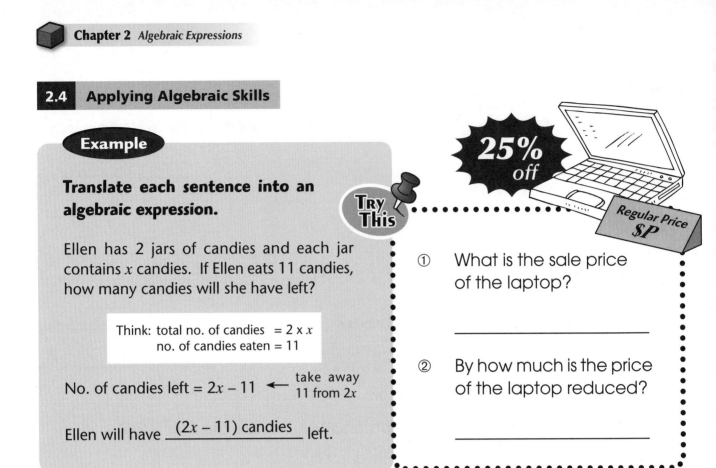

Example

Translate each sentence into an algebraic expression.

Ellen has 2 jars of candies and each jar contains x candies. If Ellen eats 11 candies, how many candies will she have left?

Think: total no. of candies = 2 x x
no. of candies eaten = 11

No. of candies left = $2x - 11$ ← take away 11 from $2x$

Ellen will have __$(2x - 11)$ candies__ left.

TRY This

25% off

Regular Price SP

① What is the sale price of the laptop?

_____

② By how much is the price of the laptop reduced?

_____

Translate each sentence into an algebraic expression.

① The length of a pool is 12 m longer than its width, w.

   a.   What is the length of the pool? _____

   b.   What is the perimeter of the pool? _____

② Marcus earns m dollars a week. Lawrence earns twice as much as Marcus.

   a.   How much does Lawrence earn in a week? _____

   b.   How much does Amy earn if her weekly salary is one third of Lawrence's? _____

③ Three bottles of different sizes contain 3 L of water in all. The first bottle contains x L of water.

   a.   The second bottle contains twice as much as the first one. How much water is there in the second bottle? _____

   b.   How much water is there in the third bottle? _____

Write an expression for each of the following. Then evaluate.

④ a. Area of the figure | Perimeter of the figure

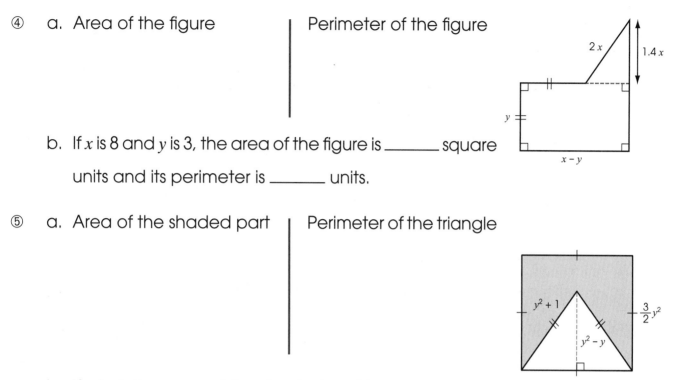

   b. If x is 8 and y is 3, the area of the figure is _____ square

   units and its perimeter is _____ units.

⑤ a. Area of the shaded part | Perimeter of the triangle

   b. If y is 4, the area of the shaded part is _____ square

   units and the perimeter of the triangle is _____ units.

⑥ Each of the equal sides of an isosceles triangle is $(x^2 - 2x)$ cm long. If the perimeter of the isosceles triangle is $3x(x - 1)$ cm, how long is the third side? If x is 8, what is the length of each side?

_____

⑦ Angles a and b are supplementary angles. The measure of angle a is $2(x + 35°)$. What is the measure of angle b? If x is 18°, what are the measures of angles a and b?

_____

⑧ Jenny has $\$(x^2 - 2x)$ and is saving at a rate of $\$(x - 3)$ per week. How much will Jenny have after 4 weeks? If x is 9, how much will she have after 4 weeks?

_____

ISBN: 978-1-77149-220-1

Solve the problems.

⑨ The length and the width of a rectangle are $(3x - 4)$ cm and $(16 - 2x)$ cm respectively.

    a. Is it possible to have 9 as the value of x? If not, suggest a possible value of x.

    b. What is the range of the possible values of x?

    c. Write an expression for the perimeter of the rectangle. Then evaluate when $x = 7$.

⑩ Winnie's savings are $\$(7n + 3.50)$ and Alice's are $\$(n^2 + 1)$.

    a. Is it possible to have -1 as the value of n? If not, suggest a possible value of n.

    b. What is the range of the possible values of n?

    c. If $n = 5$, who has more money? How much more?

    d. If $n = 8$, who has more money? How much more?

    e. If 2 girls buy a CD and share the cost equally, how much does each girl have to pay?

$\$2n(n - 2)$

ISBN: 978-1-77149-220-1

Solve the problems.

⑪   a.   Mr. Taylor buys 2 boxes of candies and a box of cereal. How much does he need to pay?

_____

b.   How much more does a box of cereal cost than a bag of marshmallows?

_____

c.   If the values of x and y are 6 and 4 respectively, how much does each item cost?

_____

⑫   The area of a rectangle is $(6x^2y^2)$ square units and its length is $(3xy)$ units.

a.   What is the width of the rectangle?   _____

b.   What is the perimeter of the rectangle?   _____

c.   If the perimeter of a regular pentagon is the same as that of the rectangle, what is the side length of the pentagon?   _____

⑬   A circular garden has a circumference of $(8x^2y\pi)$ units.

a.   What is the length of a straight path that goes through the centre of the garden?   _____

b.   What is the area of the garden?   _____

c.   Determine the area of each garden in terms of π.

Garden	A	B	C	D	E
x	$\dfrac{1}{2}$	2	-1	$\dfrac{2}{\pi}$	2π
y	3	$\dfrac{1}{2}$	$\dfrac{1}{2}$	π	$\dfrac{1}{\pi}$
Area					

ISBN: 978-1-77149-220-1

3 Polynomials and Equations

Example

Is the expression a monomial (with one term), a binomial (with two terms), or a trinomial (with three terms)? Find the coefficient of each term and identify the constant term.

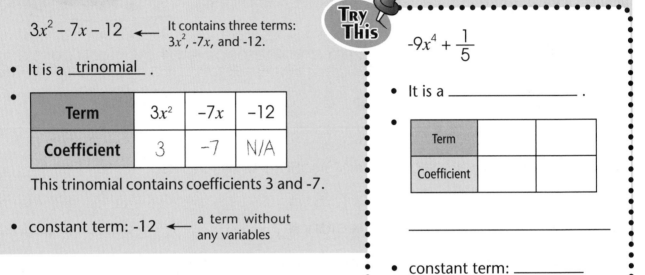

$3x^2 - 7x - 12$ ← It contains three terms: $3x^2$, $-7x$, and -12.

- It is a __trinomial__ .

Term	$3x^2$	$-7x$	-12
Coefficient	3	-7	N/A

This trinomial contains coefficients 3 and -7.

- constant term: -12 ← a term without any variables

Try This

$-9x^4 + \dfrac{1}{5}$

- It is a _____ .

Term		
Coefficient		

- constant term: _____

Write how many terms each polynomial has. Name each polynomial. Then fill in the blanks.

	No. of Terms	Type of Polynomial	Coefficients	Constant Term
① $-5x^4 + 6xy + 9$	_____	_____	_____	_____
② $\dfrac{1}{3}y^3 - 2y^2 - 4$	_____	_____	_____	_____
③ $-2xy^2 - 6$	_____	_____	_____	_____
④ $8x^2y$	_____	_____	_____	_____
⑤ $-3y^2 + 4x + \dfrac{1}{3}$	_____	_____	_____	_____

Circle the like terms in each group.

⑥ $3m^2$, $-\dfrac{1}{2}mn$, $0.8m^2$, $\dfrac{1}{m^2}$

⑦ $-8yx$, xy, $\dfrac{2y}{x}$, $0.5xy^2$

⑧ $8.5ab$, $3b^2a$, $-0.9a^2b$, $\dfrac{1}{8}ab^2$

⑨ $-2w^3$, $3w^{-2}$, $-\dfrac{1}{8}w^3y$, $\dfrac{w^3}{4}$

ISBN: 978-1-77149-220-1

Remove the brackets. Then simplify.

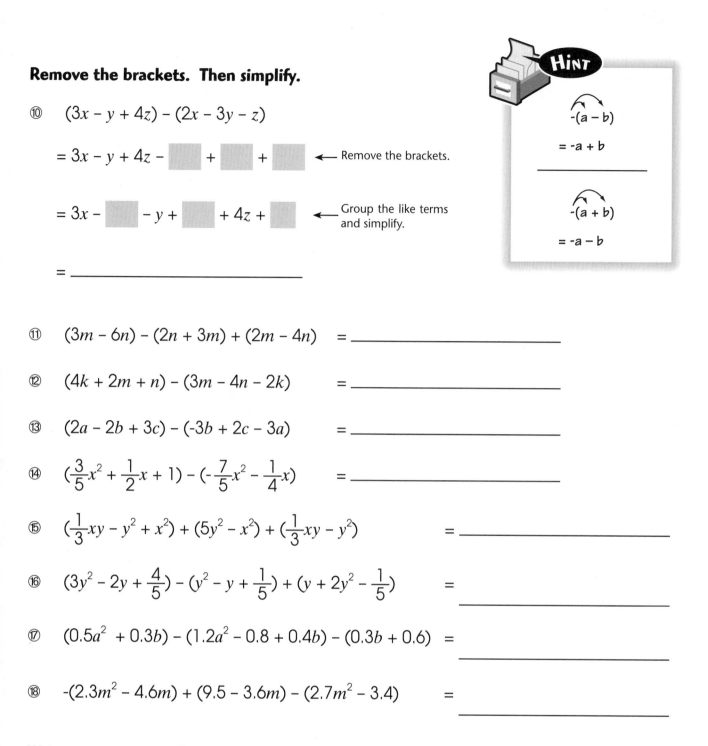

⑩ $(3x - y + 4z) - (2x - 3y - z)$

= $3x - y + 4z -$ ☐ $+$ ☐ $+$ ☐ ⟵ Remove the brackets.

= $3x -$ ☐ $- y +$ ☐ $+ 4z +$ ☐ ⟵ Group the like terms and simplify.

= _____

HINT

$-(a - b)$

$= -a + b$

_____

$-(a + b)$

$= -a - b$

⑪ $(3m - 6n) - (2n + 3m) + (2m - 4n)$ = _____

⑫ $(4k + 2m + n) - (3m - 4n - 2k)$ = _____

⑬ $(2a - 2b + 3c) - (-3b + 2c - 3a)$ = _____

⑭ $(\frac{3}{5}x^2 + \frac{1}{2}x + 1) - (-\frac{7}{5}x^2 - \frac{1}{4}x)$ = _____

⑮ $(\frac{1}{3}xy - y^2 + x^2) + (5y^2 - x^2) + (\frac{1}{3}xy - y^2)$ = _____

⑯ $(3y^2 - 2y + \frac{4}{5}) - (y^2 - y + \frac{1}{5}) + (y + 2y^2 - \frac{1}{5})$ = _____

⑰ $(0.5a^2 + 0.3b) - (1.2a^2 - 0.8 + 0.4b) - (0.3b + 0.6)$ = _____

⑱ $-(2.3m^2 - 4.6m) + (9.5 - 3.6m) - (2.7m^2 - 3.4)$ = _____

Write an expression for each problem.

⑲ The length of a rectangular field is $(4y + 3x)$ m and the width is $(2y - x)$ m. Write an expression to show the perimeter of the rectangular field.

_____

⑳ Joe has $\$(5a + a^2)$ and Katie has $4 more than Joe. Write an expression to show the total amount that the children have.

_____

Expand.

> **HINT**
>
> **Distributive Property**
>
> a(b + c) = a x b + a x c
>
> e.g. 2(3x – 4) Multiply each term by 2.
>
> = 2(3x) – 2(4)
>
> = 6x – 8

㉑ $2(4 - a)$ = ______

㉒ $3(b + 5)$ = ______

㉓ $-4(m + 3)$ = ______

㉔ $-3(2 - p)$ = ______

㉕ $-(2x + 5)$ = ______

㉖ $2(-5 + k)$ = ______

㉗ $-0.8(4 - mn + 5m^2)$ = ______

㉘ $-0.1(10p - 20q + 100pq)$ = ______

㉙ $-4(5m^2 - 4m + 2)$ = ______

㉚ $3(-y^2 - x^2 + xy)$ = ______

㉛ $2(3a^2 - 2ab + b^2)$ = ______

㉜ $-(3p - q + 4pq)$ = ______

㉝ $0.5(2x + y - 9)$ = ______

㉞ $2.5(-6 + 7c + 2d)$ = ______

㉟ $2(-5 + p - q)$ = ______

㊱ $-3(x - 2 + y)$ = ______

Expand and simplify.

㊲ $5(-2x + y) - 2(3x - y)$

=

㊳ $-4(p - q) + 3(-p - q)$

=

㊴ $\frac{1}{3}(12a + 6b) - \frac{1}{5}(5a)$

=

㊵ $3(x - y + 3) - 6(y - x) + 2(x - 4)$ = ______

㊶ $\frac{2}{5}(15a - 10b) + \frac{1}{5}(10 - 20b + 10a)$ = ______

㊷ $\frac{1}{2}(4a^2 - 8b^2) + \frac{1}{3}(9b^2 - 12b - 3a^2)$ = ______

㊸ $\frac{1}{2}(8m - 6n + 2) - \frac{1}{2}(4m - 1) + \frac{1}{4}(16 - 8n)$ = ______

ISBN: 978-1-77149-220-1

Find the missing polynomial.

㊹ $(4x^2 - 3xy + 9) + (2xy - 2x^2 - 6) + ($ _____ $) = 2x^2 + 5$

㊺ $($ _____ $) + (3a^2b - ab^2 - 8) + (a^2b - 2ab^2 - 5) = a^2b - 6ab^2$

㊻ $($ _____ $) + (\dfrac{10mn - 5m^2 + n^2}{5}) + (\dfrac{25m^2 + 4n^2}{5}) = 2m^2 + n^2 - 6$

Solve the problems.

㊼ Ryan earns $8.75 an hour on weekdays and $y more an hour on weekends. Ryan works 2 hours on Monday, x hours each day from Tuesday to Friday, and 3 hours each day on the weekend. Write an expression for his earnings this week.

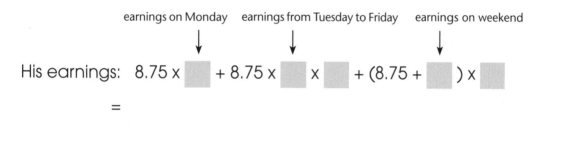

earnings on Monday   earnings from Tuesday to Friday   earnings on weekend

His earnings: $8.75 \times \boxed{} + 8.75 \times \boxed{} \times \boxed{} + (8.75 + \boxed{}) \times \boxed{}$

= _____

_____

㊽ Write an expression for the area of the shaded part.

$(a^2 + b)$ m

$(3b - \dfrac{1}{2}a^2)$ m

2 m   3 m

_____

Challenge

A robot consumes 6.84 L of gasoline on Monday and increases its consumption by y L every day. Write an expression to show how much gasoline it consumes every day on average in a week.

Make a chart to help you solve the problem.

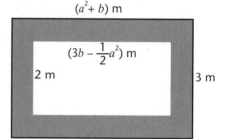

Day	Amount of Gasoline (L)
Mon	6.84
Tue	6.84 + y
Wed	6.84 + ▢ y

ISBN: 978-1-77149-220-1

3.2 Expanding, Simplifying, and Factoring Polynomials

Words TO LEARN

Factoring: rewriting an expression as a product of 2 or more expressions

(Take out the common factor of an expression from each term, and then multiply the remaining expressions.)

e.g.　　$2x^2y + 8xy$

　　$= 2xy(x) + 2xy(4)$

　　$= \underline{2xy(x + 4)}$

$2x^2y = \boxed{2} \cdot \boxed{x} \cdot x \cdot \boxed{y}$

$8xy = \boxed{2} \cdot 2 \cdot 2 \cdot \boxed{x \cdot y}$ ⟵ Factor each term of the polynomial.

G.C.F. = $2xy$

Example

Expand and simplify.

1.　$-5(4y^2 - 2y + 7)$

　$= (-5)(4y^2) + (-5)(-2y) + (-5)(7)$

　$= \underline{-20y^2 + 10y - 35}$　　Multiply each term by -5.

2.　$3x(-2x^2 + 6x)$

　$= 3x(-2x^2) + 3x(6x)$　⟵ Multiply each term by the monomial.

　$= \underline{-6x^3 + 18x^2}$

Hint

Distributive Property

• Multiply each term in the brackets by a factor outside the brackets.

$$a(b + c) = ab + ac$$

Try This

① 　$3(4m^2 - 6)$

　$= 3(\boxed{}) + 3(\boxed{})$

　$= \underline{\hspace{3cm}}$

② 　$2n(-3mn + 5m)$

　$= 2n(\boxed{}) + 2n(\boxed{})$

　$= \underline{\hspace{3cm}}$

Expand.

① 　$-3(x^2 - y + xy)$ 　　$= \underline{\hspace{3cm}}$

② 　$\dfrac{3}{5}(10m^2 + 5m)$ 　　$= \underline{\hspace{3cm}}$

③ 　$0.7(2p^2 - 5q)$ 　　$= \underline{\hspace{3cm}}$

④ 　$1.8y(y^2 - 4y + 3)$ 　　$= \underline{\hspace{3cm}}$

⑤ 　$-\dfrac{1}{2}n(n^2 - 6n - 4)$ 　　$= \underline{\hspace{3cm}}$

⑥ 　$-\dfrac{1}{3}k(-2k + k^2 - 3)$ 　　$= \underline{\hspace{3cm}}$

⑦ 　$-1\dfrac{1}{3}u(6uv - 9u^2v)$ 　　$= \underline{\hspace{3cm}}$

⑧ 　$2\dfrac{2}{5}w(10xy - 15w^2y)$ 　　$= \underline{\hspace{3cm}}$

Expand and simplify.

⑨ $3x(2x^2 - xy + y) - 2y(x + x^2)$ ← Rewrite as $3x(2x^2 - xy + y) + (-2y)(x + x^2)$.

$= 3x() + 3x() + 3x() + (-2y)() + (-2y)()$

$= \underline{\hspace{8cm}}$

$= \underline{\hspace{4cm}}$

⑩ $4m(2n^2 - 3mn + m^2) - 2n(5m^2 - 3nm) + nm(n - m) = \underline{\hspace{5cm}}$

⑪ $0.3u(uv + v^2 - u^2) - 0.1uv(v + u) + 0.2(u^2v + u^3) = \underline{\hspace{5cm}}$

⑫ $\dfrac{1}{3}abc(a + b) + \dfrac{1}{2}b(a^2c + ac^2) + \dfrac{1}{6}c(ab^2 + a^2b) = \underline{\hspace{5cm}}$

$\underline{\hspace{5cm}}$

⑬ $-\dfrac{5}{12}jk(i + j + k) + \dfrac{1}{6}ij(k + i) - \dfrac{1}{6}(jk^2 + i^2j) = \underline{\hspace{5cm}}$

$\underline{\hspace{5cm}}$

Expand.

⑭ $\dfrac{6x^2y^3 - 3xy^2}{3} = \dfrac{}{3} - \dfrac{}{3}$

$= \underline{\hspace{3cm}}$

⑮ $\dfrac{10a^2b - 5ab}{-5b} = \underline{\hspace{3cm}}$

⑯ $\dfrac{9m^2n + 6mn^2 - 12mn}{3m} = \underline{\hspace{3cm}}$

⑰ $\dfrac{4st - 8s^2t^2 - 12st^2}{4} = \underline{\hspace{3cm}}$

⑱ $\dfrac{12uv^2 - 8u^2v + 6uv}{2uv} = \underline{\hspace{3cm}}$

⑲ $\dfrac{32p^2qr + 4q^2r - 8pr}{-4r} = \underline{\hspace{3cm}}$

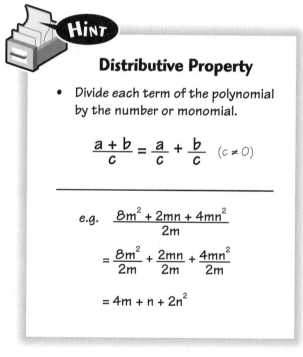

HINT

Distributive Property

- Divide each term of the polynomial by the number or monomial.

$$\dfrac{a + b}{c} = \dfrac{a}{c} + \dfrac{b}{c} \quad (c \neq 0)$$

e.g. $\dfrac{8m^2 + 2mn + 4mn^2}{2m}$

$= \dfrac{8m^2}{2m} + \dfrac{2mn}{2m} + \dfrac{4mn^2}{2m}$

$= 4m + n + 2n^2$

ISBN: 978-1-77149-220-1

Write an expression for the area of each shape. Expand and evaluate.

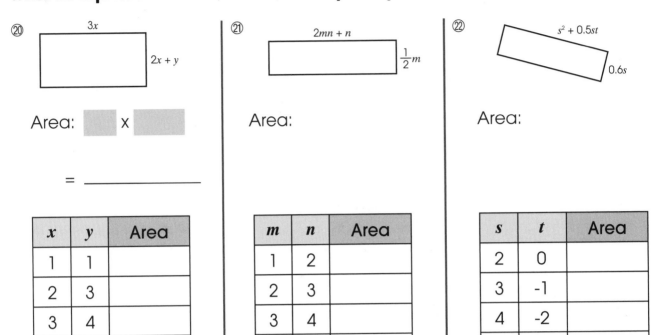

⑳ 3x

2x + y

Area: ☐ X ☐

= _____

x	y	Area
1	1	
2	3	
3	4	
5	9	

㉑ 2mn + n

$\frac{1}{2}m$

Area:

m	n	Area
1	2	
2	3	
3	4	
4	5	

㉒ $s^2 + 0.5st$

0.6s

Area:

s	t	Area
2	0	
3	-1	
4	-2	
5	-3.5	

Find the unit rate. Then solve the problems.

㉓ 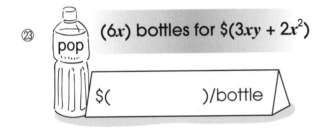 $(6x)$ bottles for $\$(3xy + 2x^2)$

$(_____)/bottle

a. How much do $(12y)$ bottles cost?

_____

b. Determine the cost of 1 bottle if $x = 3$ and $y = 1$.

_____

㉔ 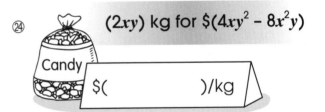 $(2xy)$ kg for $\$(4xy^2 - 8x^2y)$

Candy

$(_____)/kg

a. How much do $(3y)$ kg of candies cost?

_____

b. Determine the cost of 1 kg of candies if $x = 0.8$ and $y = 2.4$.

_____

ISBN: 978-1-77149-220-1

Write the greatest common factor. Then factor.

㉕ $6mn^2 + 3m^2n^2$

= _____

= _____

$6mn^2 = 2\cdot\underline{\ \ \ }\cdot\underline{\ \ \ }\cdot n\cdot n$

$3m^2n^2 = 3\cdot m\cdot\underline{\ \ \ }\cdot\underline{\ \ \ }\cdot n$

the G.C.F. = _____

㉖ $2p^2q - 10pq^3$

= _____

= _____

$2p^2q = $ _____

$10pq^3 = $ _____

the G.C.F. = _____

㉗ $-15a^3b - 20a^2b^2$

= _____

= _____

$-15a^3b = $ _____

$-20a^2b^2 = $ _____

the G.C.F. = _____

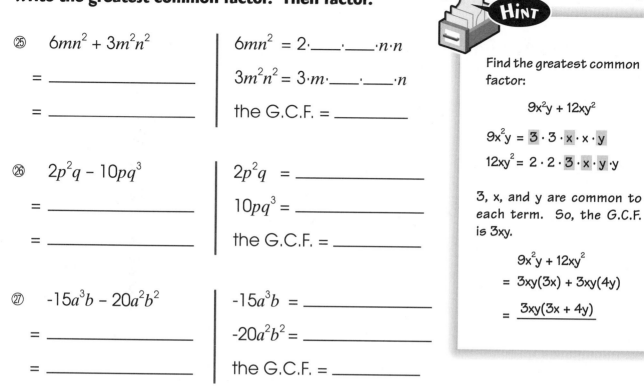

Find the greatest common factor:

$$9x^2y + 12xy^2$$

$9x^2y = \boxed{3}\cdot 3\cdot\boxed{x}\cdot x\cdot\boxed{y}$

$12xy^2 = 2\cdot 2\cdot\boxed{3}\cdot\boxed{x}\cdot\boxed{y}\cdot y$

3, x, and y are common to each term. So, the G.C.F. is 3xy.

$$9x^2y + 12xy^2$$
$$= 3xy(3x) + 3xy(4y)$$
$$= \underline{3xy(3x + 4y)}$$

Factor each polynomial.

㉘ $a^3 - 2a^2 + a$ = _____

㉙ $2b^4 + 8b^2 - 16b$ = _____

㉚ $9x^4 + 81x^3 - 18x^2$ = _____

㉛ $-mn^4 + m^2n^2 - mn^3$ = _____

㉜ $5pq^3 - 20p^3q + 10p^2q^2$ = _____

㉝ $-7x^2y^2 + 14x^3y^3 - 28x^2y^3$ = _____

㉞ $6s^3t^4 + 5s^2t^5 - s^3t^5$ = _____

㉟ $-10uv^2 + u^4v^3 + 5u^2v^2$ = _____

㊱ $4xyz^3 + 20x^2yz^4$ = _____

㊲ $-16p^2q^2r - 24pq^3r^2$ = _____

Find the missing terms.

㊳ $3xy^2 - 9x^2y^2 + \boxed{} = 3xy(y - \boxed{} + 4x)$

㊴ $\boxed{} + 14p^3q^2 - 7p^2q^3 = 7p^2q^2(3pq + 2p - \boxed{})$

㊵ $16a^4b^2c^3 - 12a^3b^4c^2 - \boxed{} = 4a^2bc^2(4a^2bc - \boxed{} - a)$

㊶ $3n^4 - 27m^2n^3 + \boxed{} = 3n^2(n^2 - \boxed{} + 6m^3n^4)$

ISBN: 978-1-77149-220-1

Simplify each expression. Then factor.

㊷ $4x^2y - 3x^2 + 3x^2y + 6x^2 - x^2$

   $= \underline{\quad} x^2y + \underline{\quad} x^2$

   $= \underline{}$

㊸ $2x(3x - y) + 4y(x - 2y)$

   $=$

㊹ $3m^2n^2 - 6mn - 4m^2n^2 - 6m^2n^2 - mn$

   $=$

㊺ $3(6x^2 + 8xy) - x(2x + 4y)$

   $=$

㊻ $-5m(n - m + nm) + 6n(m^2 - 3m)$ $= \underline{}$

㊼ $-3(a^3 - 2a + 1) + a(a^2 - a) + 3(1 - 2a^3)$ $= \underline{}$

㊽ $\dfrac{4x^2 + 8xy + 6y^2x}{2x} + \dfrac{3xy - 12y^2 - 9y^3}{3y}$ $= \underline{}$

㊾ $\dfrac{15pq + 20p^2q - 10pq^2}{5} - \dfrac{4p^2q + 8p^3q}{2p}$ $= \underline{}$

㊿ $\dfrac{16uv^3 - 8u^2v^2 + 4u^3v^3}{4uv} + \dfrac{6u^3v^2 - 18u^2v^3}{3u}$ $= \underline{}$

Factor the expression for the area of each rectangle. Then find the length.

㈜ Area: $3w^2y + 12wy^2$ $3wy$

Area: $\underline{}$

Length: $\underline{}$

㈤ Area: $6a^2b + 2ab + 8ab^2$ $4ab$

Area: $\underline{}$

Length: $\underline{}$

Write an algebraic expression to represent the rate of each robot. Then answer the questions.

(53)

a.

Robot	Performance	Rate (no. of plates/hour)
Sonic	$(6x^2y + 2x^3 - 2xy^2)$ plates in $(2x)$ hours	
Coleman	$(3xy^2 - 6x^2y + 24y^3)$ plates in $(3y)$ hours	
Lucas	$(\frac{1}{4}y^2 + 1\frac{1}{4}x^2 - \frac{3}{4}xy)$ plates in 15 minutes	
Emma	$(\frac{1}{3}x^2 - 2xy + 6y^2)$ plates in 20 minutes	

b. Determine the rate of each robot if $x = 4$ and $y = 2$.

Sonic: ______ plates/h Coleman: ____________

Lucas: ____________ Emma: ____________

c. Which has the highest rate? ____________

Solve the problem. Factor the expression.

(54) Amy has $(6mn^2 - 8mn + 12m^2n)$ marbles and Joe has $(6mn - 4mn^2 + 2m^2n)$.

a. How many marbles do the children have in all?

____

b. If the children divide their marbles into $(2m)$ equal groups, how many marbles are there in each group?

____

c. Determine the number of marbles in each group if

- $m = 2$ and $n = 8$ ______
- $m = 4$ and $n = 5$ ______

ISBN: 978-1-77149-220-1

3.3 Applying Polynomials

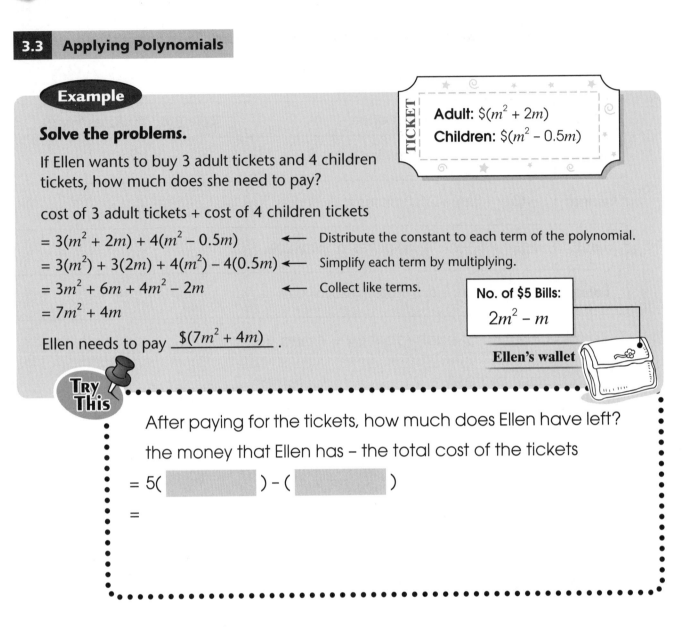

Example

Solve the problems.

TICKET
Adult: $\$(m^2 + 2m)$
Children: $\$(m^2 - 0.5m)$

If Ellen wants to buy 3 adult tickets and 4 children tickets, how much does she need to pay?

cost of 3 adult tickets + cost of 4 children tickets

$= 3(m^2 + 2m) + 4(m^2 - 0.5m)$ ← Distribute the constant to each term of the polynomial.

$= 3(m^2) + 3(2m) + 4(m^2) - 4(0.5m)$ ← Simplify each term by multiplying.

$= 3m^2 + 6m + 4m^2 - 2m$ ← Collect like terms.

$= 7m^2 + 4m$

No. of $5 Bills:
$2m^2 - m$

Ellen needs to pay $\underline{\$(7m^2 + 4m)}$.

Ellen's wallet

TRY THIS

After paying for the tickets, how much does Ellen have left?

the money that Ellen has – the total cost of the tickets

$= 5($ _____ $) - ($ _____ $)$

$=$

Solve the problems. Simplify the answers.

① The area of Eva's bedroom is $(6x^2 + 3xy)$ m^2.

a. If the width of the room is $(3x)$ m, what is the length?

_____

b. If Eva wants to put a molding around the top of the walls, what will be the length of the molding?

_____

② The cost of a paperback book is $\$(y^2 + 5)$.

a. What is the minimum cost of a paperback book?

_____

b. If a hardcover book costs $\$(y^2 + y)$ more than a paperback book, how much is a hardcover book?

_____

Factor each expression. Answer the questions.

③ a. Find the speed of each means of transport.

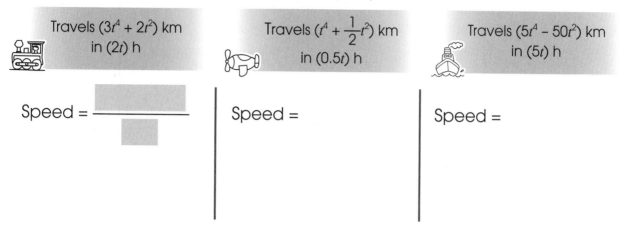

Travels $(3t^4 + 2t^2)$ km in $(2t)$ h

Speed = ⬜/⬜

Travels $(t^4 + \frac{1}{2}t^2)$ km in $(0.5t)$ h

Speed =

Travels $(5t^4 - 50t^2)$ km in $(5t)$ h

Speed =

b. Which means of transport has the highest speed? Explain.

c. If $t = 5$, what is the speed of each means of transport?

④ The cost of a dining table is $\$2m(m^2 - 6)$ and the cost of a chair is $\$m(5m + 3)$.

a. What is the cost of a dining set, including a dining table and four chairs?

b. If Mr. Taylor buys a dining set and pays for it with m equal installments, how much does he need to pay for each installment?

c. How much does Mr. Taylor need to pay for each installment and what is the total cost of the dining set if

• $m = 6$?   Each installment = _____   Total cost = _____

• $m = 8$?   Each installment = _____   Total cost = _____

• $m = 15$?   Each installment = _____   Total cost = _____

ISBN: 978-1-77149-220-1

Find the measurements. Factor each expression and evaluate.

⑤   Area = $6x^2y + 6y^2$ What is the height of the triangle?   If $y = 9$,

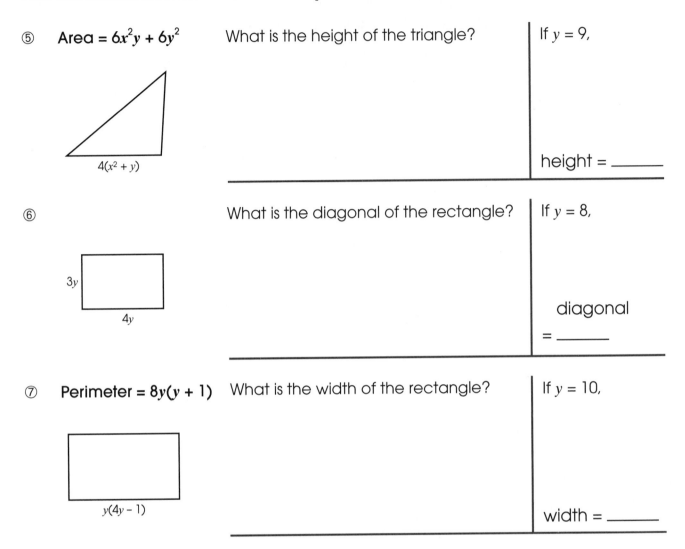

4($x^2 + y$)

height = _____

⑥   What is the diagonal of the rectangle?   If $y = 8$,

3y

4y

diagonal

= _____

⑦   Perimeter = $8y(y + 1)$ What is the width of the rectangle?   If $y = 10$,

$y(4y - 1)$

width = _____

⑧   The perimeter of the square and the triangle are the same.

a.   What is the length of the base of the triangle?

$3p(p + q)$

b.   If $p = 4$ and $q = 3$, what is the height of the triangle?

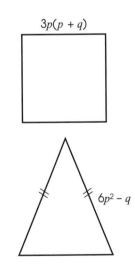

$6p^2 - q$

ISBN: 978-1-77149-220-1

Solve the problems.

⑨ a. The cost of n kg of oranges is $\$(4n^2 - n)$. How much does 1 kg of oranges cost?

_____

   b. The cost of $(\frac{1}{2}n)$ kg of peaches is $\$n(2n + \frac{1}{2})$.

       How much does 1 kg of peaches cost?

_____

   c. Which kind of fruit is more expensive? How much more?

_____

   d. If Paige buys $2n$ kg of oranges and $2n$ kg of peaches, how much does she need to pay?

_____

⑩ Kevin and Alice were on a road trip. They drove $x(x + 2y)$ km on the first day, $(2x^2 - xy)$ km on the second day, and $x(5y - x)$ km on the last day.

   a. How far did they travel in the 3 days?

_____

   b. If they drove at an average speed of $(8x)$ km/h, how many hours did they spend driving?

_____

   c. If they drove at a speed that was $(2x)$ km/h faster than their average speed, how many hours would they spend driving? How many hours would be saved?

_____

⑪   a. What is the area of the kitchen?

_____

Kitchen $-2pr$

                                               b. If Mrs. White wants to cover the entire floor with square tiles of side length r m, how many tiles does she need?

_____

ISBN: 978-1-77149-220-1

3.4 Solving First-degree Equations

Example

Make a table of values to find the unknowns for each equation.

$$3x + y = 10$$

Set up a table of values showing solutions. Substitute a value for x and then solve the equation for y.

x	y
0	10
1	7
2	4

When $x = 0$,
$3(0) + y = 10$
$y = 10$

When $x = 1$,
$3(1) + y = 10$
$3 + y = 10$
$y = 7$

When $x = 2$,
$3(2) + y = 10$
$6 + y = 10$
$y = 4$

The points (0,10), (1,7), and (2,4) are the solutions to the equation.

Try This

① $y = 4x - 1$

x	y
0	
1	
2	

$y = 4(0) - 1$
$y = 4(1) - 1$
$y = 4(2) - 1$

The solutions to the equation are _____.

② $2x - 3y = -1$

x	y
1	
4	
7	

$2(1) - 3y = -1$
$2(4) - 3y = -1$
$2(7) - 3y = -1$

The solutions to the equation are _____.

Find the values of the unknowns for each equation.

① $2x - 3y = -1$

x	y
0	
2	
4	
6	

② $y - 3x = 4$

x	y
1	
3	
5	
7	

③ $x - y = \dfrac{1}{2}$

x	y
0	
2	
4	
6	

ISBN: 978-1-77149-220-1

Set up an equation for each problem. Then solve it.

④ A small box can hold 5 chocolates and a big box can hold 12 chocolates. A factory produces 600 chocolates and packs them into boxes.

a. Write an equation to describe this situation.

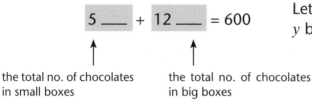

Let x be the no. of small boxes and y be the no. of big boxes.

the total no. of chocolates in small boxes

the total no. of chocolates in big boxes

b. If the factory owner uses 40 big boxes, how many small boxes does he use?

Substitute $y = 40$ into $5x + 12y = 600$.

$$5x + 12\ (\quad) = 600$$

_____ small boxes are used.

⑤ Sam has $5 bills and Leo has toonies. Sam always has $14 more than Leo. If Leo has 8 toonies, how many $5 bills does Sam have?

_____

⑥ Mrs. Lynn puts every 6 girls or 5 boys in a group. There are 235 children in all. If there are 25 groups of girls, how many groups of boys are there?

_____

Solve each equation.

⑦ $2m = 10$ _____

⑧ $4 + y = 5$ _____

⑨ $a - 2 = 9$ _____

⑩ $\frac{1}{2}u = 4$ _____

⑪ $n \div 4 = 16$ _____

⑫ $d \div 2 = -5$ _____

⑬ $0.6m = 3$ _____

⑭ $x + 1.4 = -5$ _____

⑮ $n + \frac{3}{5} = 2$ _____

Solve the equations. Show your work and check the answers.

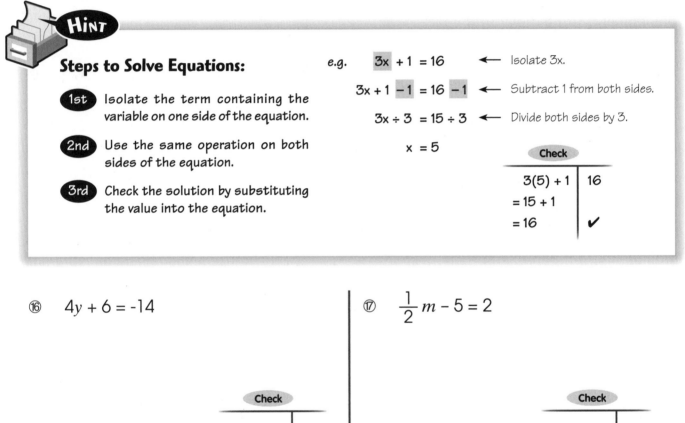

HINT

Steps to Solve Equations:

1st   Isolate the term containing the variable on one side of the equation.

2nd   Use the same operation on both sides of the equation.

3rd   Check the solution by substituting the value into the equation.

e.g. $\boxed{3x} + 1 = 16$ ⟵ Isolate 3x.

$3x + 1 \boxed{-1} = 16 \boxed{-1}$ ⟵ Subtract 1 from both sides.

$3x \div 3 = 15 \div 3$ ⟵ Divide both sides by 3.

$x = 5$

Check

$3(5) + 1$	16
$= 15 + 1$	
$= 16$	✔

⑯ $4y + 6 = -14$

Check

⑰ $\frac{1}{2}m - 5 = 2$

Check

⑱ $6 - 2k = 18$

Check

⑲ $13 = -11 + 2n$

Check

ISBN: 978-1-77149-220-1

Solve each equation.

⑳ $2y + 1 = 9$ _____

㉑ $-12 + 8x = 4$ _____

㉒ $5b + 1 = 0$ _____

㉓ $7 = -12c + 1$ _____

㉔ $-3k - 2 = -1$ _____

㉕ $-4 = 2 + 9m$ _____

Solve the problems by using equations. Then check the answers.

㉖ Chocolate chip cookies are sold in boxes of 6 and plain cookies are sold in boxes of 8. If Nancy buys 3 boxes of plain cookies and a few boxes of chocolate chip cookies to have 144 cookies in total, how many boxes of chocolate chip cookies does she buy?

Check

_____

㉗ 12 big marbles are 24 g heavier than a bag of small marbles that weighs 288 g. How heavy is each big marble?

Check

_____

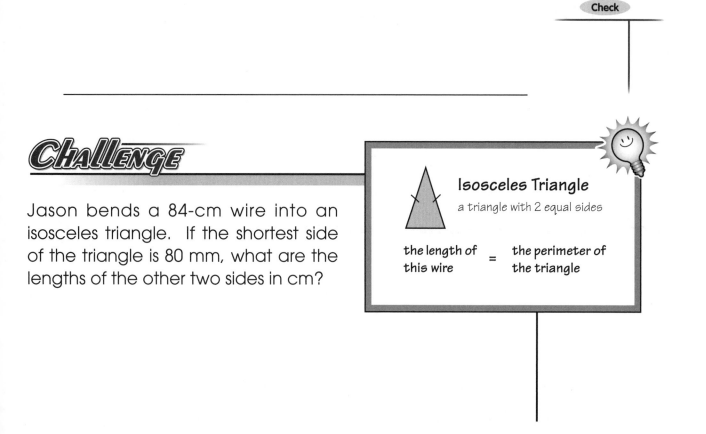

Challenge

Jason bends a 84-cm wire into an isosceles triangle. If the shortest side of the triangle is 80 mm, what are the lengths of the other two sides in cm?

Isosceles Triangle
a triangle with 2 equal sides

the length of = the perimeter of
this wire   the triangle

3.5 Solving and Rearranging First-degree Equations

Words TO LEARN

Equation: a mathematical statement showing two equal expressions

e.g. $y + 1 = 5$, $3x^2 + 4 = 16$

BEDMAS: a mnemonic for the order of operations

Brackets, **E**xponents, **D**ivision, **M**ultiplication, **A**ddition, and **S**ubtraction

Example

Use algebraic expressions or equations to represent each situation.

Amir's age ← Use a symbol or letter to represent Amir's age. _____ y _____

Ron is twice as old as Amir. ← Ron's age is 2 times Amir's. _____ $2y$ _____

The sum of Amir's and Ron's ages is 27. ← Use addition. _____ $y + 2y = 27$ _____

Try This

width of a rectangle _____

The length of the rectangle doubles the width. _____

The perimeter of the rectangle is 64 cm. _____

Convert the statements to algebraic expressions or equations.

①　a number _____

the number plus 5 _____

three times the number _____

The sum of the number plus 5 and
three times the number is 60. _____

② a number _____

double the number _____

3 less than twice the number is 9. _____

Twice the number decreased by 4 is 8. _____

③ height of a triangle _____

The base of the triangle is $\frac{1}{3}$ of the height. _____

The area of the triangle is 8 cm². _____

Solve the equations.

④ $8d = 32$

$d =$ _____

⑤ $i - 2 = 9$

$i =$ _____

⑥ $p + 8 = 14$

$p =$ _____

⑦ $5x = 55$

$x =$ _____

⑧ $g \div 5 = 10$

$g =$ _____

⑨ $13 = 6 + j$

$j =$ _____

⑩ $4y + 3 = 11$

> **HINT**
>
> We can use opposite operations to solve the equations.
>
> e.g. $2x - 1 = 5$ — If we have "−", react with
> $2x = 5 + 1$ "+" on the other side.
> $2x = 6$
> $x = 6 \div 2$ — If we have "×", react with
> $x = 3$ "÷" on the other side.

⑪ $6 = 3t - 6$

⑫ $-3m + 4 = -17$ $m =$ _____

⑬ $19 - 3k = 3 + k$ $k =$ _____

⑭ $3x - 3 = 15$ $x =$ _____

⑮ $b + 7b = 12 - 24$ $b =$ _____

ISBN: 978-1-77149-220-1

Check the answer of each equation by substitution. Check the circle if it is correct; otherwise, put a cross and find the correct answer.

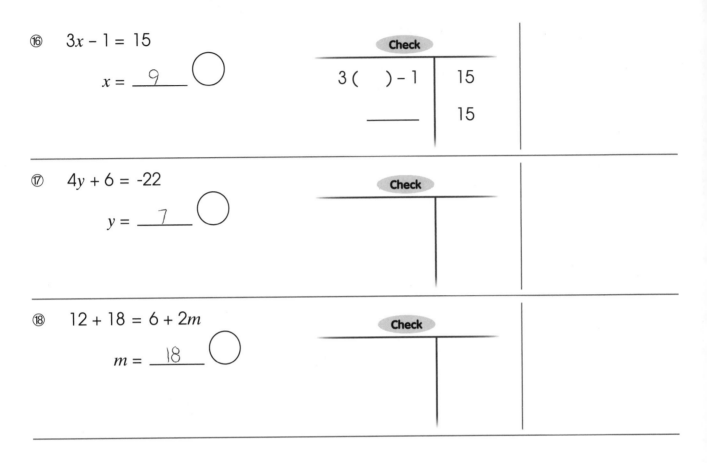

⑯ $3x - 1 = 15$

   $x = $ ___9___ ◯

   Check

   $3 (\quad) - 1$ | 15

   _____ | 15

⑰ $4y + 6 = -22$

   $y = $ ___7___ ◯

   Check

⑱ $12 + 18 = 6 + 2m$

   $m = $ ___18___ ◯

   Check

Use equations to solve the problems. Then check the answers by substitution.

⑲ Each mug costs $2.40. Jackie paid $30 for a box of mugs with $1.20 change. How many mugs did Jackie buy?

_____

⑳ The sum of complementary angles is 90°. Angles A and B are complementary. If A is 3 times as big as B, what are their measures?

_____

ISBN: 978-1-77149-220-1

Find the least common denominator of the highlighted fractions. Solve equations by multiplying the L.C.D. Then check the answers.

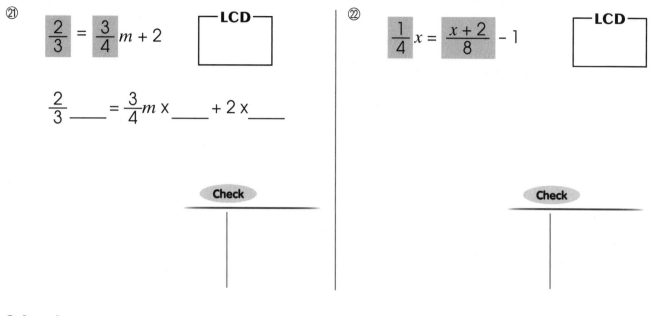

㉑
$$\frac{2}{3} = \frac{3}{4}m + 2$$

LCD

$$\frac{2}{3} \underline{\quad} = \frac{3}{4}m \times \underline{\quad} + 2 \times \underline{\quad}$$

Check

㉒
$$\frac{1}{4}x = \frac{x+2}{8} - 1$$

LCD

Check

Solve the equations.

㉓ $\dfrac{2x}{5} = 1 + \dfrac{7}{5}$ _____

㉔ $\dfrac{1}{2}x + 3 = 13$ _____

㉕ $\dfrac{6y}{7} = 3 + y$ _____

㉖ $\dfrac{4}{5}m - \dfrac{1}{3}m = 14$ _____

㉗ $\dfrac{3}{4} - y = -2y$ _____

㉘ $\dfrac{3}{10}m = 16 - \dfrac{1}{5}m$ _____

㉙ $\dfrac{10k}{3} = k + 14$ _____

㉚ $\dfrac{1}{3}x + 10 - \dfrac{1}{2}x = \dfrac{5}{6}x$ _____

㉛ $7 - p = \dfrac{p+8}{3}$ _____

㉜ $\dfrac{3y+14}{2} - 3 = \dfrac{y+18}{2} - 2$ _____

㉝ $5n = \dfrac{n}{2} - 18$ _____

㉞ $\dfrac{x-1}{6} = \dfrac{3x+9}{6} - 1$ _____

㉟ $\dfrac{i-3}{4} = 2i + 1$ _____

㊱ $8 = \dfrac{5m+3}{10} + \dfrac{3m}{5}$ _____

Example

Solve the equation with brackets.

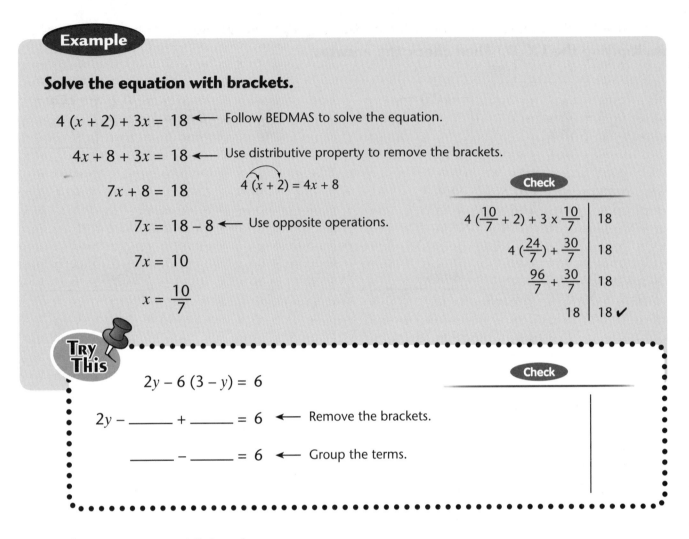

$4(x + 2) + 3x = 18$ ⟵ Follow BEDMAS to solve the equation.

$4x + 8 + 3x = 18$ ⟵ Use distributive property to remove the brackets.

$7x + 8 = 18$ $4(x + 2) = 4x + 8$

Check

$7x = 18 - 8$ ⟵ Use opposite operations.

$7x = 10$

$x = \dfrac{10}{7}$

$4(\frac{10}{7} + 2) + 3 \times \frac{10}{7}$	18
$4(\frac{24}{7}) + \frac{30}{7}$	18
$\frac{96}{7} + \frac{30}{7}$	18
18	18 ✔

TRY This

$2y - 6(3 - y) = 6$

Check

$2y - \underline{\hspace{1cm}} + \underline{\hspace{1cm}} = 6$ ⟵ Remove the brackets.

$\underline{\hspace{1cm}} - \underline{\hspace{1cm}} = 6$ ⟵ Group the terms.

Solve the equations with brackets.

③⑦ $4(2y + 1) - (3 - y) = 7$ _____

③⑧ $5x - (x - 3) = 2(x - 1)$ _____

③⑨ $(6m - 3)\,2 = 4 - 2(m + 1)$ _____

④⓪ $\dfrac{2}{3}(4b - 5) = \dfrac{1}{9}(6 - 3b)$ _____

④① $\dfrac{-3a + 2}{5} + a = \dfrac{3}{10}(3 - a)$ _____

④② $\dfrac{1}{4}k - \dfrac{k + 5}{2} = \dfrac{5}{8} + k$ _____

④③ $\dfrac{12(m + 3)}{5} - 2(m + 3) = 4(\dfrac{m + 1}{5})$ _____

④④ $\dfrac{-x}{8} + \dfrac{3x + 7}{4} = \dfrac{3(2x + 1)}{5}$ _____

   ISBN: 978-1-77149-220-1

Rearrange the formulas to isolate x.

HINT

Formulas are equations with more than one variable. To solve formulas, isolate the required variable on one side of the equation.

e.g.   Isolate x.

$$3(x + y) = h$$

$$x + y = \frac{h}{3} \quad \longleftarrow \quad \text{Divide both sides by 3.}$$

$$x = \frac{h}{3} - y \quad \longleftarrow \quad \text{Take away } y \text{ from both sides.}$$

45    $h = 2(x + y)$

46    $px + 4y = 3$

47    $g = \dfrac{ax}{6}$

48    $\dfrac{4}{3}kx = 8q$

49    $\dfrac{xb}{3} + 1 = p$

Isolate each variable in the formula "$p + qc - v = 4$". Then solve it.

50   a. $p =$ _____

    b. If $q = 3$, $c = 2$, and $v = 5$,

       then $p =$ _____ .

51   a. $q =$ _____

    b. If $p = 1$, $c = -2$, and $v = 2$,

       then $q =$ _____ .

52   a. $c =$ _____

    b. If $p = 1$, $q = 2$, and $v = -1$,

       then $c =$ _____ .

53   a. $v =$ _____

    b. If $p = q = c = -1$,

       then $v =$ _____ .

Example

Formula for finding the area of a trapezoid:

$A = \dfrac{(a + b)}{2}h$

Solve it for b.

$2A = (a + b)\, h$ ← Multiply both sides by 2.

$\dfrac{2A}{h} = a + b$ ← Divide both sides by h.

$b = \dfrac{2A}{h} - a$ ← Subtract a from both sides.

If $A = 16$ cm^2, $h = 2$ cm, $a = 4$ cm,

then $b = \dfrac{2 \times 16}{2} - 4$

$= 12$ (cm)

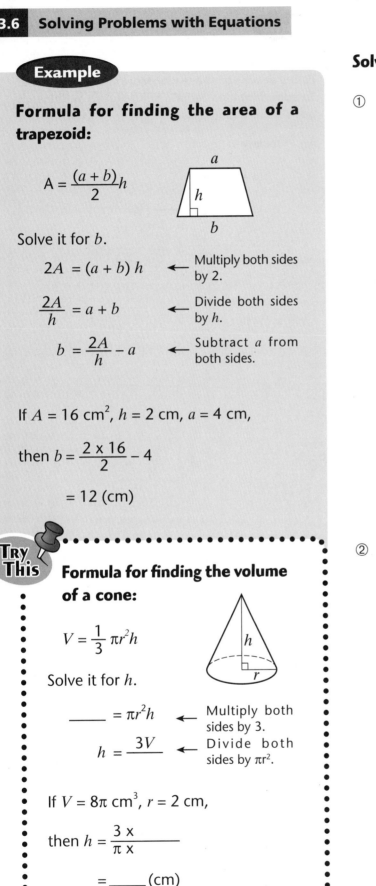

Try This

Formula for finding the volume of a cone:

$V = \dfrac{1}{3} \pi r^2 h$

Solve it for h.

_____ $= \pi r^2 h$ ← Multiply both sides by 3.

$h = \dfrac{3V}{}$ ← Divide both sides by πr^2.

If $V = 8\pi$ cm^3, $r = 2$ cm,

then $h = \dfrac{3 \times}{\pi \times}$

$=$ _____ (cm)

Solve the problems.

① $P = 2(l + w)$,

where P = perimeter of a rectangle,
  l = length, w = width

a. Find the formula for l.

_____

b. If $P = 24$ cm and $w = 4$ cm, what is l?

_____

② $C = \dfrac{5}{9}(F - 32°)$,

where C = Celsius temp.
  F = Fahrenheit temp.

a. Find the formula for F.

_____

b. If $C = 20°$, what is F?

_____

ISBN: 978-1-77149-220-1

Write an equation to solve each problem.

③ Mia earns $40 per day plus $4 for every ticket she sells. How many tickets does she need to sell each day to earn $100?

Let x be the number of tickets sold.

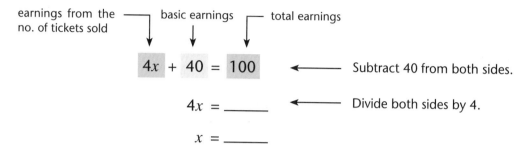

earnings from the no. of tickets sold ⟶ basic earnings ⟶ total earnings

$$4x + 40 = 100$$ ⟵ Subtract 40 from both sides.

$$4x = \underline{\hspace{1.5cm}}$$ ⟵ Divide both sides by 4.

$$x = \underline{\hspace{1.5cm}}$$

Mia needs to sell _____ tickets.

④ A taxi fare is made up of 2 charges: an initial fee of $3 plus 75¢ per km. How many kilometres can you ride with $8.25?

_____

⑤ If Uncle Tim travels at a speed of 85 km/h, how far can he go in 6 hours and 30 minutes?

_____

⑥ The temperature in Nunavut has been increasing by 0.12°C every year. If the temperature in June 2000 was 4°C, what temperature would you expect for June 2025?

_____

⑦ We need 3 eggs for every cake. How many cakes can we make with 72 eggs?

_____

ISBN: 978-1-77149-220-1

Write an equation to solve each problem.

⑧ Anna works at a furniture store. She earns commissions of 4% for selling appliances and 6% for furniture. Today she earned $120. What was her furniture sale if she sold $1800 worth of appliances?

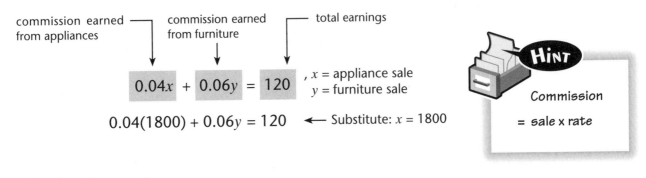

commission earned from appliances — commission earned from furniture — total earnings

$0.04x + 0.06y = 120$, x = appliance sale
y = furniture sale

$0.04(1800) + 0.06y = 120$ ← Substitute: $x = 1800$

HINT

Commission

= sale x rate

Her furniture sale was _____ .

⑨ George has a piggy bank containing dimes and nickels that are worth $3.50. If there are 25 dimes, how many nickels are there?

_____

⑩ Kelly is a technician. It takes her 3 hours to assemble a computer and 5 hours to assemble a set of stereos. Kelly worked 42 hours last week and assembled 9 computers. How many sets of stereos did she assemble?

_____

⑪ Gloria invested her money in two different stocks, $2000 in AIV and the rest in ENE. The rate of return for AIV was 5% and ENE was 12%. Last year she earned $550 from both investments. How much did she invest in ENE?

_____

ISBN: 978-1-77149-220-1

Use equations to solve the problems.

⑫   In Mrs. Shukster's class, there are 12 fewer girls than twice the number of boys. If the number of students is 33, how many girls are there?

_____

⑬   Reza is twice her sister Tammy's age. Tammy is 8 years older than Jenny. In 4 years, Reza will be 4 times Jenny's age. How old are they now?

_____

⑭   The sum of 3 consecutive odd integers is 51. What are the numbers?

_____

⑮   The ratio of white buttons to black buttons is 3:1. If there are 120 buttons in total, how many black buttons are there?

_____

⑯   An isosceles triangle and a square have the same perimeter and their total area is 42 cm². If the height of the triangle is 6 cm and the side length of the square is 4.5 cm, what is the length of one of the equal sides of the triangle?

_____

⑰   Billal earns $8/h painting and $9.50/h cutting grass. Last week he earned $162. If Billal spent 12 h on cutting grass, how much time did he spend on painting?

_____

⑱   Last Saturday the total sales of V&M Buffet were $1948.14. If 108 customers were adults, how many children were there?

_____

4 Linear Relations

4.1 Graphs and Relations

Example

Marianne walked her dog. This graph shows her distance from home during her walk. Describe her walk.

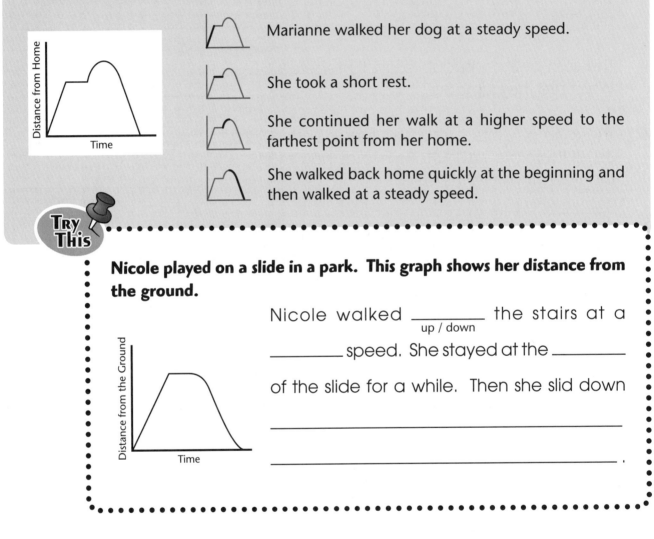

Marianne walked her dog at a steady speed.

She took a short rest.

She continued her walk at a higher speed to the farthest point from her home.

She walked back home quickly at the beginning and then walked at a steady speed.

Try This

Nicole played on a slide in a park. This graph shows her distance from the ground.

Nicole walked _____ the stairs at a
up / down

_____ speed. She stayed at the _____

of the slide for a while. Then she slid down

_____

_____ .

Match each graph with the correct description. Write the letter.

① ◯   Throw a ball in the air. It reaches a maximum height and then falls.

◯   Buy some books. The more you buy, the more you pay.

◯   Record the temperatures from 2:00 p.m. to midnight.

ISBN: 978-1-77149-220-1

Consider each situation. Describe the graph.

② the charges for a birthday party in relation to the number of guests

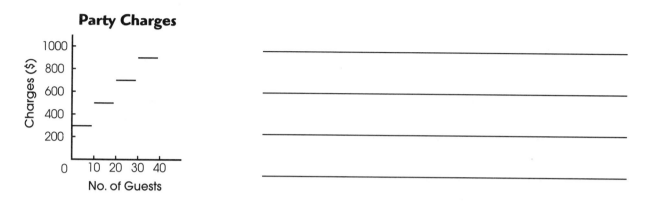

Party Charges

(graph: Charges ($) on y-axis from 200 to 1000, No. of Guests on x-axis from 0 to 40, step-shaped segments)

_____

_____

_____

_____

③ the number of bacteria reproduced in a rotten egg

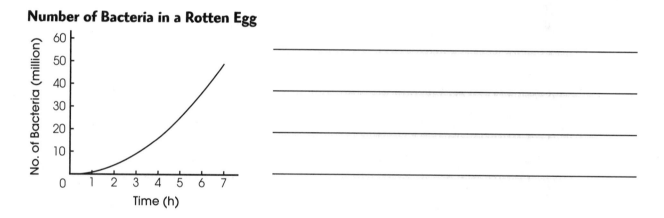

Number of Bacteria in a Rotten Egg

(graph: No. of Bacteria (million) on y-axis from 10 to 60, Time (h) on x-axis from 0 to 7, upward curve)

_____

_____

_____

_____

Make a table of values and draw a graph to show the relationship between the number of loaves and the amount of flour. Then answer the question.

④ $2\frac{1}{2}$ cups of flour are needed to bake 2 loaves of bread.

No. of Cups of Flour	No. of Loaves
$2\frac{1}{2}$	

⑤ How much flour is needed to make 10 loaves of bread? _____

Write each equation for *y* in terms of *x*. Make a table of values and draw a graph. Then fill in the blanks.

⑥ $2x + 2y = 3$

Rewrite: $2x + 2y = 3$

$$2y = \underline{\qquad} + 3$$

$$y = \underline{\qquad} + \underline{\qquad}$$

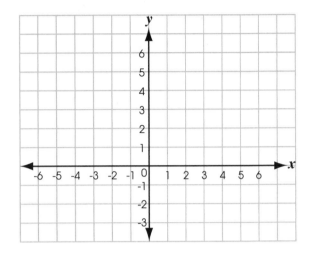

x	*y*	*(x,y)*
-4		
0		
4		

- when $x = 1$, $y = \underline{\quad}$
- when $y = \dfrac{1}{2}$, $x = \underline{\quad}$

⑦ $-y + 3x = 2$

Rewrite: _____

x	*y*	*(x,y)*
-1		
0		
2		

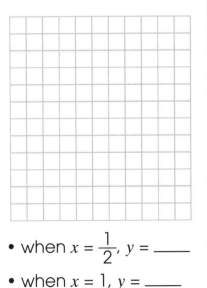

- when $x = \dfrac{1}{2}$, $y = \underline{\quad}$
- when $x = 1$, $y = \underline{\quad}$

⑧ $2x - 3y = 1$

Rewrite: _____

x	*y*	*(x,y)*
-4		
0		
2		

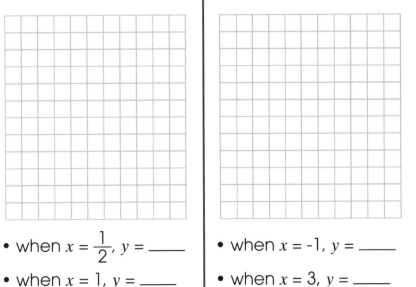

- when $x = -1$, $y = \underline{\quad}$
- when $x = 3$, $y = \underline{\quad}$

⑨ $-1 = 2y - x$

Rewrite: _____

x	*y*	*(x,y)*
-3		
-1		
5		

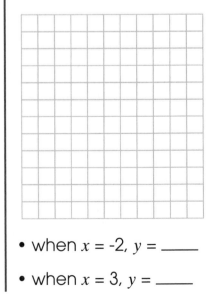

- when $x = -2$, $y = \underline{\quad}$
- when $x = 3$, $y = \underline{\quad}$

   ISBN: 978-1-77149-220-1

Trace the dotted lines to show the rise and run of each line. Complete the table. Then answer the question.

⑩

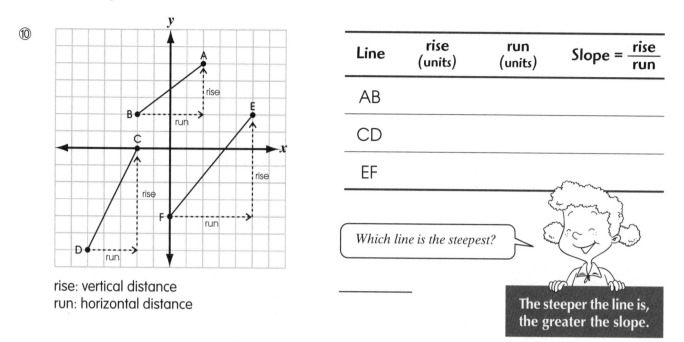

Line	rise (units)	run (units)	Slope = $\dfrac{rise}{run}$
AB			
CD			
EF			

rise: vertical distance
run: horizontal distance

Which line is the steepest?

_____

The steeper the line is, the greater the slope.

Find the slope of each line. Then fill in the blanks.

⑪

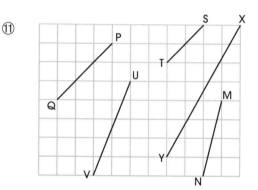

Slope   MN: _____   ST: _____   PQ: _____

UV: _____   XY: _____

Which two lines have the same slope?

_____

CHALLENGE

A ladder is leaning against the wall with a slope of 3. The foot of the ladder is x m from the wall. Find the value of x to determine the distance between the top of the ladder and the ground.

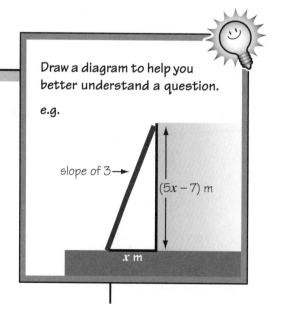

Draw a diagram to help you better understand a question.

e.g.

slope of 3 → $(5x - 7)$ m

x m

ISBN: 978-1-77149-220-1   COMPLETE MATHSMART (GRADE 9)   **73**

4.2 Linear and Non-linear Relations

WOrds TO LEARN

Linear relation: the relationship exhibited by two variables that appears as a straight line when graphed on a coordinate system

Non-linear relation: the relationship exhibited by two variables that does not fit a straight line when graphed on a coordinate system

Example

Plot the points on the grids. Then answer the questions.

The points (4,1), (1,4), and (4,7) are the vertices of a square. What are the coordinates of the fourth vertex of the square?

This is the 4th vertex. Its coordinates are (7,4).

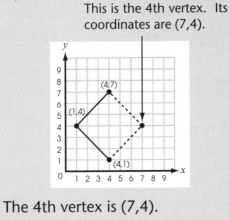

The 4th vertex is (7,4).

Try This

The line joining the points (5,0) and (5,8) is the hypotenuse of a right triangle. What are the possible coordinates of the third vertex of the right triangle?

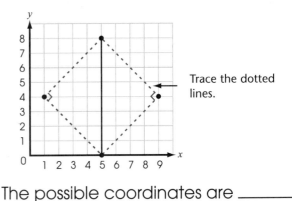

Trace the dotted lines.

The possible coordinates are _____

_____ .

Plot the points on the grid. Then write what geometric figure is formed by each group of points.

① (1,10), (5,9), (7,4), (2,6) _____

② (1,4), (4,6), (4,0), (1,1) _____

③ (8,8), (11,8), (12,5), (11,2), (8,2), (9,5)

_____

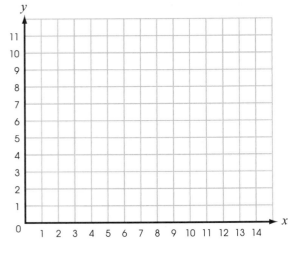

ISBN: 978-1-77149-220-1

Plot the points on the grid. Then answer the questions.

④ Plot these points on the grid. Then join the points.

A(-6,-4)   B(-4,4)   C(-2,-4)   D(0,4)   E(2,-4)   F(4,4)

a.

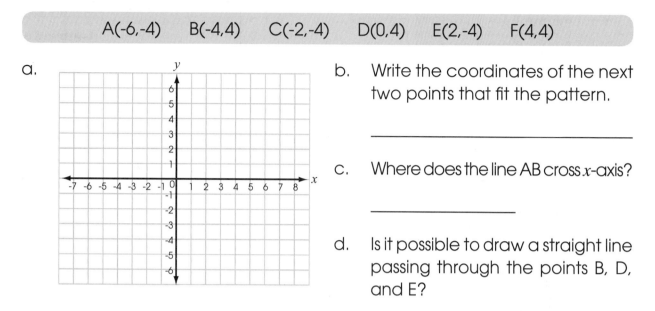

b. Write the coordinates of the next two points that fit the pattern.

_____

c. Where does the line AB cross x-axis?

_____

d. Is it possible to draw a straight line passing through the points B, D, and E?

_____

⑤ Plot each group of points on the grid. Then join the points to form the right triangles.

Triangle A
(-3,4), (3,4), (3,-4)

Triangle B
(-6,4), (-2,-2), (-6,-2)

Triangle C
(4,0), (7,-4), (4,-4)

a.

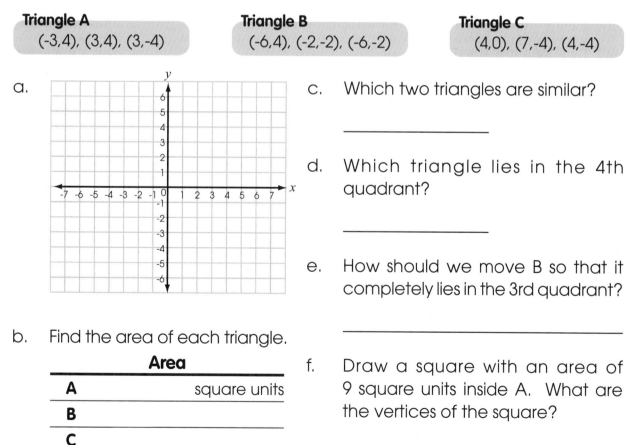

c. Which two triangles are similar?

_____

d. Which triangle lies in the 4th quadrant?

_____

e. How should we move B so that it completely lies in the 3rd quadrant?

_____

b. Find the area of each triangle.

	Area	
A		square units
B		
C		

f. Draw a square with an area of 9 square units inside A. What are the vertices of the square?

_____

ISBN: 978-1-77149-220-1

State whether each graph shows a linear or non-linear relationship.

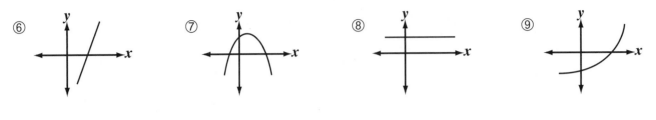

⑥ _____ ⑦ _____ ⑧ _____ ⑨ _____

Complete the table of values and graph the relations. Then answer the questions.

⑩ Movie tickets cost $9.00 each.

a.

No. of Tickets	Total Cost ($)
0	0
1	9
2	
3	
4	

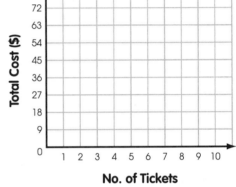

Cost of Movie Tickets

b. Describe the graph.

_____

c. What is the total cost of 7 tickets?   _____

⑪ Jasmine walks 0.15 km/min.

a.

Time (min)	Distance Travelled (km)
0	0
1	0.15
2	
3	
4	

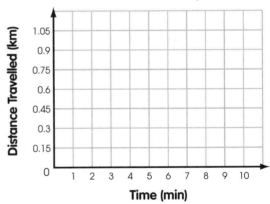

Distance Travelled by Jasmine

b. Describe the graph.

_____

c. How far can Jasmine walk in 5 min?   _____

d. How long does it take Jasmine to walk 0.9 km?   _____

ISBN: 978-1-77149-220-1

⑫ Here are the points: A(-2,9), B(-1,8), C(1,6), D(2,5), E(4,3), F(6,1).

a.   Find the sum of the coordinates of each ordered pair. What do you notice?

sum of the coordinates: A: ___   B: ___   C: ___   D: ___   E: ___   F: ___

_____

b.   Plot the points on the grid. Then describe the graph.

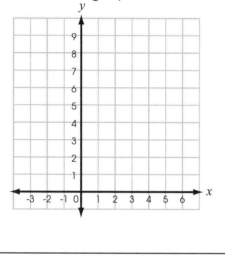

_____

_____

c.   Does the point (8,-2) fit the pattern?

_____

d.   Write the coordinates of two other points that fit the pattern.

_____

e.   Check the equation that matches the graph.

Ⓐ $y - x = 7$

Ⓑ $x + y = 7$

Ⓒ $x = 7 + y$

⑬ Eddie uses 24 1-cm sticks to build rectangles.

a.   Find the possible widths and lengths of different rectangles. Then graph the relation.

Width (cm)	Length (cm)
1	11
2	
3	
4	
5	
6	

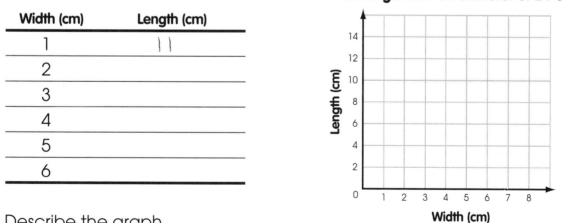

Rectangle with a Perimeter of 24 cm

b.   Describe the graph.

_____

c.   Does the line intersect the *x*-axis or the *y*-axis? Explain.

_____

ISBN: 978-1-77149-220-1

Example

For each relationship, make a table of values. Then graph the relation and describe it.

Graph $y = 10 - 2x$. Use -2, 0, and 2 for the x-coordinates.

Table of Values:

x	y	$\leftarrow 10 - 2x$
-2	14	$\leftarrow 10 - 2(-2) = 14$
0	10	$\leftarrow 10 - 2(0) = 10$
2	6	$\leftarrow 10 - 2(2) = 6$

Plot the points:

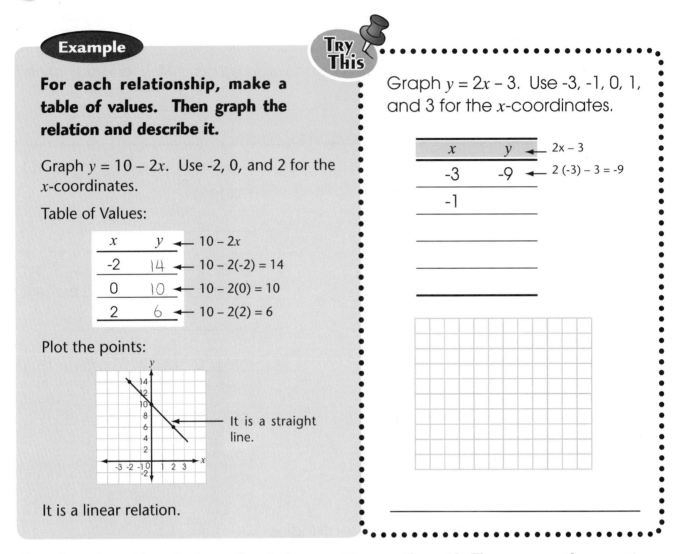

It is a straight line.

It is a linear relation.

Try This

Graph $y = 2x - 3$. Use -3, -1, 0, 1, and 3 for the x-coordinates.

x	y	$\leftarrow 2x - 3$
-3	-9	$\leftarrow 2(-3) - 3 = -9$
-1		

_____

Complete the tables of values. Graph the equations on the grid. Then answer the questions.

⑭

$y = x - 1$

x	-3	0	3
y			

$y = x + 1$

x	-3	0	3
y			

$y = x + 3$

x	-3	0	3
y			

Describe the lines on the grid.

_____

_____

  ISBN: 978-1-77149-220-1

For each relationship, make a table of values and graph it. Then find the *x*-intercept and *y*-intercept.

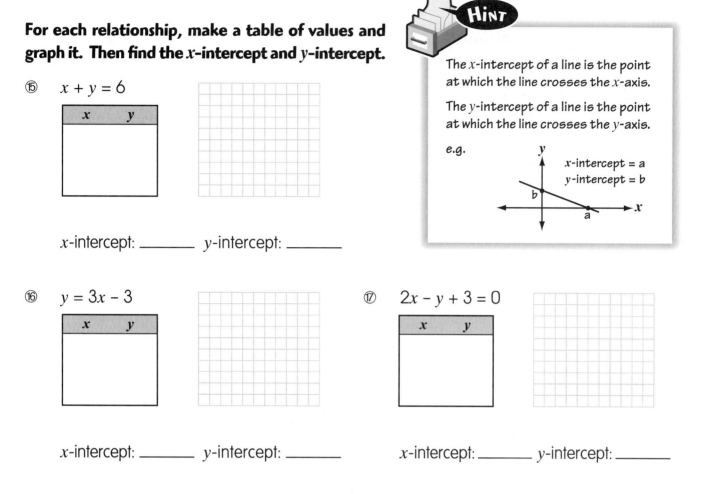

⑮ $x + y = 6$

x	*y*

x-intercept: _____   *y*-intercept: _____

HINT

The *x*-intercept of a line is the point at which the line crosses the *x*-axis.

The *y*-intercept of a line is the point at which the line crosses the *y*-axis.

e.g.

x-intercept = a
y-intercept = b

⑯ $y = 3x - 3$

x	*y*

x-intercept: _____   *y*-intercept: _____

⑰ $2x - y + 3 = 0$

x	*y*

x-intercept: _____   *y*-intercept: _____

Solve the problems.

⑱   A bag of mixed nuts containing peanuts and almonds weighs 9 kg. Make a table of values to graph their relationships.

a. $x + y = 9$, where *x* – amount of peanuts
                          y – amount of almonds

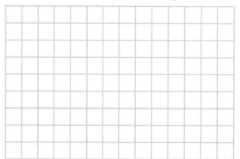

x	*y*

_____

Amount of Peanuts and Almonds in a Bag

b.   What do the *x*-intercept and *y*-intercept of the line mean in this situation?

4.3 Direct and Partial Variations

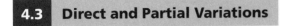

WORDS TO LEARN

Direct variation:

a relation where two variable quantities have a constant ratio called the constant of variation. The formula for direct variation is $y = kx$, where k = constant of variation.

$y = kx$

• a straight line passing through the origin

Partial variation:

a relation where one variable is a constant of the other, plus another constant. The formula for partial variation is $y = kx + c$, where k = constant of variation and $c \neq 0$.

$y = kx + c$

• a straight line passing through the y-axis at c

Example

Look at the lines on the graph. State whether it shows a direct variation, a partial variation, or neither.

$L_1 \longleftarrow$ a straight line intersecting the y-axis

$L_2 \longleftarrow$ a straight line passing through the origin

L_1: ___a partial variation___ L_2: ___a direct variation___

TRY THIS

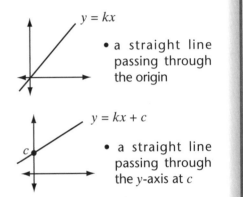

L_1: _____

L_2: _____

L_3: _____

L_4: _____

State whether each equation represents a direct or partial variation. Then find the constant of variation and constant term.

	Variation	Constant of Variation	Constant Term
① $y = \dfrac{1}{3}x + 6$	_____	_____	_____
② $4y = -16x$	_____	_____	_____
③ $2x - y = 9$	_____	_____	_____
④ $\dfrac{1}{2}x + 10 - y = 6$	_____	_____	_____

ISBN: 978-1-77149-220-1

Write an algebraic equation to match each situation. Then state each situation as a direct or partial variation.

⑤ The cost of staying in a hotel is $89/night.

$$\boxed{} = 89\ \boxed{}\ ,\quad \text{where } y = \text{the total cost} \atop \text{and } x = \text{no. of nights}$$

It is a _____ variation.

⑥ The cost of renting a car is $50/day plus $25 service charge.

_____

⑦ The speed of sound in air is 331.4 m/s plus 0.6 m/s for each degree Celsius above zero.

_____

⑧ There are 16 floor tiles in each row.

_____

Make a table of values for each of the situations above. Then graph it and state whether it is a linear or non-linear relation.

⑨
Total Cost

x	y
0	
2	
4	

It is a _____ relation.

⑩
Cost of Renting

x	y
1	
2	
3	

It is a _____ relation.

⑪
Speed of Sound

x	y
0	
10	
20	

It is a _____ relation.

⑫
Total No. of Tiles

x	y
0	
4	
8	

It is a _____ relation.

Complete the difference table for each table of values. Then state whether the data represents a linear or non-linear relationship.

⑬

x	y	Δy
1	6	
2	11	11 – 6 =
3	16	16 – 11 =
4	21	

a _____ relationship

⑭

x	y	Δy
2	11	
4	15	15 – 11 =
6	26	
8	43	

a _____ relationship

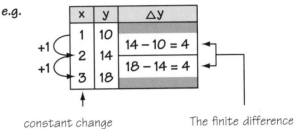

HINT

A table of values represents a linear relationship if the finite differences are the same for each row in the difference table*.

e.g.

x	y	Δy
1	10	14 – 10 = 4
2	14	18 – 14 = 4
3	18	

+1, +1 constant change

The finite difference is always 4.

So, this relationship is linear.

* Make sure that the values for the independent variables are put in order from smallest to largest.

⑮

x	4	2	3	1
y	8	24	11	5

x	y	Δy

a _____ relationship

⑯

x	4	3	6	5
y	24	18	36	30

x	y	Δy

a _____ relationship

Identify the data above that has a linear relationship. Graph it. Then state whether it shows a direct or partial variation.

⑰

_____

_____

ISBN: 978-1-77149-220-1

Complete the difference table to show that the relationship is linear. Then find and use the equation of the relationship to solve the problems.

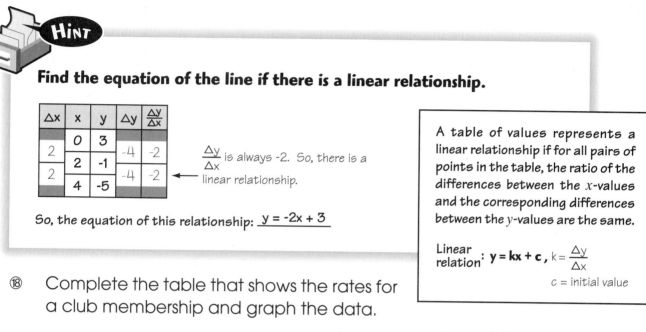

HINT

Find the equation of the line if there is a linear relationship.

Δx	x	y	Δy	$\frac{\Delta y}{\Delta x}$
	0	3		
2			-4	-2
	2	-1		
2			-4	-2
	4	-5		

$\frac{\Delta y}{\Delta x}$ is always -2. So, there is a linear relationship.

So, the equation of this relationship: $\underline{y = -2x + 3}$

A table of values represents a linear relationship if for all pairs of points in the table, the ratio of the differences between the x-values and the corresponding differences between the y-values are the same.

Linear relation: $\mathbf{y = kx + c}$, $k = \frac{\Delta y}{\Delta x}$

c = initial value

⑱ Complete the table that shows the rates for a club membership and graph the data.

a.

Δx	x	y	Δy	$\frac{\Delta y}{\Delta x}$
	0	90		
	3	135		
	6	180		
	9	225		

x: no. of months y: membership fees

Rates of Membership

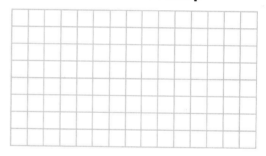

b. The equation of this relationship:

_____

c. The membership fees for 1 year:

_____

⑲ Complete the table that shows the cost of renting a party room and graph it.

a.

Δx	x	y	Δy	$\frac{\Delta y}{\Delta x}$
	5	60		
	10	120		
	15	180		
	20	240		

x: no. of guests y: total cost

Cost of Renting a Party Room

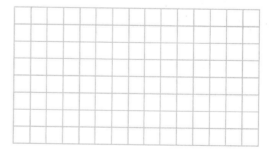

b. The equation of this relationship:

_____

c. The total cost for 30 guests:

_____

ISBN: 978-1-77149-220-1

Plot a scatter plot for each group of data. Tell whether it indicates a positive or negative correlation. Draw the line of best fit. Then check the most appropriate equation to match the line.

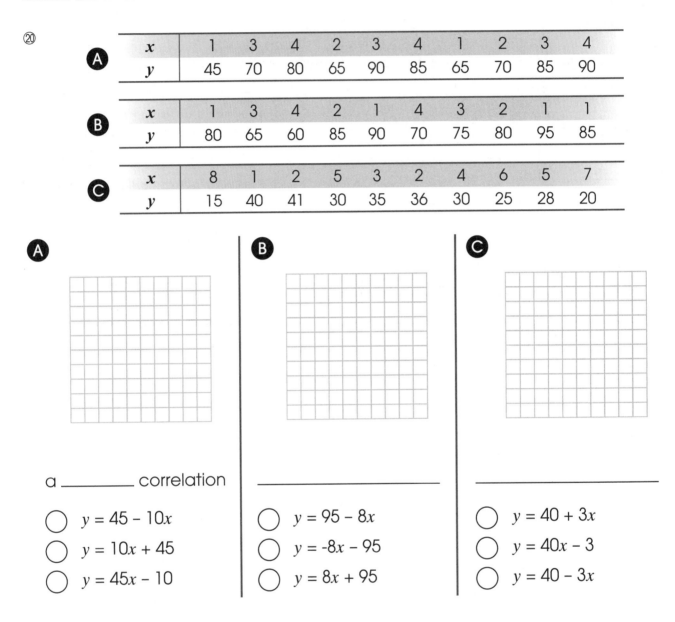

㉑

x	1	3	4	2	3	4	1	2	3	4
y	45	70	80	65	90	85	65	70	85	90

Ⓑ

x	1	3	4	2	1	4	3	2	1	1
y	80	65	60	85	90	70	75	80	95	85

Ⓒ

x	8	1	2	5	3	2	4	6	5	7
y	15	40	41	30	35	36	30	25	28	20

Ⓐ

a _____ correlation

○ $y = 45 - 10x$
○ $y = 10x + 45$
○ $y = 45x - 10$

Ⓑ

_____

○ $y = 95 - 8x$
○ $y = -8x - 95$
○ $y = 8x + 95$

Ⓒ

_____

○ $y = 40 + 3x$
○ $y = 40x - 3$
○ $y = 40 - 3x$

Find the missing number of the equation of the line of best fit that matches each group of data.

㉑

x	y
1	3
2	4
3	4.8
5	8
6	7.5

$y = x + \boxed{}$

㉒

x	y
1	3.1
2	6.4
3	9
4	13
5	14.6

$y = \boxed{} x$

㉓

x	y
1	-4.1
2	-2
4	0
5	1.2
7	2.8

$y = x - \boxed{}$

ISBN: 978-1-77149-220-1

Plot the points on a scatter plot. Tell whether the plot indicates a positive or negative correlation. Then draw the line of best fit and answer the questions.

㉔

a.

Red Wine

Age (years)	Price ($)
1	12
2	24
3	34
2	23
5	60
4	50
3	33
4	47
5	62
1	13
3	35

Price of a Bottle of Red Wine and its Age

Price ($)

Age of Wine (Year)

b. This indicates a _____ correlation.

c. Suggest an equation in the form $y = kx$ for the line of best fit. _____

d. If the price of a bottle of wine is about $83, predict the age of the wine. _____

㉕

a.

Speed (km/h)	Time (h)
60	5.6
65	5.2
70	4.9
40	8.5
50	7
60	5.7
90	3.6
80	4.3
85	4
90	3.9
45	7.6

Time Taken to Drive from Town A to Town B at Different Speeds

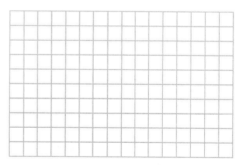

b. This indicates a _____ correlation.

c. Suggest an equation in the form $y = kx + 12$ for the line of best fit. _____

d. If the speed of the car is 75 km/h, predict how long it takes to drive from Town A to Town B. _____

ISBN: 978-1-77149-220-1

4.4 Applying Linear Models

Example

Explain what the coordinates of all points on each line have in common.

1. **the x-axis**

   The y-coordinates of all the points on the x-axis are 0.

   e.g. (5,0) and (-3,0) are the points on the x-axis.

2. **any horizontal line**

   The y-coordinates of all the points on the same horizontal line are the same.

   e.g. (4,5) and (-3,5) are on the same horizontal line.

TRY This

① the y-axis

_____

_____

_____

② any vertical line

_____

_____

_____

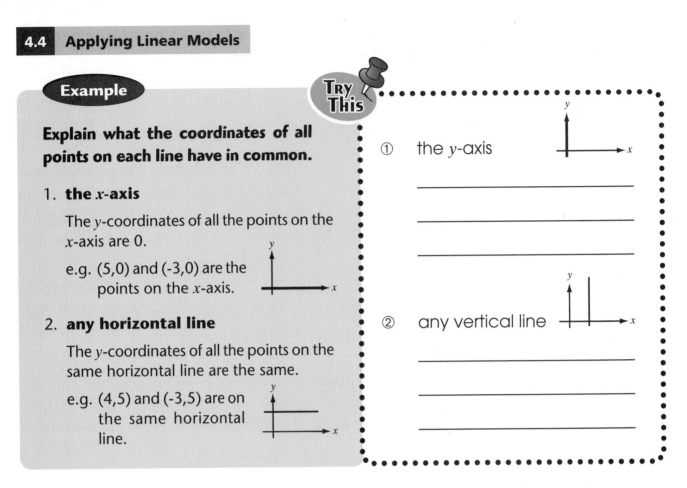

Plot the points on the grid. Join the points in order. Then answer the questions.

① (-7,0), (-2,-1), (-1,-6), (-6,-5)

a.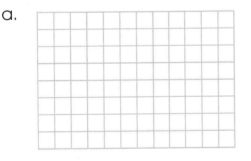

b. What geometric figure is formed?

_____

c. Draw the diagonal lines. What are the coordinates of the point of intersection?

_____

② (-3,-3), (-3,-1), (-1,-1), (-1,1), (1,1)

a.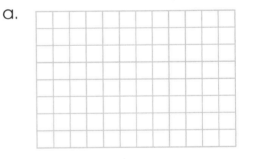

b. Write the coordinates of the two points that come next.

_____

c. How long is each line segment?

_____

ISBN: 978-1-77149-220-1

Check the equations that show either a direct or partial variation. Then write scenarios to match with the equations.

③   (A) $y = 3x$ _____

    (B) $y = x^2 + 6$ _____

    (C) $y = 5 - 2x$ _____

    (D) $x + x^2 = y$ _____

Solve the problems.

④   An apple orchard charges a flat fee of $4.00 plus $1.25/kg of apples picked.

    a.   Write an algebraic equation for this relation.

        _____

    b.   Is this relation a direct or partial relation? Explain.

        _____

    c.   Use the equation to find the charge for apples picked.

        • 5 kg   _____

        • 12 kg   _____

        • 30 kg   _____

⑤   Riders have two options to buy tickets. Write the algebraic equations for both options. Then make the tables of values and graph the data.

    a.   Option A: Pay $1.50 per ride

        _____

        Option B: Pay $8.00 plus $0.50 per ride

        _____

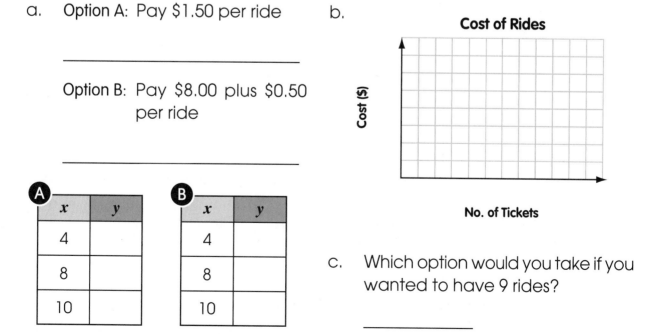

    b.   **Cost of Rides**

        Cost ($) / No. of Tickets

A	x	y
	4	
	8	
	10	

B	x	y
	4	
	8	
	10	

    c.   Which option would you take if you wanted to have 9 rides?

        _____

ISBN: 978-1-77149-220-1

Plot a scatter plot. Tell whether it indicates a positive or negative correlation. Draw the line of best fit and fill in the missing numbers in the equation of the line of best fit that matches the plot.

⑥

x	4	1	0	5	2	3	4	2	0	3	1	1
y	31	65	73	38	54	40	35	56	78	46	62	60

a.

b. It indicates a _____ correlation.

c. The equation of the line of best fit:

$$y = \boxed{} \; x + \boxed{}$$

Plot the points on a scatter plot. Then answer the questions.

⑦ The table shows the prices of some magazines in Canada and in the United States.

Magazine	Price	
	CAD $	USD $
Puppy Palace	5.00	4.50
Cat Craze	4.60	4.25
Healthy Eating	4.10	3.75
Fashion World	6.20	5.60
Design & Decor	8.25	7.40
Games Day	8.90	8.25
Tekkies	7.05	6.45
Home & Garden	5.50	5.25
Kidds	6.85	6.00

a.

Price of Magazine

Price in US $

Price in Canadian $

b. Is there a positive or negative correlation between the 2 variables? _____

c. Draw a line of best fit on the scatter plot. Then write a possible equation for the line of best fit. _____

d. If a magazine costs 7.75 Canadian dollars, how much does it cost in US dollars? _____

ISBN: 978-1-77149-220-1

Solve the problems.

⑧ If y varies directly with x and $y = 30$ when $x = 6$, find y when $x = 2$.

_____

⑨ If y varies directly with x and the constant of variation is 12, find y when $x = 9$.

_____

⑩ If y varies partial directly with x, the constant of variation is 4, and the constant term is 3, find y when $x = 6$.

_____

⑪ If y varies partial directly with x, the constant of variation is $\frac{1}{2}$, and $y = 18$ when $x = 20$, find the constant term.

_____

⑫ Complete the table that shows the earnings of Uncle Tim and graph the data.

a.

Δx	x	y	Δy	$\dfrac{\Delta y}{\Delta x}$
	0	500		
	10	620		
	20	740		
	30	860		

x: no. of hours y: total earnings ($)

Uncle Tim's Earnings

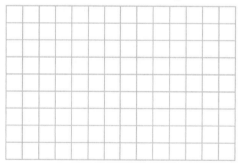

b. What is the basic salary of Uncle Tim? What is his hourly rate?

_____

c. The equation of this relationship: _____

d. Use the equation to find the earnings of Uncle Tim if he works for 60 hours.

_____

e. If the basic salary of Uncle Tim is $600, how much will he earn in 50 hours?

_____

ISBN: 978-1-77149-220-1

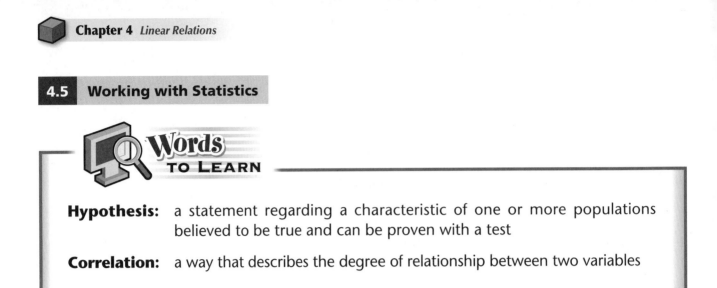

4.5 Working with Statistics

Words TO LEARN

Hypothesis: a statement regarding a characteristic of one or more populations believed to be true and can be proven with a test

Correlation: a way that describes the degree of relationship between two variables

Example

Determine the hypothesis, primary, and secondary data from each situation.

Connie operates a small restaurant serving lunch and dinner. She thinks ← hypothesis
that adding breakfast could bring in more profit. Before doing so,
however, Connie surveys her customers. She also gathers data and ← primary data
information from magazines and the Internet. Then she organizes the ← secondary data
data by putting them in charts and graphs to help her reach a conclusion.

 Try This

Highlight the sentences with the specified highlighters.

red – hypothesis   **yellow** – primary data
green – secondary data

A battery manufacturer claims that its batteries, used on a specified MP3 player, last at least 8 hours longer than other batteries. Jason performs experiments to test the lifetime of this brand and three other brands. He also collects information from consumer reports. Then he organizes the data and makes a conclusion.

Write a hypothesis for each situation.

① amount of water, height of a tree

_____

② number of hours watching TV, scores on a Science test

_____

Use cluster and stratified sampling methods to select a sample for the situation.

③ Find the favourite computer games for kids 7–10 years old in your area.

- **Cluster Sampling**

_____

_____

_____

- **Stratified Sampling**

Cluster Sampling

These groups of samples have common locations or features. For example, in a survey of a school, randomly select 2 classes and ask every student in those classes.

Stratified Sampling

The population is divided into groups and then 5–10% of each group is surveyed.

_____

_____

_____

Which types of graphs have the specified characteristics? Write "Bar graphs", "Circle graphs", or "Broken line graphs" on the lines. Then use an appropriate graph to show the data.

④ _____ : showing changes in data over time

_____ : showing the frequencies of different categories

_____ : showing what percent a particular item represents a part of a set of data

The Change in Gasoline Prices*
in a Week in February (*per Litre)

Day	Price ($)
Sun	1.07
Mon	1.10
Tue	1.02
Wed	1.03
Thu	1.01
Fri	1.09
Sat	1.12

Describe the correlation of data that each scatter plot shows.

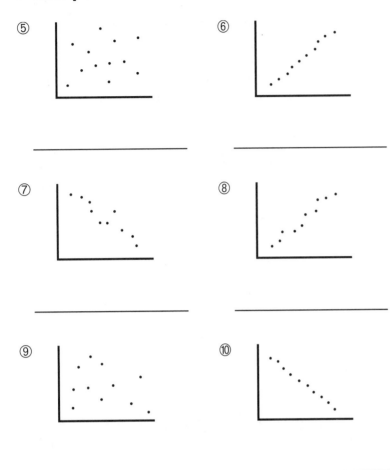

⑤ _____

⑥ _____

⑦ _____

⑧ _____

⑨ _____

⑩ _____

Scatter Plots

- A graph that shows the relationship between a dependent variable and an independent variable

Correlation of Data

- Strong Positive Correlation

- Weak Positive Correlation

- Strong Negative Correlation

- Weak Negative Correlation

- No Correlation

Draw a scatter plot to show the data. Then describe the correlation and fill in the blanks.

⑪ The average height of children of different ages:

Age (year)	4	5	6	7	8	9	10
Average Height (cm)	103	109	114	120	126	130	139

x-axis (independent variable): _____

y-axis (dependent variable): _____

⑫ It shows a _____ correlation. As the children get older,

_____ .

ISBN: 978-1-77149-220-1

Draw the line of best fit. Then describe the correlation and answer the questions.

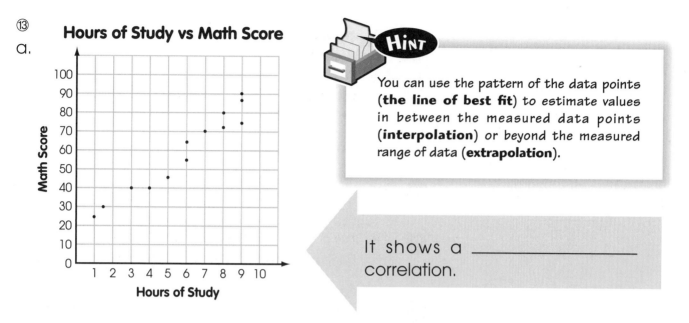

⑬

a. **Hours of Study vs Math Score**

It shows a _____
correlation.

b. Describe the trend shown in the data.

_____

c. How many hours of study will be needed to get 100 marks on the Math test? Did you use interpolation or extrapolation to find the answer?

_____

Make a scatter plot and draw the line of best fit. Then describe the correlation and answer the question.

⑭

Concentration (%)	0	5	10	15	20	25	30	35	40
Decrease (%) in Mosquito Population	2	7	13	20	27	31	35	39	43

a.

b. It shows a _____ correlation.

c. Predict the decrease in population when the concentration is at 23%. Did you use interpolation or extrapolation to find the answer?

_____

_____

Match each distance-time graph with the correct description. Write the letter.

⑮

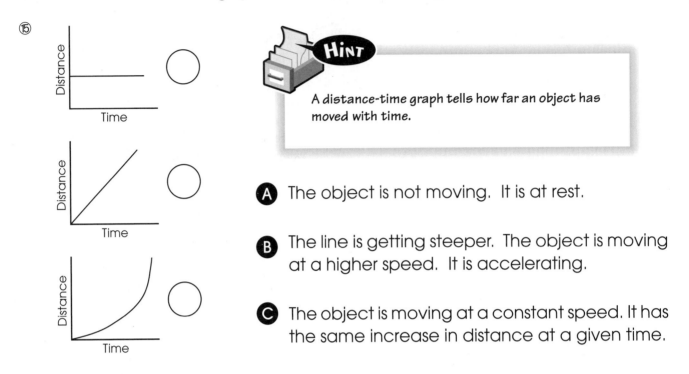

A distance-time graph tells how far an object has moved with time.

A The object is not moving. It is at rest.

B The line is getting steeper. The object is moving at a higher speed. It is accelerating.

C The object is moving at a constant speed. It has the same increase in distance at a given time.

Sketch a distance-time graph to match each description.

⑯ Michael walked at a steady speed to school and stayed at his school for a while. Then he went back home at a higher speed.

⑰ Mr. Smith drove at a steady speed to his office for half an hour. Then he increased his speed gradually until he arrived at his office.

⑱ Tim and Tiffany started racing to a park. They both ran at a constant speed, but Tim's speed was higher.

⑲ A bus accelerates when it leaves the station. Then it moves at a steady speed. Afterwards, it decelerates to stop.

Look at the distance-time graph. Answer the questions.

A Race among 3 Runners

⑳ How long was the race? Which runner won the race?

_____

㉑ Write a description of each runner and tell how long it took each of them to complete the race.

Wayne: _____

_____

Sam: _____

_____

Ted: _____

_____

Draw a distance-time graph to illustrate each paragraph.

㉒ Ali left home at 7:45 a.m. yesterday and walked to school at a steady speed. Midway, he realized that he had left his lunch at home. So, he walked back home at a faster steady speed and he reached home at 8:05 a.m. He left home quickly and ran to school, increasing his speed gradually. Finally, he arrived at school at 8:20 a.m.

If Ali did not go back home and walked at a steady speed to school, at what time would he arrive at his school?

_____

ISBN: 978-1-77149-220-1

| 4.6 | **Reading and Interpreting Graphs** |

Example

TRY THIS

State a hypothesis for each situation. Then write a primary source and a secondary source to collect the data.

no. of recycle posters displayed versus the no. of the plastic bottles collected

Hypothesis: The more posters are displayed, the more plastic bottles are collected.

Primary source: Survey your friends and neighbours.

Secondary source: Do research on the Internet.

the household income versus the household expenditure

Hypothesis:

_____

_____

Primary source:

_____

_____

Secondary source:

_____

_____

State a hypothesis and describe how to obtain the primary data by using the specified sampling method to select a sample for each situation.

① the favourite comics in your age group and the prices of the comics

Hypothesis: _____

Cluster sampling: _____

② the number of students in a class versus their performance

Hypothesis: _____

_____

Stratified sampling: _____

_____

HINT

See p.91 if you are unsure about the definitions of cluster sampling and stratified sampling.

Look at the graphs. Answer the questions.

③ a. Describe the trend in ice cream sales.

_____

_____

b. Predict the amount of ice cream sales for December. Plot your prediction on the graph.

_____

_____

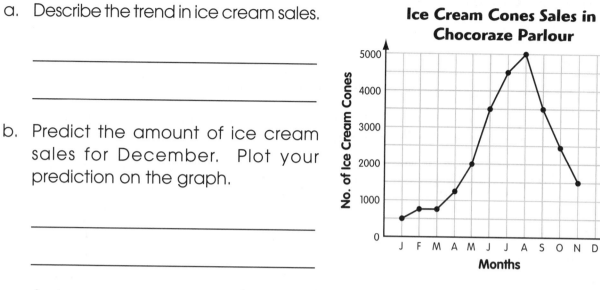

Ice Cream Cones Sales in Chocoraze Parlour

c. An ice cream cone costs $2. What was the total revenue for Chocoraze Parlour last year?

_____

d. Is it appropriate to use a broken-line graph to display the data? Explain.

_____

④ 20 Grade 9 students were surveyed to determine if there is a relationship between the number of hours of exercise and test scores. The results were plotted in a scatter plot.

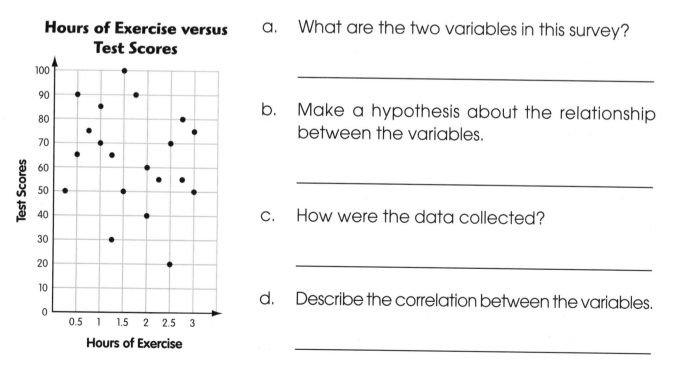

Hours of Exercise versus Test Scores

a. What are the two variables in this survey?

_____

b. Make a hypothesis about the relationship between the variables.

_____

c. How were the data collected?

_____

d. Describe the correlation between the variables.

_____

ISBN: 978-1-77149-220-1

Make a scatter plot and draw the line of best fit. Then describe the correlation and answer the questions.

⑤ The weights and heights of 10 Grade 9 students were collected. Plot the data and draw the line of best fit.

Weight (kg)	51	58	59	48	60	57	53	59	56	51
Height (cm)	150	157	157	149	164	156	154	163	154	153

a.

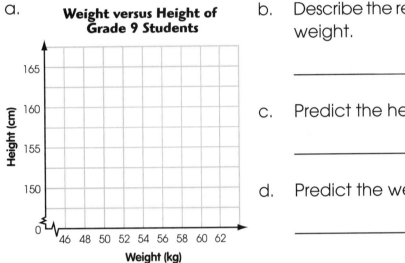

Weight versus Height of Grade 9 Students

b. Describe the relationship between height and weight.

_____

c. Predict the height of a 63-kg student.

_____

d. Predict the weight of a 155-cm-tall student.

_____

⑥ The weights of 20 6-year-old children were collected and compared to their weights at 1 month old. Plot the data and draw the line of best fit.

(weights (kg) at 1 month old versus weights (kg) at 6 years old)

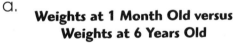

(2.7, 18.2)	(4.5, 27.3)	(4, 25)	(4.2, 22.7)	(3, 17.4)	(4, 25.8)	(4.3, 24.2)	(4, 24.6)
(5, 23.6)	(3.4, 18.5)	(3.8, 21.8)	(5, 26.4)	(3.6, 20.2)	(4.8, 24.5)	(5.5, 27.4)	(4.9, 22.8)
(4.6, 24)	(5.1, 26.2)	(4.3, 24)	(3.8, 21.8)				

a.

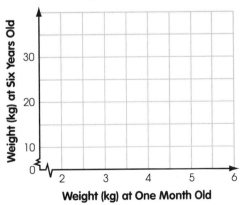

Weights at 1 Month Old versus Weights at 6 Years Old

b. Make a hypothesis about the relationship between the variables.

_____

c. Describe the correlation between the variables.

_____

d. Predict the weight of a 6-year-old child who weighed 6 kg at 1 month old.

_____

   ISBN: 978-1-77149-220-1

Solve the problems.

⑦ Esther wants to open a tutoring school. Before finding a location, she wants to gather some data to support her decision.

a. What data should Esther collect? Give 3 ideas.

- _____

- _____

- _____

b. How might she collect the data? Give some suggestions.

_____

c. Esther wants to survey the parents in the area about their views on tutoring. Suggest a question she can use to ask the parents.

_____

d. Explain how Esther can conduct a fair stratified sampling for her survey.

_____

⑧ David left home at 11:00 a.m. to meet his friends at a library yesterday. The graph shows his distance from home and the time elapsed.

a. What is the distance between the library and David's house?

_____

b. How long did David stay in the library?

_____

c. Write a description of David's journey.

_____

_____

Distance Travelled by David

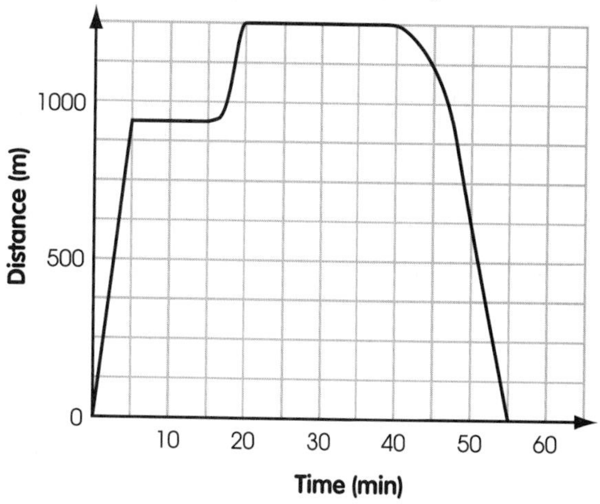

5 Analytic Geometry

5.1 Slope

Slope of a line: the slope of a line measures the steepness and shows the direction

$$\text{Slope} = \frac{\text{rise}}{\text{run}} = \frac{\text{change in } y\text{-coordinates}}{\text{change in } x\text{-coordinates}}$$

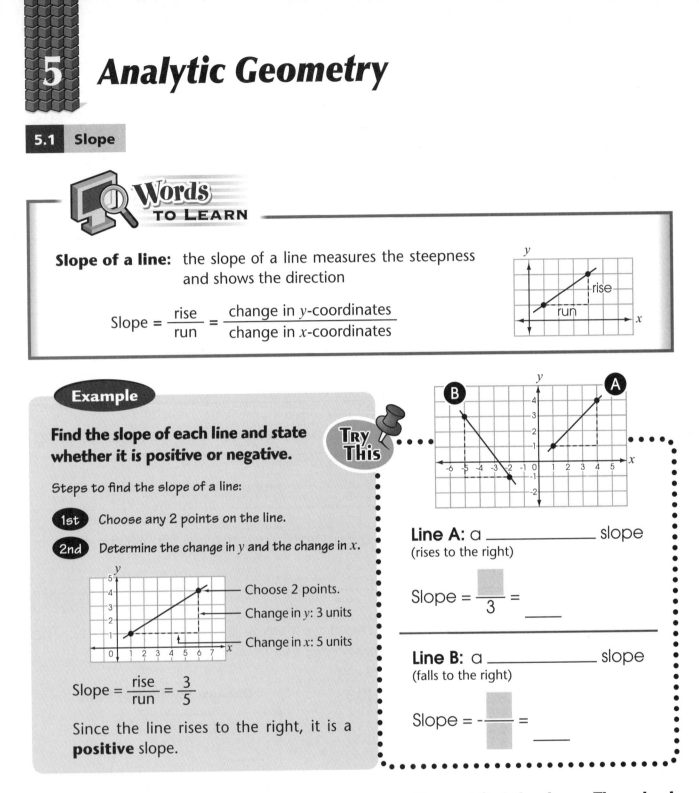

Example

Find the slope of each line and state whether it is positive or negative.

TRY This

Steps to find the slope of a line:

1st Choose any 2 points on the line.

2nd Determine the change in y and the change in x.

— Choose 2 points.
— Change in y: 3 units
— Change in x: 5 units

$$\text{Slope} = \frac{\text{rise}}{\text{run}} = \frac{3}{5}$$

Since the line rises to the right, it is a **positive** slope.

Line A: a _____ slope
(rises to the right)

$$\text{Slope} = \frac{\boxed{}}{3} = \underline{}$$

Line B: a _____ slope
(falls to the right)

$$\text{Slope} = -\frac{\boxed{}}{\boxed{}} = \underline{}$$

State whether the slope of each line is positive or negative and find the slope. Then check the steepest line.

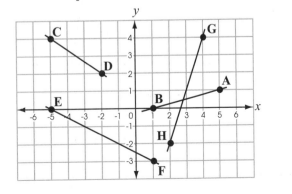

① $\overline{AB}$: a _____ slope ; _____ ◯

$\overline{CD}$: a _____ slope ; _____ ◯

$\overline{EF}$: a _____ slope ; _____ ◯

$\overline{GH}$: a _____ slope ; _____ ◯

ISBN: 978-1-77149-220-1

Complete the slope formula. Then apply the formula to find the slope of the line passing through each pair of points.

②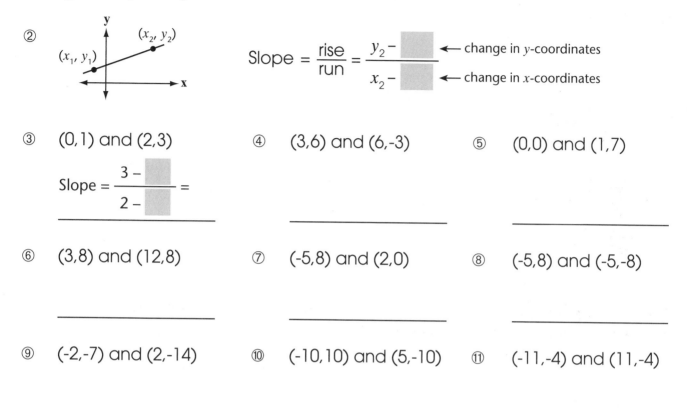

$$\text{Slope} = \frac{\text{rise}}{\text{run}} = \frac{y_2 - \boxed{}}{x_2 - \boxed{}}$$ ← change in y-coordinates
← change in x-coordinates

③ (0,1) and (2,3)

$$\text{Slope} = \frac{3 - \boxed{}}{2 - \boxed{}} = $$

——————————

④ (3,6) and (6,-3)

——————————

⑤ (0,0) and (1,7)

——————————

⑥ (3,8) and (12,8)

——————————

⑦ (-5,8) and (2,0)

——————————

⑧ (-5,8) and (-5,-8)

——————————

⑨ (-2,-7) and (2,-14)

——————————

⑩ (-10,10) and (5,-10)

——————————

⑪ (-11,-4) and (11,-4)

——————————

Draw lines on the grid. Then find the slopes of the lines.

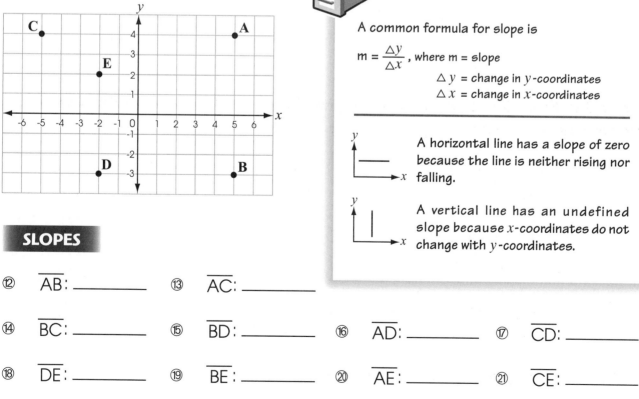

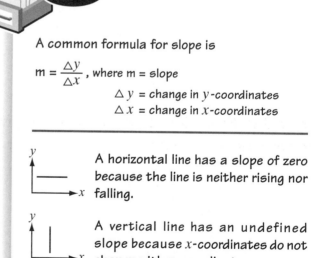

HINT

A common formula for slope is

$m = \dfrac{\triangle y}{\triangle x}$, where m = slope

$\triangle y$ = change in y-coordinates
$\triangle x$ = change in x-coordinates

A horizontal line has a slope of zero because the line is neither rising nor falling.

A vertical line has an undefined slope because x-coordinates do not change with y-coordinates.

SLOPES

⑫ $\overline{AB}$: —————

⑬ $\overline{AC}$: —————

⑭ $\overline{BC}$: —————

⑮ $\overline{BD}$: —————

⑯ $\overline{AD}$: —————

⑰ $\overline{CD}$: —————

⑱ $\overline{DE}$: —————

⑲ $\overline{BE}$: —————

⑳ $\overline{AE}$: —————

㉑ $\overline{CE}$: —————

ISBN: 978-1-77149-220-1

Find the slopes of a mountain at different sections. Then answer the questions.

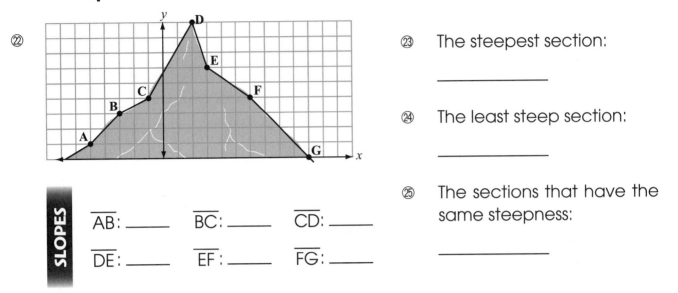

㉒

SLOPES

AB: _____   BC: _____   CD: _____

DE: _____   EF: _____   FG: _____

㉓ The steepest section:

_____

㉔ The least steep section:

_____

㉕ The sections that have the same steepness:

_____

Draw a line with each given slope and label the line. Then state the coordinates of one of the points that you start drawing the line.

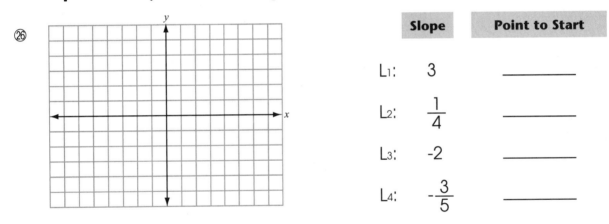

	Slope	Point to Start
L₁:	3	_____
L₂:	$\frac{1}{4}$	_____
L₃:	-2	_____
L₄:	$-\frac{3}{5}$	_____

Draw a line through each point with the given slope and label the points. Then state the coordinates of one of the points on the line.

㉗ AB: passing through A(0,0) and B _____
   with slope 4

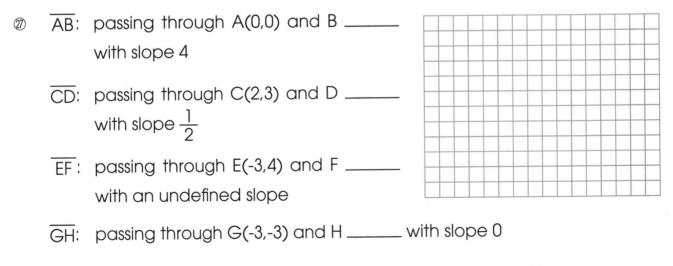

CD: passing through C(2,3) and D _____
   with slope $\frac{1}{2}$

EF: passing through E(-3,4) and F _____
   with an undefined slope

GH: passing through G(-3,-3) and H _____ with slope 0

ISBN: 978-1-77149-220-1

Draw the lines on the grid. Then answer the questions.

㉘ $\overline{AB}$: A(-2,-2) and B(2,4)

  $\overline{CD}$: C(-4,0) and D(0,6)

  $\overline{EF}$: E(-2,3) and F(1,1)

㉙ What do you notice about lines $\overline{AB}$ and $\overline{CD}$?

_____

㉚ Compare the slopes of $\overline{AB}$ and $\overline{CD}$. What do you find?

_____

㉛ What do you notice about lines $\overline{AB}$ and $\overline{EF}$?

_____

㉜ Compare the slopes of $\overline{AB}$ and $\overline{EF}$. What do you find?

_____

Find the slope of each line passing through the given points. State whether L₁ and L₂ are parallel, perpendicular, or neither.

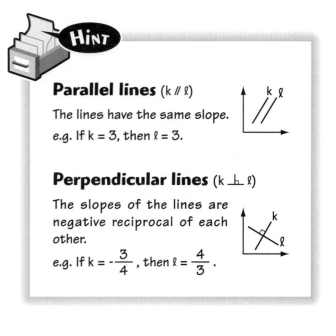

Parallel lines (k // ℓ)

The lines have the same slope.
e.g. If k = 3, then ℓ = 3.

Perpendicular lines (k ⊥ ℓ)

The slopes of the lines are negative reciprocal of each other.
e.g. If k = $-\dfrac{3}{4}$, then ℓ = $\dfrac{4}{3}$.

㉝ L₁: (2,5), (4,9), m = _____

  L₂: (4,0), (-2,3), m = _____

  L₁ & L₂: _____

㉞ L₁: (-2,1), (0,4), m = _____

  L₂: (1,3), (4,1), m = _____

  L₁ & L₂: _____

㉟ L₁: (3,2), (8,4), m = _____

  L₂: (-1,-3), (4,-1), m = _____

  L₁ & L₂: _____

㊱ L₁: (-1,3), (-1,6), m = _____

  L₂: (2,4), (3,4), m = _____

  L₁ & L₂: _____

㊲ L₁: (-2,-5), (-3,-5), m = _____

  L₂: (4,8), (7,8), m = _____

  L₁ & L₂: _____

㊳ L₁: (-2,-7), (-1,4), m = _____

  L₂: (0,-3), (3,0), m = _____

  L₁ & L₂: _____

Find the slope and *y*-intercept of each line.
Then find the equation of the line.

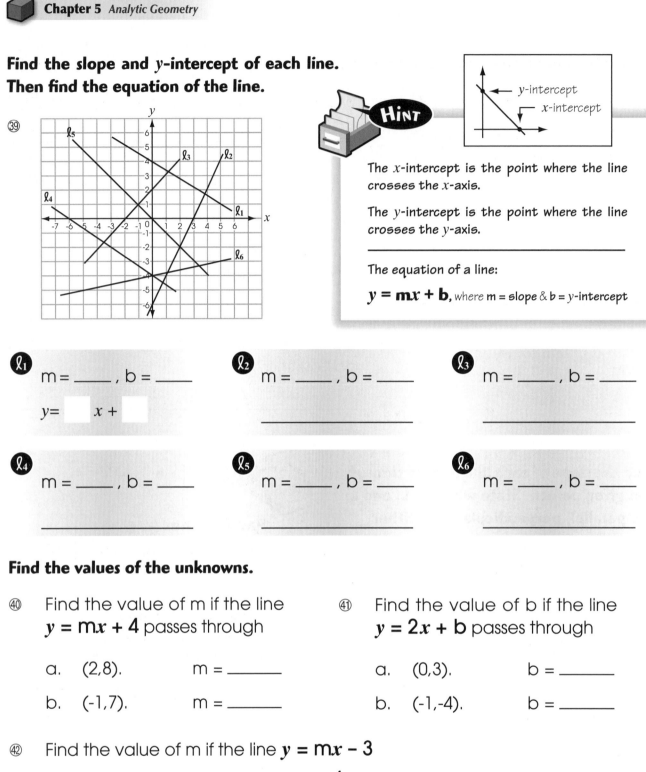

HINT

The *x*-intercept is the point where the line crosses the *x*-axis.

The *y*-intercept is the point where the line crosses the *y*-axis.

The equation of a line:

$y = mx + b$, where m = slope & b = y-intercept

ℓ₁ m = _____ , b = _____

y = ☐ x + ☐

ℓ₂ m = _____ , b = _____

_____

ℓ₃ m = _____ , b = _____

_____

ℓ₄ m = _____ , b = _____

_____

ℓ₅ m = _____ , b = _____

_____

ℓ₆ m = _____ , b = _____

_____

Find the values of the unknowns.

④⓪ Find the value of m if the line $y = mx + 4$ passes through

    a. (2,8).   m = _____

    b. (-1,7).   m = _____

④① Find the value of b if the line $y = 2x + b$ passes through

    a. (0,3).   b = _____

    b. (-1,-4).   b = _____

④② Find the value of m if the line $y = mx - 3$

    a. is perpendicular to the line $y = \frac{4}{5}x + 7$.   _____

    b. is parallel to the line $y = \frac{2}{3}x - 15$.   _____

④③ Find the values of m and b if the line $y = mx + b$

    a. is perpendicular to the line $y = -\frac{2}{3}x + 4$ and passes through (0,-1).   _____

    b. is parallel to the line $y = 4x - 5$ and passes through the origin.   _____

Find the slope and *y*-intercept of the line and interpret their meanings. Then answer the questions.

㊹ The cost of a large pizza is charged according to $y = 1.50x + 9.50$, where y is the total cost of a pizza and x is the number of toppings added.

a. Slope:

_____

b. *y*-intercept:

_____

c. What is the total cost of the pizza if there are 6 toppings?

_____

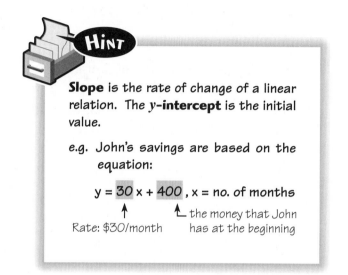

HINT

Slope is the rate of change of a linear relation. The **y-intercept** is the initial value.

e.g. John's savings are based on the equation:

$y = 30\,x + 400$, x = no. of months

Rate: $30/month ⎿ the money that John has at the beginning

㊺ The graph shows the volume of water left in the bathtub and the time elapsed.

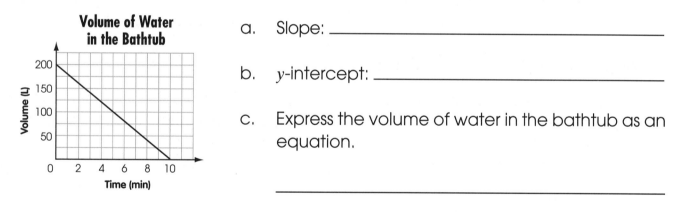

Volume of Water in the Bathtub

Volume (L)

Time (min)

a. Slope: _____

b. *y*-intercept: _____

c. Express the volume of water in the bathtub as an equation.

_____

㊻ The graph shows the number of pages read and the time elapsed.

a. Slope: _____

b. *y*-intercept: _____

c. Express the number of pages read as an equation.

_____

Pages Read

No. of Pages

Time (days)

5.2 Solving Problems Involving Rate of Change

Example

TRY THIS

Determine and explain the rate of change.

In 1996, the population of Ontario was approximately 10.8 million. In 2001, it was approximately 11.4 million. Find the rate of change in population.

Rate of Change $= \dfrac{\triangle y}{\triangle x}$ ← change in population
← change in time

$= \dfrac{11.4 \text{ million} - 10.8 \text{ million}}{2001 - 1996}$

$= 0.12$ million

There was an average of 0.12 million increase in population per year.

No. of Farms in Canada	
1996	about 274 000
2001	about 247 000

Find the rate of change in the number of farms in Canada.

Rate of Change $= \dfrac{\triangle y}{\triangle x}$ ← change in the number of farms
← change in time

$= \dfrac{\boxed{} - \boxed{}}{\boxed{} - \boxed{}}$

$= \underline{}$

There was an average of _____
_____ .

Determine and explain the rate of change.

① In 2004, the minimum wage in Ontario was $7.15. In 2008, it was $8.75.

_____

② In 1998, there were about 1200 polar bears in Manitoba. In 2008, there were 930.

_____

③ At 6:00 a.m., the temperature is 16°C. At 10:00 a.m., it is 24°C.

_____

④ At 3:28, a parachutist is 6500 m above the ground. At 3:31, he is 4400 m above the ground.

_____

⑤ In April, Sue had a balance of $500 in her account. In June, she had a balance of $640.

⑥ Jason had 160 marbles. After 4 weeks, he had 192 marbles in all.

_____

_____

ISBN: 978-1-77149-220-1

Solve the problems.

⑦ Find the slope of the line that passes through

     a.   (-1,-2) and (2,5). _____

     b.   (-7,-5) and (-4,-9). _____

     c.   (0,4) and (-3,4). _____

     d.   (6,-1) and (6,-7). _____

⑧ Draw lines on the grid and label them. Then find another point on each line.

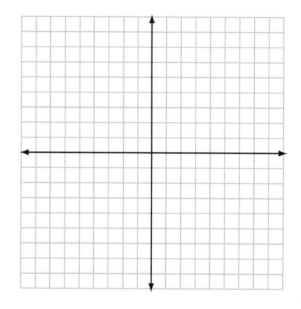

     a.   A line (L) passes through (3,8) and has a slope of $\frac{1}{4}$.

        Another point on L: _____

     b.   A line (K) passes through (0,-4) and has a slope of -2.5.

        Another point on K: _____

     c.   A line (P) intersects the x-axis at 5 and has a slope of $-\frac{2}{3}$.

        Another point on P: _____

     d.   A line (M) intersects the y-axis at 7 and has a slope of 0.

        Another point on M: _____

     e.   A line (N) is parallel to $y = 3x$ and passes through (0,5).

        Another point on N: _____

⑨ Determine whether or not each set of points are collinear.

     a.   (4,-6), (12,-8), and (16,-10)

     _____

     b.   (5,8), (15,12), and (25,16)

     _____

     c.   (1,5), (3,1), and (7,-7)

     _____

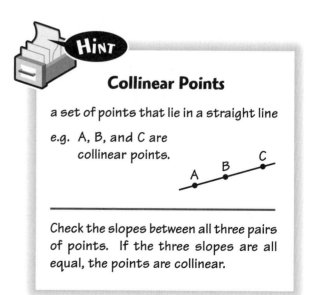

HINT

Collinear Points

a set of points that lie in a straight line

e.g. A, B, and C are collinear points.

Check the slopes between all three pairs of points. If the three slopes are all equal, the points are collinear.

Write a linear model for each problem. Then answer the questions.

⑩ Louis is paid a base salary of $500 a week and a commission of 5% on every computer he sold.

a. Write his total salary as an equation.

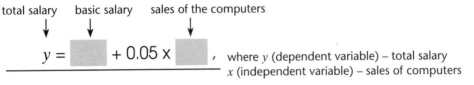

total salary   basic salary   sales of the computers

$y = \boxed{} + 0.05 \times \boxed{}$, where y (dependent variable) – total salary
x (independent variable) – sales of computers

b. Describe the rate of change for Louis' salary.

_____

c. Find the y-intercept and interpret its meaning.

_____

d. What will Louis' total salary be if the computer sales he made are $6000?

_____

⑪ The cost of renting a party room is $80 plus $5 per guest. The maximum number of guests allowed per party is 30.

a. Write the rental cost as an equation.

_____

b. Are there any restrictions to the variables? What are they?

_____

c. Describe the rate of change in rental cost.

_____

_____

d. Find the y-intercept and interpret its meaning.

_____

_____

e. Graph the equation. Then find the rental cost if there are 20 guests.

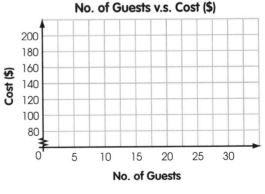

No. of Guests v.s. Cost ($)

Cost ($): 200, 180, 160, 140, 120, 100, 80

No. of Guests: 0, 5, 10, 15, 20, 25, 30

The rental cost for 20 guests: _____

ISBN: 978-1-77149-220-1

Solve the problems.

⑫ What are the *x*-intercept and *y*-intercept of each equation?

a. $y = 4x - 9$ _____

b. $y = -\frac{1}{2}x + 2$ _____

⑬ If the points (3,4), (-2,5), and (-7,*a*) are collinear, what is the value of *a*? _____

⑭ Marcus is driving from Toronto to Windsor. After an hour of driving, he notices there are 50 L of gasoline left. After another hour, there are 40 L left.

a. What is the rate of change in the amount of gasoline? _____

b. How much gasoline was there at first? _____

c. Write an equation to describe the amount of gasoline left in the tank. _____

d. How much gasoline will there be if Marcus continues to drive for another 1.5 hours? _____

⑮ A cup of boiling water was left to cool.

a. Find the slope for the line segment.

$\overline{AB}$: _____

$\overline{BC}$: _____

b. Explain the rate of change in cooling.

_____

_____

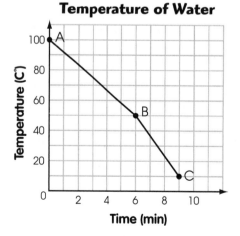

Temperature of Water

c. Is it possible for a segment on this graph to have a slope of 0? Explain.

_____

_____

5.3 Equations of Lines

Words TO LEARN

Equations of Lines in Different Forms

- **Slope-intercept form:**

  $y = mx + b$, where m is the slope and b is the y-intercept

- **Point-slope form:**

  $y - y_1 = m(x - x_1)$, where m is the slope and (x_1, y_1) is a point on the line

- **Standard form:**

  $Ax + By + C = 0$, where A, B, and C are all integers and A is positive

Example

Graph the line and write an equation for the line in slope-intercept form.

a line that has a slope of $-\frac{1}{3}$ and passes through (0,2)

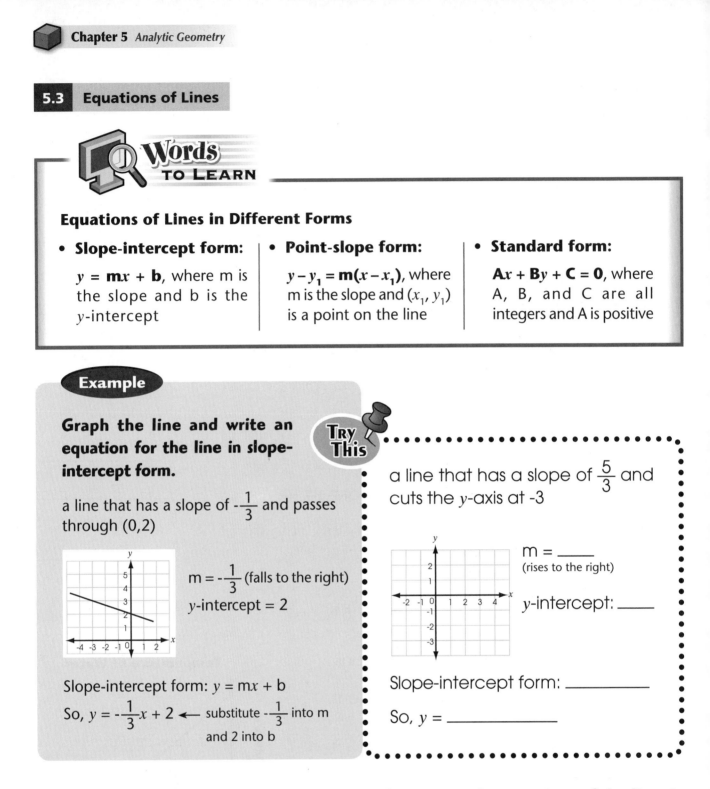

$m = -\frac{1}{3}$ (falls to the right)

y-intercept = 2

Slope-intercept form: $y = mx + b$

So, $y = -\frac{1}{3}x + 2$ ← substitute $-\frac{1}{3}$ into m and 2 into b

TRY This

a line that has a slope of $\frac{5}{3}$ and cuts the y-axis at -3

$m =$ _____ (rises to the right)

y-intercept: _____

Slope-intercept form: _____

So, $y =$ _____

Find the y-intercepts and slopes of the lines. Then write the equations of the lines in slope-intercept form.

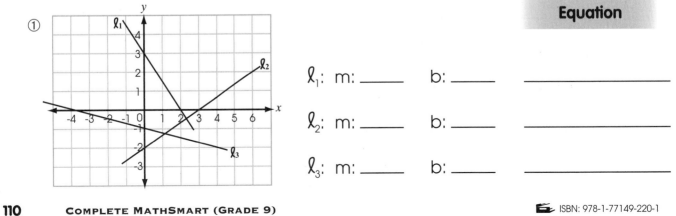

①

Equation

ℓ_1: m: _____ b: _____ _____

ℓ_2: m: _____ b: _____ _____

ℓ_3: m: _____ b: _____ _____

ISBN: 978-1-77149-220-1

Rewrite the equations of the lines in slope-intercept form. Find the slopes and *y*-intercepts of the lines. Draw them on the graph. Then answer the questions.

② L₁ $4x + y = 0$ _____ , m: _____ and b: _____

L₂ $x + 2y = -4$ _____ , m: _____ and b: _____

L₃ $y - 2x + 1 = 0$ _____ , m: _____ and b: _____

L₄ $y - 3x = 2$ _____ , m: _____ and b: _____

③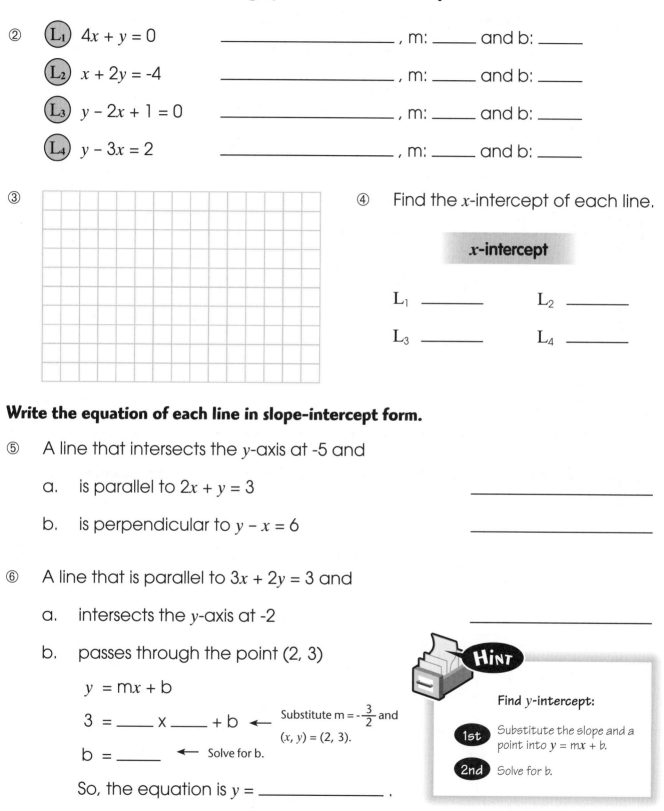

④ Find the *x*-intercept of each line.

x-intercept

L₁ _____   L₂ _____

L₃ _____   L₄ _____

Write the equation of each line in slope-intercept form.

⑤ A line that intersects the *y*-axis at -5 and

a. is parallel to $2x + y = 3$ _____

b. is perpendicular to $y - x = 6$ _____

⑥ A line that is parallel to $3x + 2y = 3$ and

a. intersects the *y*-axis at -2 _____

b. passes through the point (2, 3)

$y = mx + b$

$3 = $ _____ x _____ $+ b$ ← Substitute $m = -\frac{3}{2}$ and $(x, y) = (2, 3)$.

$b = $ _____ ← Solve for b.

So, the equation is $y = $ _____ .

HINT

Find *y*-intercept:

1st Substitute the slope and a point into $y = mx + b$.

2nd Solve for b.

c. passes through the point (-1, 4) _____

d. passes through the point $(-\frac{2}{3}, 3)$ _____

ISBN: 978-1-77149-220-1

Example

Use point-slope form to find the equation of each line.

a line that passes through (3, 1) and has a slope of 2

Point-slope form: $y - y_1 = m(x - x_1)$

$y - 1 = 2(x - 3)$ ⌐ Substitute the point (3,1) into (x_1, y_1)
                          and the slope (2) into m.

$y - 1 = 2x - 6$ ← Simplify by removing the brackets.

$y = 2x - 5$

The equation of the line is $\underline{\quad y = 2x - 5 \quad}$.

Try This

1. a line that passes through (-5,2) and has a slope of -4

    $y - \boxed{} = \boxed{} (x - (-5))$

    _____

2. a line that passes through (1,-7) and has a slope of $-\dfrac{1}{3}$

    $y - (-7) = \boxed{} (x - \boxed{})$

    _____

Use point-slope form to find the equation of each line and write each equation in slope-intercept form.

⑦   (-1, 7), m = -2

⑧   (4, -6), m = $-\dfrac{1}{3}$

⑨   (2, 3), m = $\dfrac{1}{5}$

⑩   (-5, -8), m = $\dfrac{1}{4}$

⑪   (7, 4), m = -1

⑫   origin, m = $-\dfrac{2}{3}$

⑬   a line passing through (3, -2) and parallel to $3x + y = 3$ _____

⑭   a line passing through $(\dfrac{1}{2}, \dfrac{1}{2})$ and perpendicular to $2y - 3x = 1$ _____

⑮   a line cutting the x-axis at 5 and parallel to $y = \dfrac{1}{2}x$ _____

Check the equations that are in standard form.

⑯ Ⓐ $-2x + 3y = 6$ Ⓑ $4x + 5y - 3 = 0$

Ⓒ $y = -5x - 2$ Ⓓ $\frac{1}{3}x - y - 1 = 0$

Ⓔ $y + 2x + 3 = 0$ Ⓕ $3x - \frac{1}{2}y + 1 = 0$

Ⓖ $x - 6y - 5 = 0$ Ⓗ $0 = -3y - 5 + 2x$

Ⓘ $0 = -2x - y - 1$ Ⓙ $10 - 2y + x = 0$

Ⓚ $3x + 5 = 0$ Ⓛ $-8y + x + 1 = 0$

Write the equation of each line in standard form.

⑰ $y = 4x - 5$

⑱ $y = \frac{1}{4}x + 9$

⑲ $y = -\frac{1}{2}x - 7$

⑳ $y = 2x - \frac{7}{9}$

㉑ $\frac{1}{2}x - y = 3$

㉒ $4 - y = \frac{3}{2}x$

㉓ $y - 1 = \frac{2}{5}x$ _____

㉔ $2x = 2y + \frac{3}{5}$ _____

㉕ $0.5y + 1 = x$ _____

㉖ $-0.25x - y = 16$ _____

Rewrite the equation of each line in slope-intercept form.

㉗ $x - y - 1 = 0$

㉘ $5x + 2y - 12 = 0$

㉙ $3x - 9y - 4 = 0$

㉚ $2x + 4y - 5 = 0$

㉛ $2x - 2y - 3 = 0$

㉜ $y + 2x - 1 = 0$

Find the values of the unknowns.

㉝ Each pair of lines are parallel to each other.

> For questions ㉝ – ㉞, write each equation in slope-intercept form first. Then compare their slopes to find the unknowns.
>
> ———————————
>
> • If two lines are //, their slopes are the same.
>
> • If two lines are ⊥ , their slopes are negative reciprocal of each other.

a. $2x - y = 4$ and $ax - 3y = 3$

The value of a: _____

b. $x + 2y + 1 = 0$ and $3x + ky = 1$

The value of k: _____

c. $4x - py - 1 = 0$ and $-px + y - 2 = 0$

The value of p: _____

㉞ Each pair of lines are perpendicular to each other.

a. $3x - y = 5$ and $qx + y = 3$

The value of q: _____

b. $5x + 4y - 1 = 0$ and $2x + ky = 4$

The value of k: _____

c. $3x - y + 4 = 0$ and $w^2x + 3y = 2$

The value of w: _____

d. $x = 4$ and $(s + 1)x + y = 3$

The value of s: _____

Find the equation of each line. Then answer the questions.

㉟ A line passes through (4, 6) and has a slope of $-\frac{3}{4}$. Which of the points below lie on the line?

> (8, 3)
> (6, 6)
> (-4, 12)
> (-3, 9)

_____

㊱ A line intersects the y-axis at -3 and has a slope of $\frac{1}{4}$. Which of the points below lie on the line?

> (2, 5)
> (4, -2)
> (0, -2)
> (-4, -4)

_____

ISBN: 978-1-77149-220-1

Solve the problems.

㊲ Points (-4,0) and (0,-3) are two of the vertices of a square. If the square is in the 3rd quadrant, draw the square on the grid and find the equations of the sides of the square. Write the equations in standard form as your answer.

㊳ Anna and Steve each use an equation to model their savings in terms of time. Write their equations in slope-intercept form. Graph them. Then answer the questions.

Slope-intercept Form

Anna's savings: $x - 2y + 4 = 0$

_____ , where m: ____ and b: ____

Steve's savings: $-x - y + 8 = 0$

_____ , where m: ____ and b: ____

x: no. of months y: no. of $100 bills

a. **Anna's and Steve's Savings**

b. Who has more savings at the beginning?

_____

c. After half a year, who has more savings?

_____

d. When do they have the same amount of savings?

_____

5.4 *x*- and *y*-Intercepts and Points of Intersection

Words TO LEARN

Point of Intersection: the common point where lines meet

A family of lines: lines that share a common characteristic, such as lines that have the same slope and lines that intersect at a point

e.g.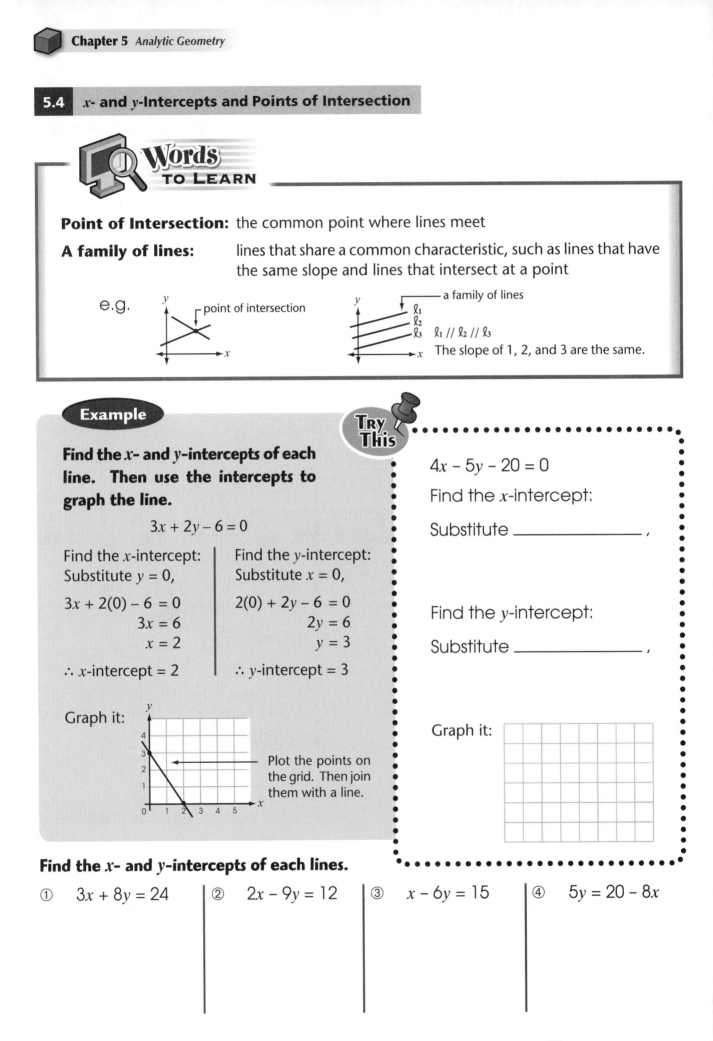

point of intersection

a family of lines

$\ell_1 // \ell_2 // \ell_3$

The slope of 1, 2, and 3 are the same.

Example

Find the *x*- and *y*-intercepts of each line. Then use the intercepts to graph the line.

$$3x + 2y - 6 = 0$$

Find the *x*-intercept:	Find the *y*-intercept:
Substitute $y = 0$,	Substitute $x = 0$,
$3x + 2(0) - 6 = 0$	$2(0) + 2y - 6 = 0$
$\quad\quad 3x = 6$	$\quad\quad 2y = 6$
$\quad\quad\ x = 2$	$\quad\quad\ y = 3$
$\therefore$ *x*-intercept = 2	$\therefore$ *y*-intercept = 3

Graph it:

Plot the points on the grid. Then join them with a line.

Try This

$$4x - 5y - 20 = 0$$

Find the *x*-intercept:

Substitute _____ ,

Find the *y*-intercept:

Substitute _____ ,

Graph it:

Find the *x*- and *y*-intercepts of each lines.

① $3x + 8y = 24$ ② $2x - 9y = 12$ ③ $x - 6y = 15$ ④ $5y = 20 - 8x$

ISBN: 978-1-77149-220-1

Find the *x*- and *y*-intercepts of each line. Use the intercepts to graph the line. Then find the slope of the line.

⑤ L_1: $2x - 5y + 10 = 0$

     x-intercept = _____   m =

     y-intercept = _____

     L_2: $7x - 3y - 21 = 0$

     x-intercept = _____   m =

     y-intercept = _____

     L_3: $7x + 6y = -42$

     x-intercept = _____   m =

     y-intercept = _____

     L_4: $2x - 3y = 6$

     x-intercept = _____   m =

     y-intercept = _____

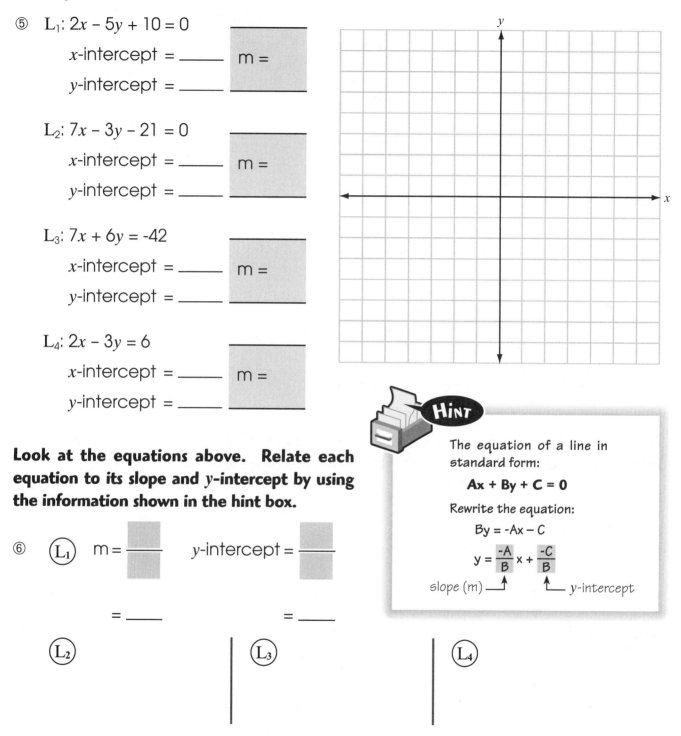

Look at the equations above. Relate each equation to its slope and *y*-intercept by using the information shown in the hint box.

HINT

The equation of a line in standard form:

$$Ax + By + C = 0$$

Rewrite the equation:

$$By = -Ax - C$$

$$y = \frac{-A}{B} x + \frac{-C}{B}$$

slope (m) ⟶   ⟵ *y*-intercept

⑥ L_1 m = $\dfrac{\quad}{\quad}$ *y*-intercept = $\dfrac{\quad}{\quad}$

         = ____   = ____

     L_2 L_3 L_4

Find the equation of each line and write it in strandard form.

⑦   m = $-\dfrac{3}{4}$, *y*-intercept = $\dfrac{2}{4}$ _____

⑧   m = $\dfrac{5}{6}$,   *y*-intercept = $\dfrac{7}{6}$ _____

⑨   m = $-1\dfrac{1}{4}$, *y*-intercept = 1   _____

ISBN: 978-1-77149-220-1

Find and compare the slopes of each pair of lines. Put a checkmark in the circle if they have a point of intersection; otherwise, put a cross.

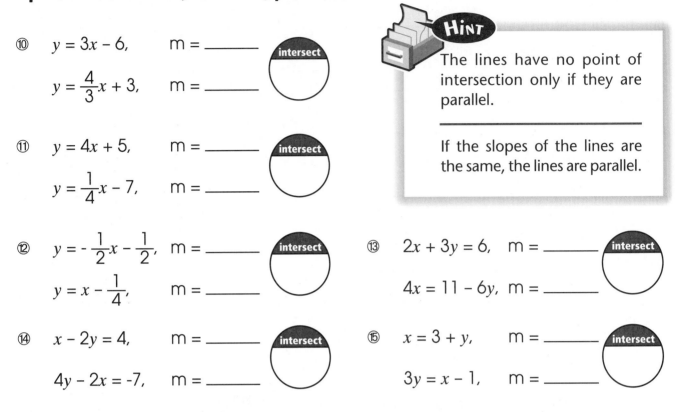

⑩ $y = 3x - 6,$ m = _____   intersect ◯

$y = \dfrac{4}{3}x + 3,$ m = _____

⑪ $y = 4x + 5,$ m = _____   intersect ◯

$y = \dfrac{1}{4}x - 7,$ m = _____

⑫ $y = -\dfrac{1}{2}x - \dfrac{1}{2},$ m = _____   intersect ◯

$y = x - \dfrac{1}{4},$ m = _____

⑬ $2x + 3y = 6,$ m = _____   intersect ◯

$4x = 11 - 6y,$ m = _____

⑭ $x - 2y = 4,$ m = _____   intersect ◯

$4y - 2x = -7,$ m = _____

⑮ $x = 3 + y,$ m = _____   intersect ◯

$3y = x - 1,$ m = _____

Does each pair of lines have a point of intersection? If it does, write its coordinates; otherwise, write "do not intersect". Then answer the questions.

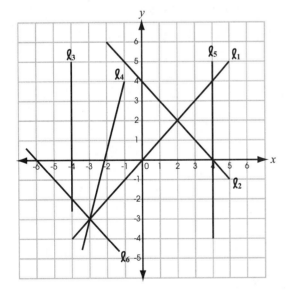

⑯ ℓ_1 and ℓ_2 : _____

⑰ ℓ_1 and ℓ_4 : _____

⑱ ℓ_1 and ℓ_5 : _____

⑲ ℓ_2 and ℓ_5 : _____

⑳ ℓ_1 and ℓ_3 : _____

㉑ ℓ_3 and ℓ_5 : _____

㉒ ℓ_2 and ℓ_6 : _____

㉓ Which lines intersect at (-4,-2)?   _____

㉔ Which lines intersect at (-3,-3)?   _____

㉕ Draw a line that intersects ℓ_3 at (-4,3) and intersects ℓ_1 at (1,1) on the grid.

Write an equation for each line represented by the table of values in slope-intercept form. Then identify the point of intersection for each pair of lines by using the table of values.

㉖

x	y
-1	-1
0	-3
1	-5
2	-7

← common point →

x	y
-1	-6
0	-3
1	0
2	3

$y =$ _____   _____

point of intersection: _____

㉗

x	y
-1	0
0	1
1	2
2	3

x	y
-1	6
0	4
1	2
2	0

_____   _____

point of intersection: _____

㉘

x	y
1	2
2	1
3	0
4	-1

x	y
1	0.5
2	0
3	-0.5
4	-1

$y =$ _____   _____

point of intersection: _____

㉙

x	y
-2	-6
-1	-5
0	-4
1	-3

x	y
-2	-9
-1	-5
0	-1
1	3

_____   _____

point of intersection: _____

Graph the lines. Then determine the coordinates of the points of intersection.

㉚ $L_1: y = 4x - 4$

$L_2: y = x + 2$

$L_3: y = \frac{5}{9}x - 5$

$L_4: y = -\frac{5}{7}x - 5$

$L_5: y = -2x - 4$

$L_6: y = 4$

Point of Intersection:

L_1 and L_2: _____ L_3 and L_4: _____ L_1 and L_5: _____

L_2 and L_5: _____ L_5 and L_6: _____ L_2 and L_6: _____

ISBN: 978-1-77149-220-1

A family of lines shares a common characteristic. Graph each group of lines. Cross the line that does not belong to the family. Then write the common characteristic that the family has.

㉛ (A) L_1: $y = -\frac{1}{2}x + 3$

(B) L_2: $y - x = 0$

(C) L_3: $4y = x - 2$

(D) L_4: $2x - y - 2 = 0$

common characteristic:

_____

㉜ (A) L_5: $2x + 3y = -12$

(B) L_6: $3y = -2x$

(C) L_7: $\frac{3}{2}y = -x + 5$

(D) L_8: $2x - 3y - 6 = 0$

common characteristic:

_____

All lines in the group belong to a family. Graph the first 2 lines to find what common characteristic each family has. Then solve for the unknowns in the other 2 lines.

㉝
- $y = \frac{2}{3}x + 1$
- $y - 1 = \frac{2}{3}(x - 3)$
- $kx - 3y + 6 = 0$, $k =$ _____
- $ay - 2x - 9 = 0$, $a =$ _____

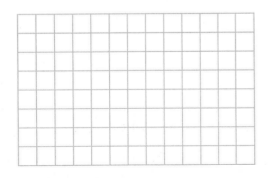

㉞
- $x + 2y = 0$
- $x - y = 3$
- $y + px = 3$, $p =$ _____
- $y = bx + 15$, $b =$ _____

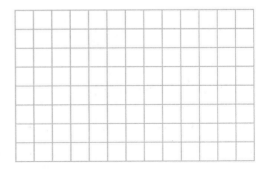

ISBN: 978-1-77149-220-1

Solve the problems.

③⑤ Find the equation of a line that passes through the origin and the point of intersection of $x - y = 1$ and $2y = x + 3$.

_____

③⑥ Find the equation of a line that passes through the point of intersection of $2y = x - 5$ and $y = 2x - 1$ and the point of intersection of $x + y + 4 = 0$ and $2y = -5x - 2$.

_____

③⑦ Find the vertices of a triangle that is bounded by the lines below.

- $3y + 8x - 21 = 0$
- $3y = x - 6$
- $3y - 21 = 10x$

_____

③⑧ For each family of lines, write one more equation that belongs to the family.

Family 1
- $3y = 2x - 4$
- $\frac{2}{3}x - y - 6 = 0$
- _____

Family 2
- $x - 2y - 5 = 0$
- $4x - 3y = 0$
- _____

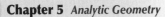

5.5 **Solving Problems with Linear Equations**

Example

Find the unknown values.

TRY This

The equation of a line is $3x - ky + 6 = 0$. If the line passes through the point (3,1), what is the value of k?

Substitute the point (3,1) into the equation.

$3(3) - k(1) + 6 = 0$ ← $x = 3$ and $y = 1$
$9 - k + 6 = 0$
$k = 15$

The value of k is __15__ .

The equation of a line is $kx - 2ky - 12 = 0$. If the line passes through (2,4), what is the value of k?

Substitute the point (2,4) into the equation.

$k(\;\;\;\;) - 2k(\;\;\;\;) - 12 = 0$ ← $x = 2$ and $y = 4$

_____

Find the values of the unknowns.

①   The equation of a line is $5x - ky - 20 = 0$. If the line has the same y-intercept as $y = -x - 5$, what is the value of k?   _____

②   The slope and the x-intercept of the line $2x + ky - p = 0$ are $\frac{2}{3}$ and 4 respectively. What are the values of k and p?   _____

③   The x-coordinate of one of the points on the line $4x - y + 2 = 0$ is one fifth of its y-coordinate. What are the coordinates of the point?   _____

④   The lines $2x + y - 1 = 0$ and $y = kx - b$ are perpendicular to each other and intersect at the point (5,3). What are the values of k and b?   _____

⑤   The line $\frac{1}{2}x + \frac{3}{4}y = 1$ is parallel to the line $px + 3y = q$ which passes through the point (3,-4). What are the values of p and q?   _____

   ISBN: 978-1-77149-220-1

Look at the triangles on the grid. Find the vertices and the equations for the sides of the triangles. Then write the equations in standard form and slope-intercept form.

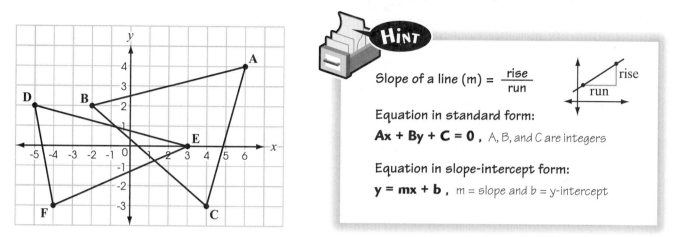

Slope of a line (m) = $\dfrac{\text{rise}}{\text{run}}$

Equation in standard form:

Ax + By + C = 0, A, B, and C are integers

Equation in slope-intercept form:

y = mx + b, m = slope and b = y-intercept

⑥ The vertices of △ABC: _____

$\overline{AB}$	$\overline{BC}$	$\overline{AC}$
equation of $\overline{AB}$	equation of $\overline{BC}$	equation of $\overline{AC}$

⑦ The vertices of △DEF: _____

$\overline{DE}$	$\overline{EF}$	$\overline{DF}$
equation of $\overline{DE}$	equation of $\overline{EF}$	equation of $\overline{DF}$

Find the equation for the fourth side and the vertices of the square.

⑧ The equations for the three sides of a square:

- $y = x + 4$
- $y + x = 4$
- $y + 2 = x$

The equation for the fourth side:

_____

The vertices:

_____

Solve the problems.

⑨ Jimmy and Lawrence are electricians. Jimmy charges a fee of $80 per service call, whereas Lawrence charges $90. In addition, they both charge $40/h for labour.

a. Write an equation for each of their total labour. Then graph them.

C_1: total service charge for Jimmy
C_2: total service charge for Lawrence
  t: no. of hours

_____

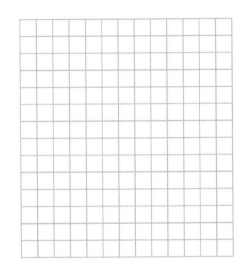

b. How are the two equations of lines related?

_____

c. Who always charges more? How much more?

d. If a job costs $320, how long does it take Jimmy to complete the work?

_____   _____

⑩ A cellular phone company offers two monthly plans.

a. Write an equation for the total cost of each monthly plan. Then graph them on the grid.

Plan A
$10/month + 25¢/minute

Plan B
$15/month + 15¢/minute

b. What are the coordinates of the point of intersection? What do they mean?

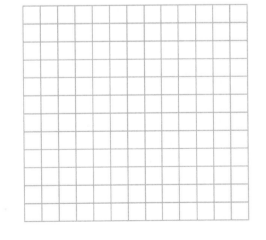

_____

c. Under what condition is Plan A a better choice?

_____

    ISBN: 978-1-77149-220-1

Solve the problems.

⑪ Find the equation for the line of symmetry of the triangle.

_____

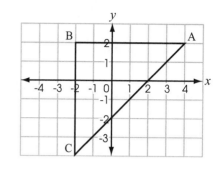

⑫ Find the equation for the line passing through the points of intersection of each pair of lines.

- $2y = x - 11$ and $3x + y = 5$
- $4x - y = 4$ and $2x = 3y + 2$

_____

⑬ State the common characteristic of this family of lines. Then write one more equation that belongs to this family.

$$5y = -2x + 5 \qquad 2x + 5y + 1 = 0 \qquad x = -\frac{5}{2}y$$

_____

⑭ David and Agnes work at two different electronic stores. David earns $300 a week and 4% commissions on the sales he makes. Agnes earns $400 a week and 3% commissions on the sales she makes.

a. Write each of their weekly salaries as an equation. Then graph them on the grid.

b. What will the amount of sales be if David and Agnes earn the same amount in a week?

_____

c. Who has a better salary plan? Explain.

_____

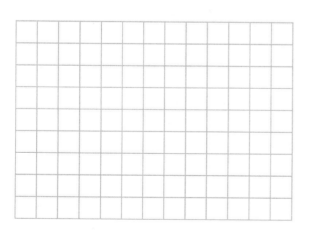

d. How much more or less did Agnes earn if each of them made $25 000 worth of total sales?

_____

ISBN: 978-1-77149-220-1

6 Properties of Two-dimensional Shapes

6.1 Angles of Polygons

Example

Find the measure of each marked angle.

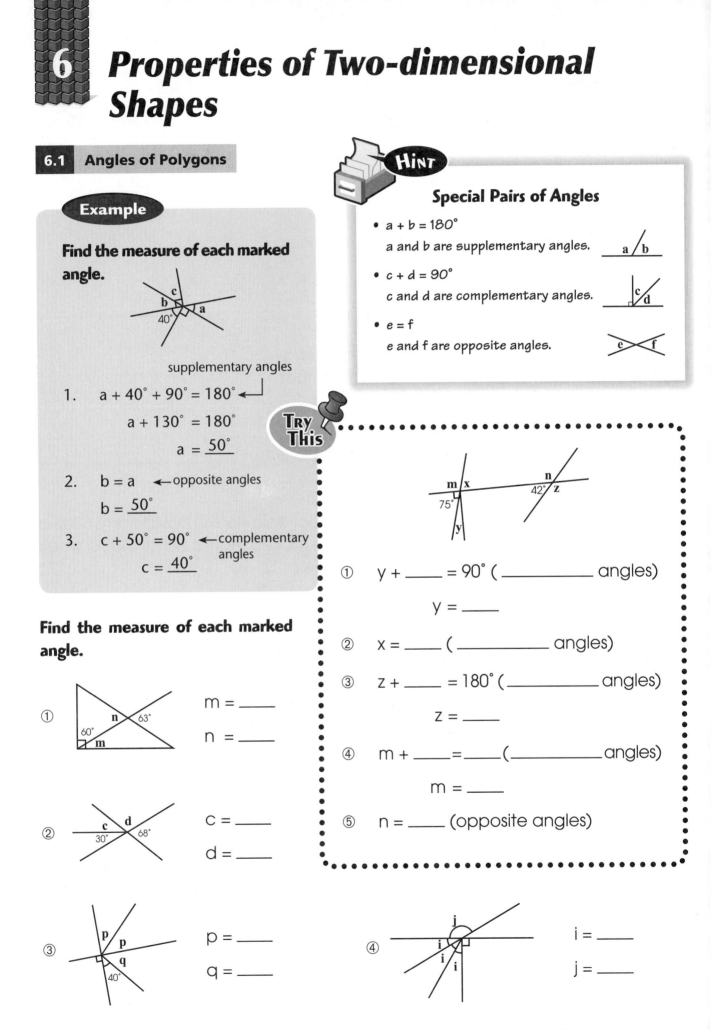

supplementary angles

1. $a + 40° + 90° = 180°$

    $a + 130° = 180°$

    $a = \underline{50}°$

2. $b = a$ ← opposite angles

    $b = \underline{50}°$

3. $c + 50° = 90°$ ← complementary angles

    $c = \underline{40}°$

HINT

Special Pairs of Angles

- $a + b = 180°$

    a and b are supplementary angles.

- $c + d = 90°$

    c and d are complementary angles.

- $e = f$

    e and f are opposite angles.

TRY THIS

① $y + \underline{\quad} = 90°$ (_____ angles)

    $y = \underline{\quad}$

② $x = \underline{\quad}$ (_____ angles)

③ $z + \underline{\quad} = 180°$ (_____ angles)

    $z = \underline{\quad}$

④ $m + \underline{\quad} = \underline{\quad}$ (_____ angles)

    $m = \underline{\quad}$

⑤ $n = \underline{\quad}$ (opposite angles)

Find the measure of each marked angle.

① m = _____

    n = _____

② c = _____

    d = _____

③ p = _____

    q = _____

④ i = _____

    j = _____

ISBN: 978-1-77149-220-1

Fill in the blanks to complete the sentences. Then find the measures of the marked angles and give reasons.

⑤ ▬▬ **Angles Associated with Parallel Lines** ▬▬▬▬▬▬

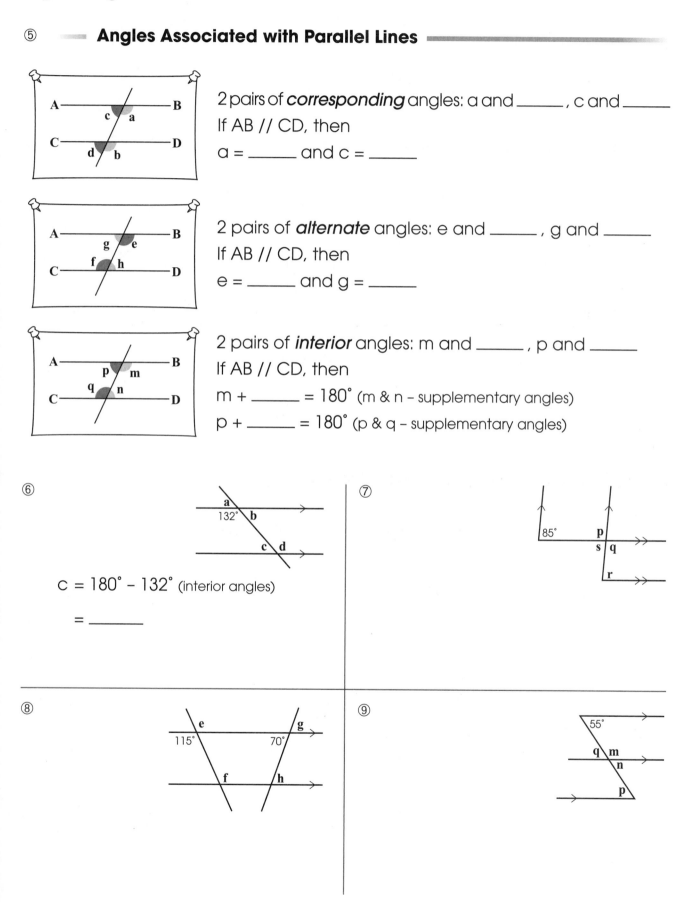

2 pairs of **corresponding** angles: a and _____ , c and _____
If AB // CD, then
a = _____ and c = _____

2 pairs of **alternate** angles: e and _____ , g and _____
If AB // CD, then
e = _____ and g = _____

2 pairs of **interior** angles: m and _____ , p and _____
If AB // CD, then
m + _____ = 180° (m & n – supplementary angles)
p + _____ = 180° (p & q – supplementary angles)

⑥

c = 180° – 132° (interior angles)

= _____

⑦

⑧

⑨

Find the measures of the marked angles.

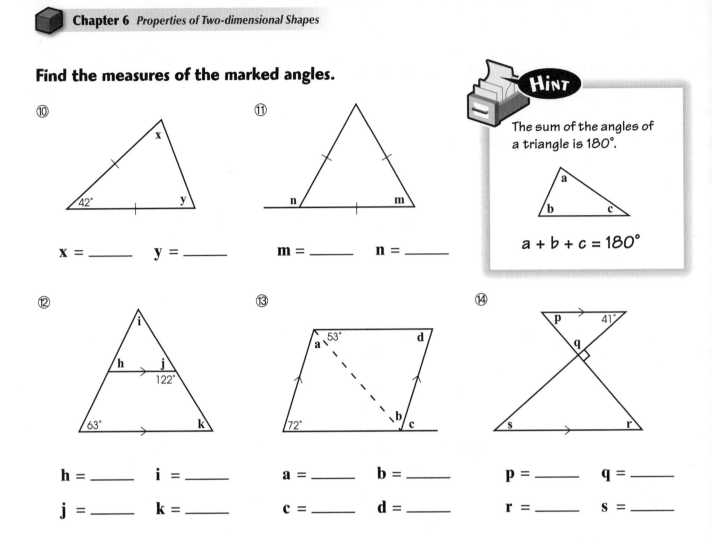

HINT

The sum of the angles of a triangle is 180°.

$$a + b + c = 180°$$

⑩

x = _____   y = _____

⑪

m = _____   n = _____

⑫

h = _____   i = _____

j = _____   k = _____

⑬

a = _____   b = _____

c = _____   d = _____

⑭

p = _____   q = _____

r = _____   s = _____

Find the measures of the marked angles. Give reasons.

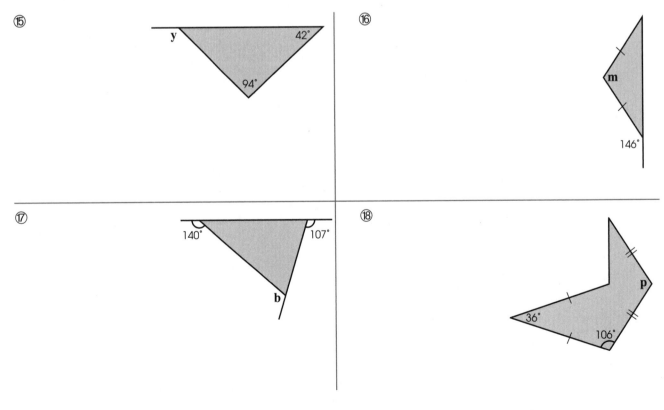

⑮

⑯

⑰

⑱

ISBN: 978-1-77149-220-1

Find the measures of the marked angles. Give reasons. Add lines to the diagrams if needed.

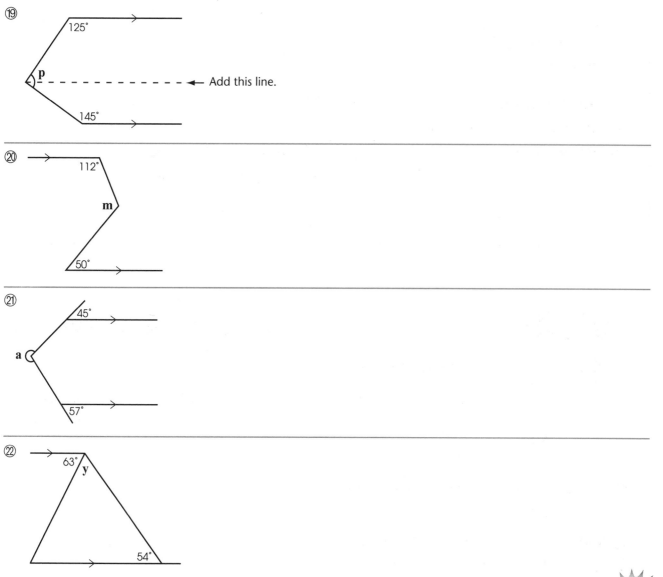

⑲

125°

p — — — — — — — — — — ← Add this line.

145°

⑳

112°

m

50°

㉑

45°

a

57°

㉒

63°
y

54°

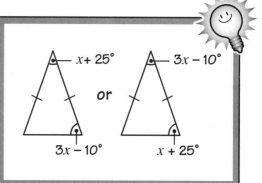

Challenge

If two of the angles of an isosceles triangles are $x + 25°$ and $3x - 10°$, what are the measures of the three angles?

$x + 25°$ **or** $3x - 10°$

$3x - 10°$ $x + 25°$

ISBN: 978-1-77149-220-1

6.2 Properties of Interior and Exterior Angles

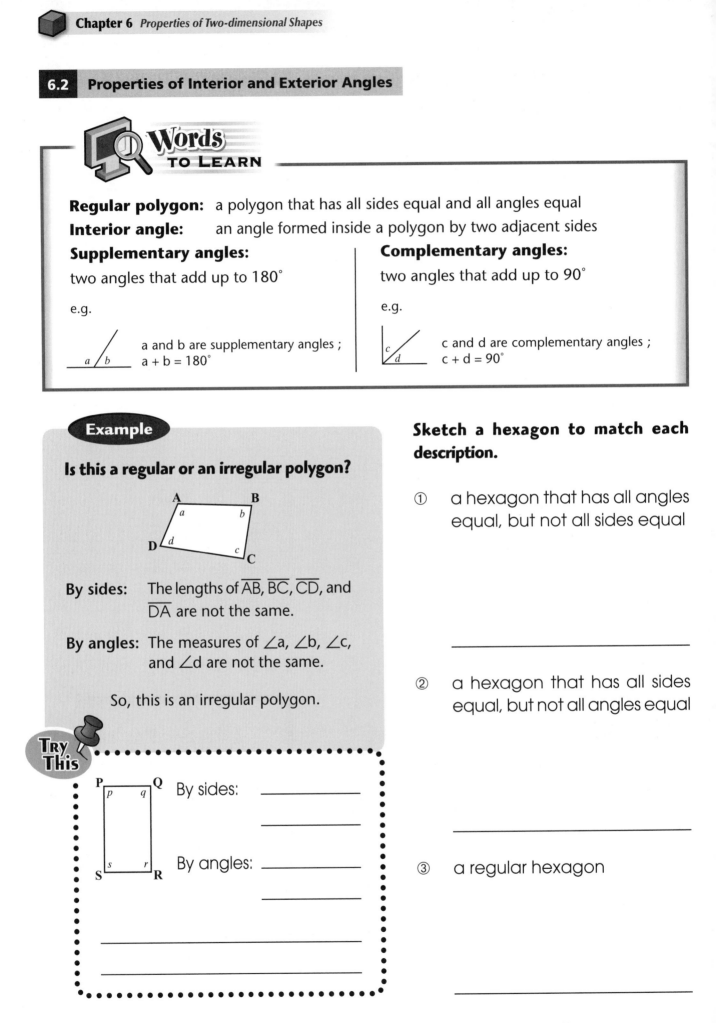

Words TO LEARN

Regular polygon: a polygon that has all sides equal and all angles equal

Interior angle: an angle formed inside a polygon by two adjacent sides

Supplementary angles:
two angles that add up to 180°

e.g.

a and b are supplementary angles ;
a + b = 180°

Complementary angles:
two angles that add up to 90°

e.g.

c and d are complementary angles ;
c + d = 90°

Example

Is this a regular or an irregular polygon?

By sides: The lengths of $\overline{AB}$, $\overline{BC}$, $\overline{CD}$, and $\overline{DA}$ are not the same.

By angles: The measures of $\angle a$, $\angle b$, $\angle c$, and $\angle d$ are not the same.

So, this is an irregular polygon.

Try This

By sides: _____

_____

By angles: _____

_____

_____

_____

Sketch a hexagon to match each description.

① a hexagon that has all angles equal, but not all sides equal

_____

② a hexagon that has all sides equal, but not all angles equal

_____

③ a regular hexagon

_____

ISBN: 978-1-77149-220-1

Draw all the diagonals from one vertex of each polygon. Then count the number of triangles formed by the diagonals. Complete the table. Then answer the questions.

④

Polygon	No. of Sides	No. of △ Formed	Sum of Measures of Interior Angles	
triangle	3	1	1 × 180°	← (3 – 2) × 180°
quadrilateral	4	2	2 × 180°	← (4 – 2) × 180°
pentagon	5	3	× 180°	← (– 2) × 180°
hexagon				← (– 2) × 180°
heptagon				← (– 2) × 180°

⑤ Derive a formula for finding the sum of the interior angles of a polygon with *n* sides. Then use the formula to find the sum of measures of interior angles of each polygon.

Formula:

_____

Sum of interior angles

- an octagon _____
- a 12-sided polygon _____
- a 20-sided polygon _____

Find the sum of the interior angles of each polygon. Then answer the question.

⑥ nonagon _____

⑦ decagon _____

⑧ hexadecagon _____

⑨ octadecagon _____

⑩ a 14-sided polygon _____

⑪ a 17-sided polygon _____

⑫ a regular polygon with 50 sides _____

⑬ an irregular polygon with 50 sides _____

⑭ There are two *n*-sided polygons, one is regular and one is irregular. Are the sums of their interior angles the same?

_____

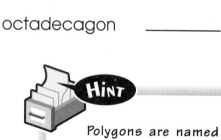

HINT

Polygons are named according to the number of sides.

e.g. nonagon - 9 sides
decagon - 10 sides
hexadecagon - 16 sides
octadecagon - 18 sides

Find the measure of each interior angle of each regular polygon.

⑮ an equilateral triangle _____

⑯ a square _____

⑰ a regular pentagon _____

⑱ a regular hexagon _____

⑲ a regular heptagon _____

⑳ a regular octagon _____

Find the measures of the marked angles in each polygon.

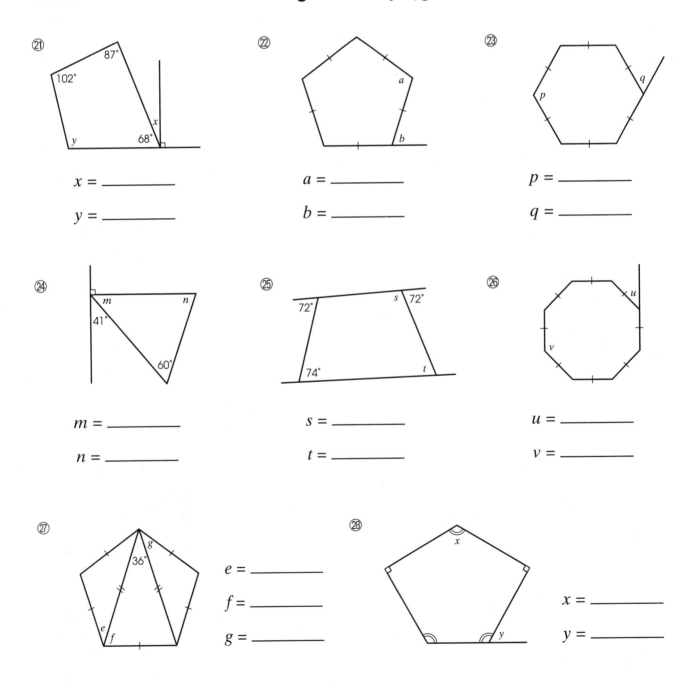

㉑
x = _____
y = _____

㉒
a = _____
b = _____

㉓
p = _____
q = _____

㉔
m = _____
n = _____

㉕
s = _____
t = _____

㉖
u = _____
v = _____

㉗
e = _____
f = _____
g = _____

㉘
x = _____
y = _____

ISBN: 978-1-77149-220-1

Set up an equation to find the value of x. Then find the measure of each interior angle.

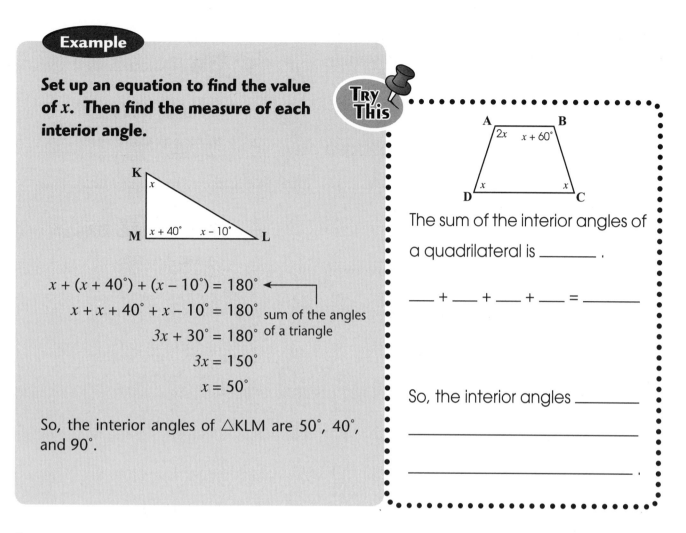

$x + (x + 40°) + (x - 10°) = 180°$

$x + x + 40° + x - 10° = 180°$ sum of the angles

$3x + 30° = 180°$ of a triangle

$3x = 150°$

$x = 50°$

So, the interior angles of △KLM are 50°, 40°, and 90°.

Try This

The sum of the interior angles of a quadrilateral is _____ .

___ + ___ + ___ + ___ = _____

So, the interior angles _____

_____

_____ .

Set up an equation to find the value of x. Then find the measure of each interior angle.

㉙

4x + 6°

5x - 2°

6x - 4°

㉚

2x + 16°   100°

2x - 16°   72°

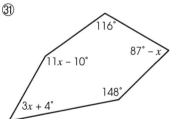

㉛

116°

11x - 10°

87° - x

148°

3x + 4°

Find the measures of the angles or lengths of each pair of similar triangles. Give reasons.

Similar Triangles

- corresponding angles equal
- corresponding sides proportional

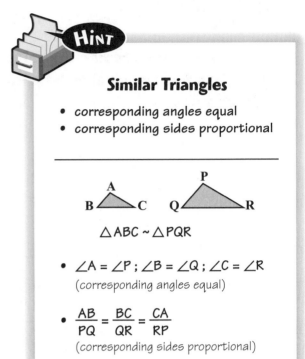

$\triangle ABC \sim \triangle PQR$

- $\angle A = \angle P$; $\angle B = \angle Q$; $\angle C = \angle R$
  (corresponding angles equal)

- $\dfrac{AB}{PQ} = \dfrac{BC}{QR} = \dfrac{CA}{RP}$
  (corresponding sides proportional)

㉜

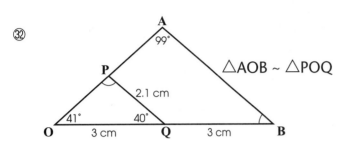

$\triangle AOB \sim \triangle POQ$

$\angle P =$ _____ ; $\angle B =$ _____ (corresponding angles equal)

$\dfrac{AB}{2.1} = \dfrac{6}{\ \ \ }$ (corresponding sides proportional)

$AB =$ _____

㉝

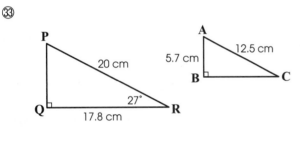

$\triangle PQR \sim \triangle ABC$

$\angle A =$ _____

$\angle C =$ _____

$BC =$ _____

$PQ =$ _____

㉞

$\angle O =$ _____

$\angle C =$ _____

$\angle B =$ _____

$OC =$ _____

$DB =$ _____

ISBN: 978-1-77149-220-1

Solve the problems.

㉟ △ABC and △DEF are similar triangles. The lengths of AB, BC, and CA are 5 cm, 4 cm, and 6 cm respectively. If the length of DF is 11.2 cm, what are the lengths of DE and EF?

_____

㊱ A 1.8-m-tall man casts a 2.7-m-long shadow at the same time that a tree casts a 6.48-m-long shadow. How tall is the tree?

_____

㊲ The lengths of the sides of four triangles are listed as follows. Which two triangles are similar? Explain.

Ⓐ 5 cm, 6 cm, 8 cm

Ⓑ 6 cm, 7 cm, 8 cm

Ⓒ 8 cm, 10 cm, 12 cm

Ⓓ 12 cm, 15 cm, 18 cm _____

㊳ If the feet of the sign are 28.6 cm apart, how long is the wire?

_____

6.3   Angle Properties of Parallel Lines

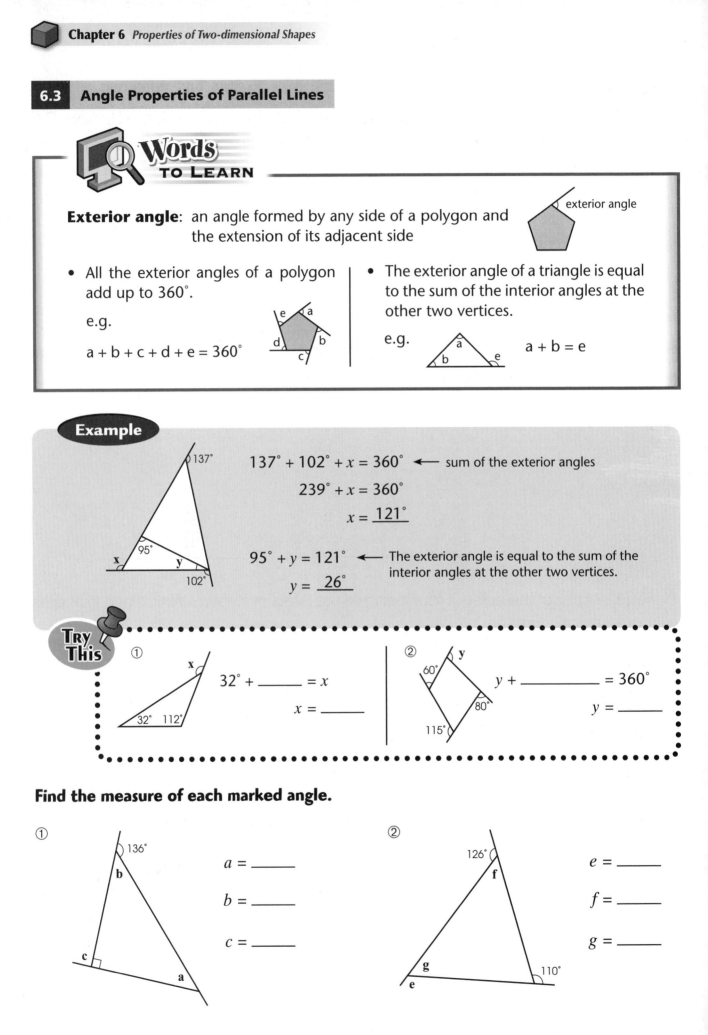

Words TO LEARN

Exterior angle: an angle formed by any side of a polygon and the extension of its adjacent side

exterior angle

- All the exterior angles of a polygon add up to 360°.

  e.g.

  a + b + c + d + e = 360°

- The exterior angle of a triangle is equal to the sum of the interior angles at the other two vertices.

  e.g.

  a + b = e

Example

137° + 102° + x = 360° ← sum of the exterior angles

239° + x = 360°

x = __121°__

95° + y = 121° ← The exterior angle is equal to the sum of the interior angles at the other two vertices.

y = __26°__

Try This

① 32° + _____ = x

x = _____

② y + _____ = 360°

y = _____

Find the measure of each marked angle.

① 136°

a = _____

b = _____

c = _____

② 126°

e = _____

f = _____

g = _____

110°

ISBN: 978-1-77149-220-1

③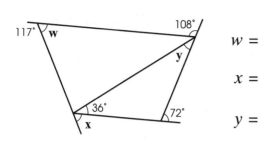

$w = $ _____

$x = $ _____

$y = $ _____

④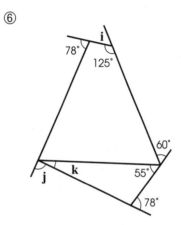

$s = $ _____

$t = $ _____

$u = $ _____

⑤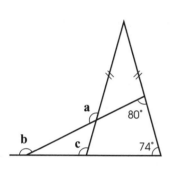

$a = $ _____

$b = $ _____

$c = $ _____

⑥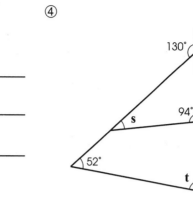

$i = $ _____

$j = $ _____

$k = $ _____

⑦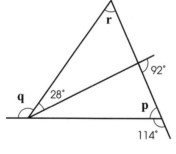

$p = $ _____

$q = $ _____

$r = $ _____

⑧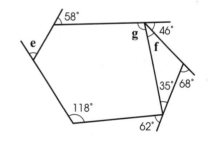

$e = $ _____

$f = $ _____

$g = $ _____

⑨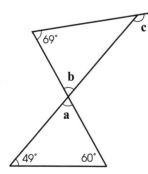

$a = $ _____

$b = $ _____

$c = $ _____

⑩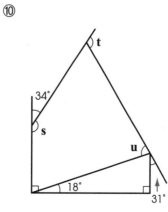

$s = $ _____

$t = $ _____

$u = $ _____

ISBN: 978-1-77149-220-1

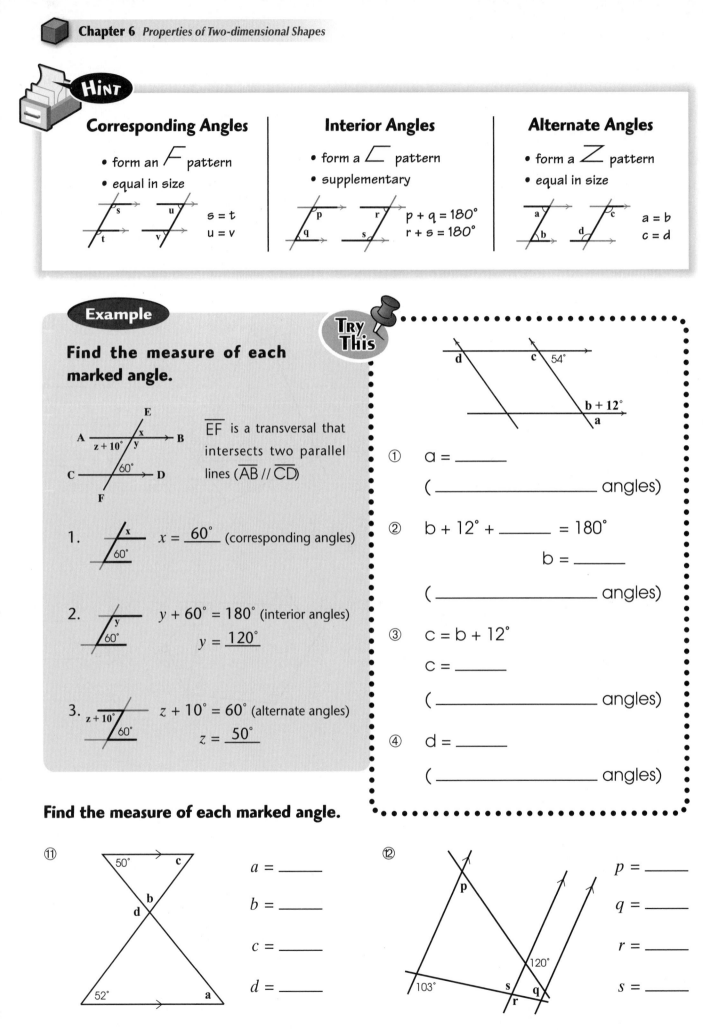

HINT

Corresponding Angles
- form an F pattern
- equal in size

$s = t$
$u = v$

Interior Angles
- form a $\sqsubset$ pattern
- supplementary

$p + q = 180°$
$r + s = 180°$

Alternate Angles
- form a Z pattern
- equal in size

$a = b$
$c = d$

Example

Find the measure of each marked angle.

$\overline{EF}$ is a transversal that intersects two parallel lines ($\overline{AB} // \overline{CD}$)

1. $x = \underline{60°}$ (corresponding angles)

2. $y + 60° = 180°$ (interior angles)
   $y = \underline{120°}$

3. $z + 10° = 60°$ (alternate angles)
   $z = \underline{50°}$

TRY THIS

① $a = \underline{\hphantom{xxxx}}$
   ($\underline{\hspace{3cm}}$ angles)

② $b + 12° + \underline{\hphantom{xx}} = 180°$
   $b = \underline{\hphantom{xx}}$
   ($\underline{\hspace{3cm}}$ angles)

③ $c = b + 12°$
   $c = \underline{\hphantom{xx}}$
   ($\underline{\hspace{3cm}}$ angles)

④ $d = \underline{\hphantom{xx}}$
   ($\underline{\hspace{3cm}}$ angles)

Find the measure of each marked angle.

⑪

$a = \underline{\hspace{2cm}}$

$b = \underline{\hspace{2cm}}$

$c = \underline{\hspace{2cm}}$

$d = \underline{\hspace{2cm}}$

⑫

$p = \underline{\hspace{2cm}}$

$q = \underline{\hspace{2cm}}$

$r = \underline{\hspace{2cm}}$

$s = \underline{\hspace{2cm}}$

Find the value of x. Then find the measure of each unknown angle.

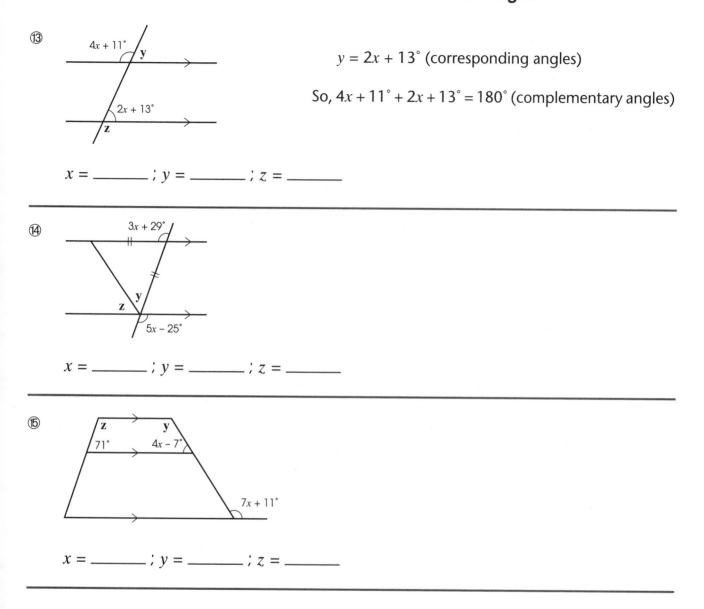

⑬

$y = 2x + 13°$ (corresponding angles)

So, $4x + 11° + 2x + 13° = 180°$ (complementary angles)

$x =$ _____ ; $y =$ _____ ; $z =$ _____

⑭

$x =$ _____ ; $y =$ _____ ; $z =$ _____

⑮

$x =$ _____ ; $y =$ _____ ; $z =$ _____

Find the values of x and y.

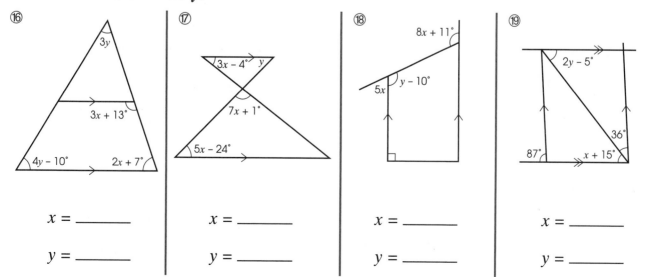

⑯

$x =$ _____

$y =$ _____

⑰

$x =$ _____

$y =$ _____

⑱

$x =$ _____

$y =$ _____

⑲

$x =$ _____

$y =$ _____

ISBN: 978-1-77149-220-1

Tell whether each statement is true or false. Draw a diagram to help explain your choice.

⑳

(A) The exterior angles of an acute triangle are obtuse. _____

(B) A right angle can be a base angle of an isosceles triangle. _____

(C) A pentagon with five equal sides is regular. _____

(D) The sum of the exterior angles of any polygon is 360˚. _____

Diagram and Explanation

(A)

(B)

(C)

(D)

Identify the parallel lines. Explain why they are parallel.

㉑

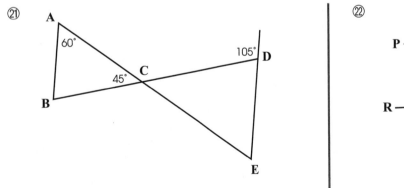

㉒

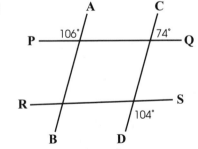

ISBN: 978-1-77149-220-1

Draw a diagram to illustrate each question. Then solve the question.

㉓ The measures of the angles of a quadrilateral are in the ratio of 1:2:3:4. Find the measure of each angle.

_____

㉔ The diagonal of a square is the slant side of a parallelogram. The height of the parallelogram is the side length of the square. What are the measures of the angles of the parallelogram?

_____

㉕ One of the angles of a parallelogram has a supplementary angle of 36°. What are the measures of the angles of the parallelogram?

_____

㉖ One of the angles of a rhombus is 118°. If the rhombus is cut into 2 congruent acute triangles, what are the measures of the angles of the triangle?

_____

ISBN: 978-1-77149-220-1

6.4 Applying Geometry Knowledge

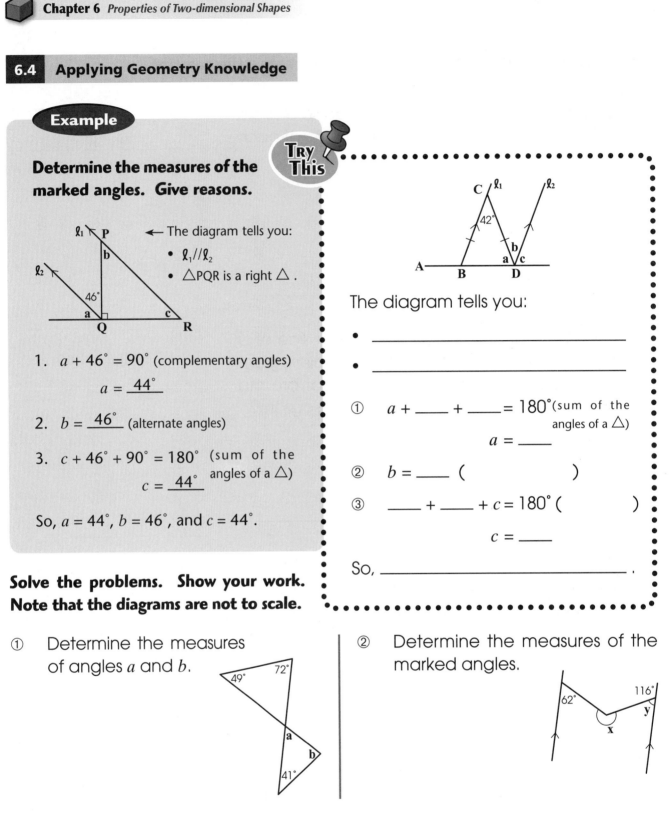

Example

Determine the measures of the marked angles. Give reasons.

← The diagram tells you:
- $\ell_1 // \ell_2$
- $\triangle PQR$ is a right $\triangle$.

1. $a + 46° = 90°$ (complementary angles)

   $a = \underline{44°}$

2. $b = \underline{46°}$ (alternate angles)

3. $c + 46° + 90° = 180°$ (sum of the angles of a $\triangle$)

   $c = \underline{44°}$

So, $a = 44°$, $b = 46°$, and $c = 44°$.

TRY This

The diagram tells you:

- _____
- _____

① $a + \underline{\quad} + \underline{\quad} = 180°$ (sum of the angles of a $\triangle$)

   $a = \underline{\quad}$

② $b = \underline{\quad}$ ($\qquad\qquad$)

③ $\underline{\quad} + \underline{\quad} + c = 180°$ ($\qquad$)

   $c = \underline{\quad}$

So, _____ .

Solve the problems. Show your work. Note that the diagrams are not to scale.

① Determine the measures of angles a and b.

② Determine the measures of the marked angles.

③ If the measures of ∠EYG and ∠EPT are 118° and 106° respectively, what is the measure of ∠YEP?

④ Determine the measures of angles *a*, *b*, and *c*.

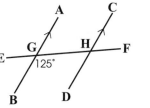

⑤ Are ℓ_1 and ℓ_2 parallel? Explain.

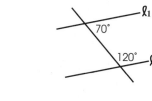

⑥ Identify three angles with a measure of 55°. Then explain.

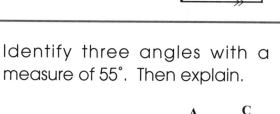

⑦ Tell the relationship between angles *x* and *y*.

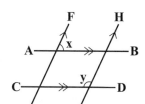

⑧ Is △ABC an isosceles triangle? Explain.

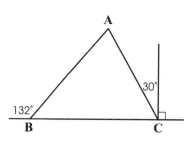

⑨ Are △AOB and △POQ similar triangles? Give reasons.

⑩ What are the measures of the exterior angles of △ABC?

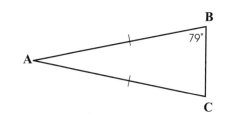

Solve the problems using equations.

⑪ Two of the angles of a quadrilateral are congruent. The third angle is one third of the sum of the congruent angles. The exterior angle of the fourth angle is 44°. What are the measures of the angles of the quadrilateral?

Let x be the measure of one of the congruent angles.

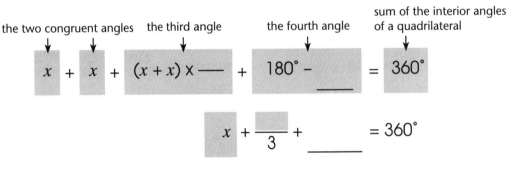

The measures of the angles are _____ .

⑫ An isosceles triangle has a vertex angle of $6x$ and the supplementary angle of a base angle is $21x$. What are the measures of the angles of the isosceles triangle?

⑬ The exterior angles of a triangle are $(3x - 4°)$, $(5x - 20°)$, and $4x$. What are the measures of the angles of the triangles?

⑭ Name the triangles that are similar. Then find the lengths of CD and DB.

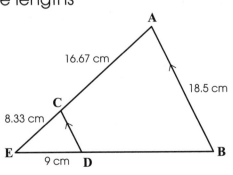

ISBN: 978-1-77149-220-1

Solve the problems.

⑮ What is the measure of an exterior angle of a regular dodecagon?

_____

⑯ The ratio of the measure of the exterior angle to the measure of the adjacent interior angle of a regular polygon is 1:8. How many sides does this regular polygon have?

_____

⑰ The measures of a pair of interior angles between two parallel lines are $3x - 2°$ and $x + 16°$. What are the measures of the interior angles?

_____

⑱

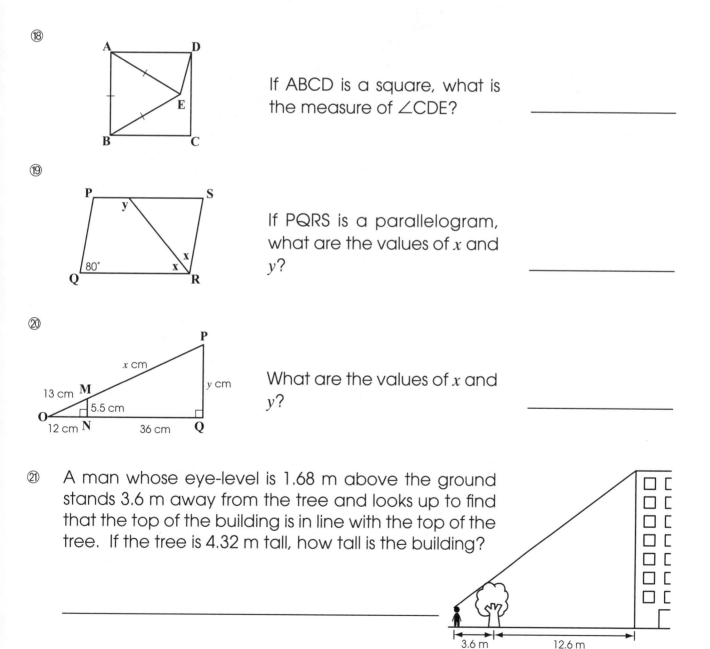

If ABCD is a square, what is the measure of ∠CDE?

_____

⑲ If PQRS is a parallelogram, what are the values of x and y?

_____

⑳ What are the values of x and y?

_____

㉑ A man whose eye-level is 1.68 m above the ground stands 3.6 m away from the tree and looks up to find that the top of the building is in line with the top of the tree. If the tree is 4.32 m tall, how tall is the building?

_____

7 Measurement Relationships in Three-dimensional Figures

7.1 The Pythagorean Theorem

Example

Find the length of the third side of each triangle.

3 cm / 5 cm

$c^2 = a^2 + b^2$ (the Pythagorean Theorem)
$c^2 = 3^2 + 5^2$
$c^2 = 34$
$c = 5.83$ (rounded to 2 decimal places)

The length of the third side is 5.83 cm.

HINT

The Pythagorean Theorem

For any right triangle,

$$a^2 + b^2 = c^2$$

hypotenuse — c / a / b

Try This

① $h^2 = \underline{\quad}^2 + \underline{\quad}^2$

$h^2 = \underline{\qquad}$

$h = \underline{\quad}$

h cm / 8 cm / 6 cm

The length of the third side is _____ cm.

② $\underline{\quad}^2 = y^2 + \underline{\quad}^2$

$\underline{\quad} = y^2 + \underline{\quad}$

$y^2 = \underline{\quad}$ ← Isolate y.

$y = \underline{\quad}$

5 cm / y cm / 12 cm

The length of the third side is _____ cm.

Find the length of the third side of each triangle. Write each answer to 2 decimal places.

①

9 cm
4.2 cm

②
7 cm
10 cm

③
4 cm
6.8 cm

④
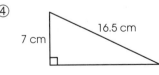
16.5 cm
7 cm

ISBN: 978-1-77149-220-1

Find the length of the hypotenuse and the perimeter of each triangle.

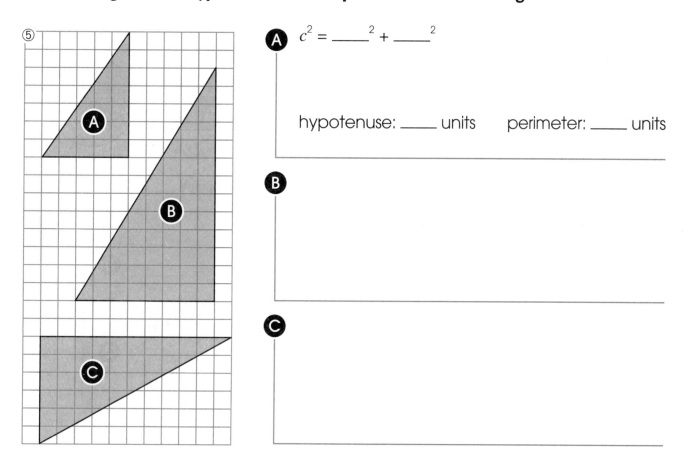

A $c^2 =$ ____^{2} + ____^{2}

hypotenuse: ____ units   perimeter: ____ units

B

C

Find the perimeter of each triangle. Show your work.

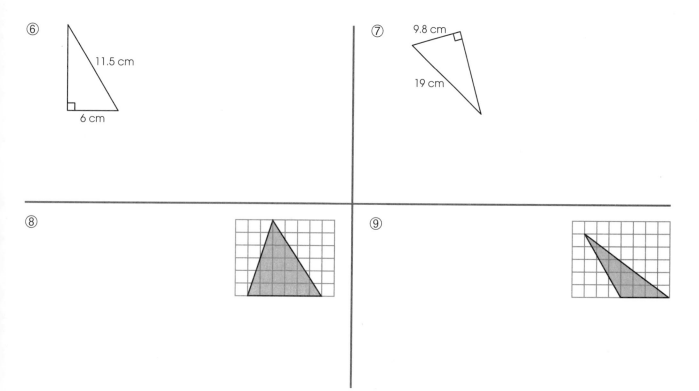

⑥ 11.5 cm 6 cm

⑦ 9.8 cm 19 cm

⑧

⑨

ISBN: 978-1-77149-220-1

Draw one of the diagonals on each rectangle. Then find its length.

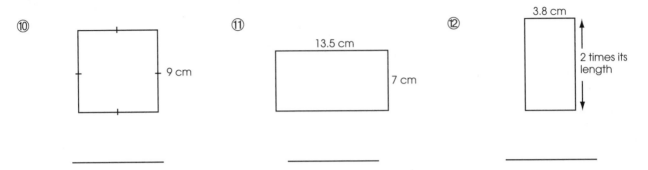

⑩ 9 cm

⑪ 13.5 cm   7 cm

⑫ 3.8 cm   2 times its length

_____   _____   _____

Find the perimeter of each shape.

⑬ 21 cm   10 cm   15 cm

⑭ 4.5 cm   12 cm   6 cm   10 cm

⑮ 9.8 cm   4 cm   5 cm   13 cm

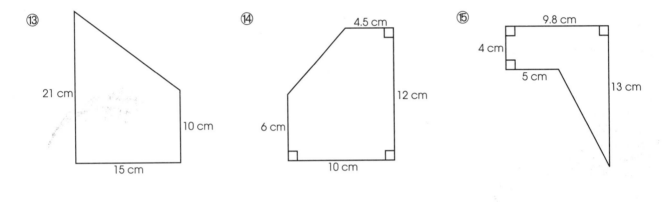

_____   _____   _____

Find the length of the side in bold of each shape.

⑯

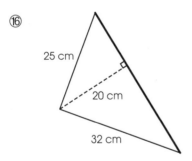

25 cm   20 cm   32 cm

$25^2 = 20^2 + y^2$

$y =$ _____

$32^2 =$ _____$^2 + x^2$

$x =$ _____

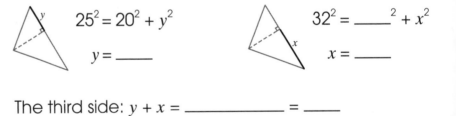

The third side: $y + x =$ _____ = _____

The third side is _____ cm.

⑰

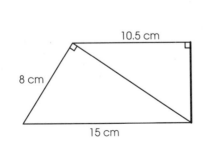

10.5 cm   8 cm   15 cm

ISBN: 978-1-77149-220-1

Find the perimeter of each shape.

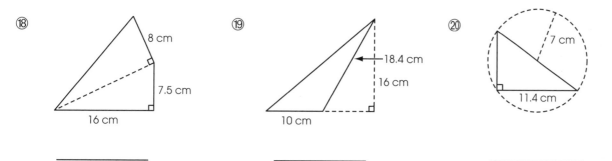

⑱ 8 cm 7.5 cm 16 cm

_____

⑲ 18.4 cm 16 cm 10 cm

_____

⑳ 7 cm 11.4 cm

_____

Solve the problems.

㉑ Judy has two sticks. If she wants to make a right triangle, what are the possible lengths of the third stick?

9.4 cm   12.8 cm

_____

㉒ A 5-m ladder leans against the wall. What is the distance from the top of the ladder to the base of the wall?

_____

㉓ If the ladder is pulled 0.4 m further away from the wall, what is the distance from the top of the ladder to the base of the wall now?

1.2 m

_____

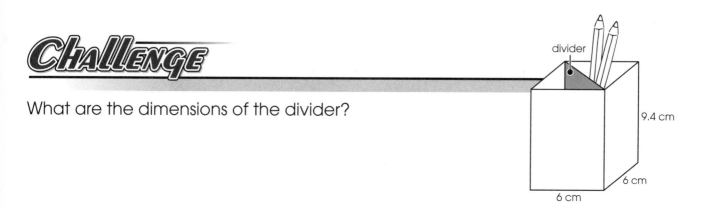

CHALLENGE

What are the dimensions of the divider?

divider

9.4 cm

6 cm

6 cm

ISBN: 978-1-77149-220-1

7.2 Perimeters and Areas of Composite Figures

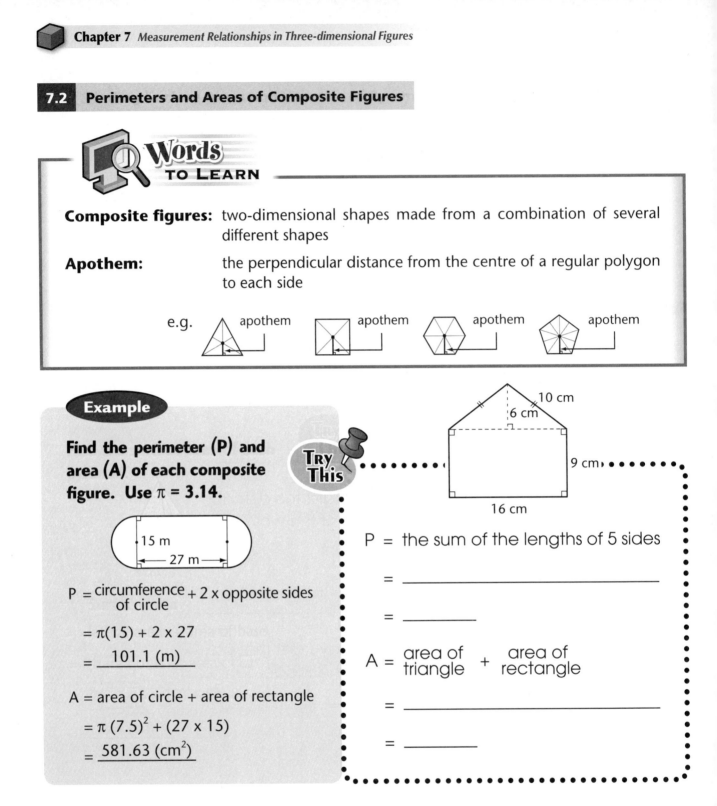

Words TO LEARN

Composite figures: two-dimensional shapes made from a combination of several different shapes

Apothem: the perpendicular distance from the centre of a regular polygon to each side

e.g.

Example

Find the perimeter (P) and area (A) of each composite figure. Use π = 3.14.

15 m
27 m

$P = \text{circumference} + 2 \times \text{opposite sides}$ of circle

$= \pi(15) + 2 \times 27$

$= \underline{101.1}$ (m)

A = area of circle + area of rectangle

$= \pi (7.5)^2 + (27 \times 15)$

$= \underline{581.63}$ (cm^2)

TRY THIS

10 cm
6 cm
9 cm
16 cm

P = the sum of the lengths of 5 sides

= _____

= _____

$A = \begin{matrix}\text{area of} \\ \text{triangle}\end{matrix} + \begin{matrix}\text{area of} \\ \text{rectangle}\end{matrix}$

= _____

= _____

Find the perimeter and area of each polygon.

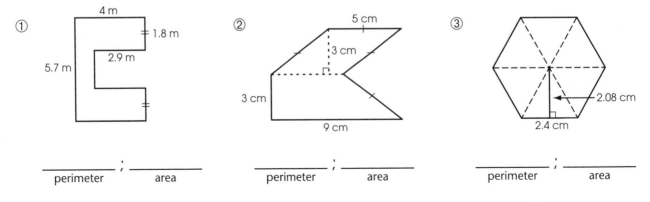

① 4 m
1.8 m
2.9 m
5.7 m

_____ ; _____
perimeter   area

② 5 cm
3 cm
3 cm
9 cm

_____ ; _____
perimeter   area

③ 2.08 cm
2.4 cm

_____ ; _____
perimeter   area

ISBN: 978-1-77149-220-1

Find the perimeter and area of each composite figure. Round the answers to the nearest hundredth. Use π = 3.14.

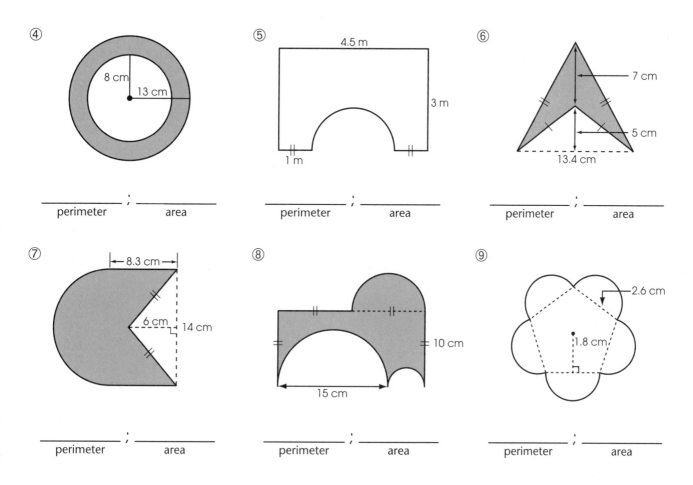

④ 8 cm 13 cm

_____ ; _____
perimeter   area

⑤ 4.5 m   3 m   1 m

_____ ; _____
perimeter   area

⑥ 7 cm   5 cm   13.4 cm

_____ ; _____
perimeter   area

⑦ 8.3 cm   6 cm   14 cm

_____ ; _____
perimeter   area

⑧ 10 cm   15 cm

_____ ; _____
perimeter   area

⑨ 2.6 cm   1.8 cm

_____ ; _____
perimeter   area

Solve the problems. Round the answers to the nearest hundredth. Use π = 3.14.

⑩ If the area of this triangle is 196 cm², what is its perimeter?

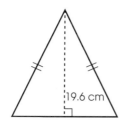

19.6 cm

_____

⑪ If the perimeters of the flower and the leaf are 62.8 cm and 15.7 cm respectively, what are their areas?

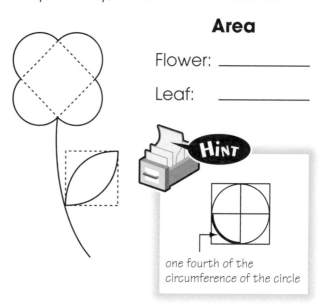

Area

Flower: _____

Leaf: _____

HINT

one fourth of the circumference of the circle

ISBN: 978-1-77149-220-1

Draw a diagram to illustrate each problem. Round the answers to the nearest hundredth. Use π = 3.14.

⑫ Jasmine is knitting a scarf that has the shape of an isosceles triangle. If the scarf has a base of 1.2 m and a height of 0.8 m, how long does the piping along the edge of the scarf need to be?

⑬ Carl is making a hexagon and an octagon with cardboard. The hexagon has a side length of 10.6 cm and its apothem is 9.18 cm. The octagon has a side length of 8.4 cm and its apothem is 10.14 cm. Which shape has a greater area? By how much?

⑭ A string is hung on a rod from one end to the other to make 3 identical semi-circles with the radius of 24.5 cm. How long is the string?

⑮ The vertices of a triangle on a graph are (1,4), (-2,1), and (6,-1). What are the perimeter and area of the triangle?

⑯ Michelle cuts out the biggest circle from a rectangular cardboard measuring 16 cm by 25 cm. What is the area of the remaining cardboard?

 ISBN: 978-1-77149-220-1

Using whole numbers, for the length and width, complete each table to determine which dimensions give the maximum area.

A gardener wants to fence a rectangular garden patch with 20 m of rope. Help him find all the possible rectangles and their areas.

Rectangle*	Width (m)	Length (m)	Area (m²)
A	1	9	9
B	2	8	16
C	3	7	21
D	4	6	24
E	5	5	25

1 m
9 m

* Each has a perimeter of 20 m.

the greatest

The patch measuring 5 m by 5 m gives the maximum area of 25 m². It is in the shape of a square.

Try This

Fence: 24 m →

Flowerbed

A landscaper wants to surround a rectangular flowerbed with a 24-m fence. Find all the possible rectangles and their areas.

Rectangle*	Width (m)	Length (m)	Area (m²)
A	1	11	11
B			

* Each has a perimeter of 24 m.

The flowerbed measuring _____

_____

_____ .

Use the results from above to answer the questions.

⑰ If a rectangle with a given perimeter gives the maximum area, it is in the

shape of a _____ .

⑱ Write an equation to find the maximum area of the rectangle with a given perimeter.

⑲ If the perimeter of a rectangle is 96 cm, what is the maximum area?

Find the measurements of the rectangles in whole numbers. Complete the tables and answer the questions.

⑳ **Case I** **A Rectangular Pig Pen**

A pig farmer wants to fence a pen of an area of 64 m² using the least amount of fencing.

Rectangle*	Width (m)	Length (m)	Perimeter (m)
A	1	64	

*Each has an area of 64 m².

The minimum perimeter: _____

The dimensions of the rectangle:

_____

Case II **A Daycare Centre**

Mr. Smith wants to fence a rectangular playground of an area of 36 m² using the least amount of fencing.

Rectangle*	Width (m)	Length (m)	Perimeter (m)

*Each has an area of 36 m².

The minimum perimeter: _____

The dimensions of the rectangle:

_____

Use the results from above to answer the questions.

㉑ If a rectangle with a given area has the minimum perimeter, it is in the

shape of a _____ .

㉒ Describe the relationship between the dimensions of the rectangle and the area when the perimeter is minimized.

_____

㉓ Write an equation to find the minimum perimeter of the rectangle with a given area. Then use the equation to find the minimum perimeter if the area of a rectangle is 64 cm².

_____

ISBN: 978-1-77149-220-1

Solve the problems. Round the answers to the nearest hundredth.

㉔   Find the perimeter and area of each figure. Then find which figure has the greatest perimeter and which figure has the greatest area.

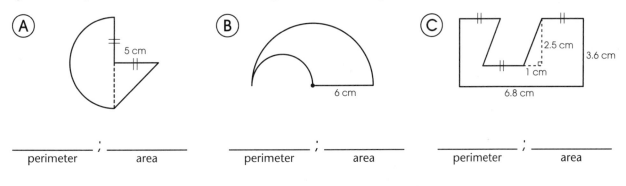

_____ ; _____
  perimeter   area

_____ ; _____
  perimeter   area

_____ ; _____
  perimeter   area

_____ has the greatest perimeter and _____ has the greatest area.

㉕   Melvin is making a rectangle with 56 1-cm sticks. What is the maximum area of the rectangle?

_____

㉖   Each turf measures 1 m by 1 m. What is the minimum perimeter of the rectangular garden that is covered by 100 turfs?

_____

㉗   Leo ran 870.66 m. How many laps did he run?

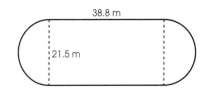

_____

㉘   Mr. Hutton has to paint 15 doors. If he paints 0.6 m^2 in one minute, how long does it take him to complete the job?

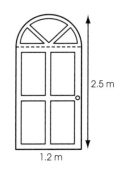

_____

7.3 Solving Problems Involving Perimeters and Areas

Example

Solve the problems.

If the area of this floor plan is 65 m², what is the length of the kitchen?

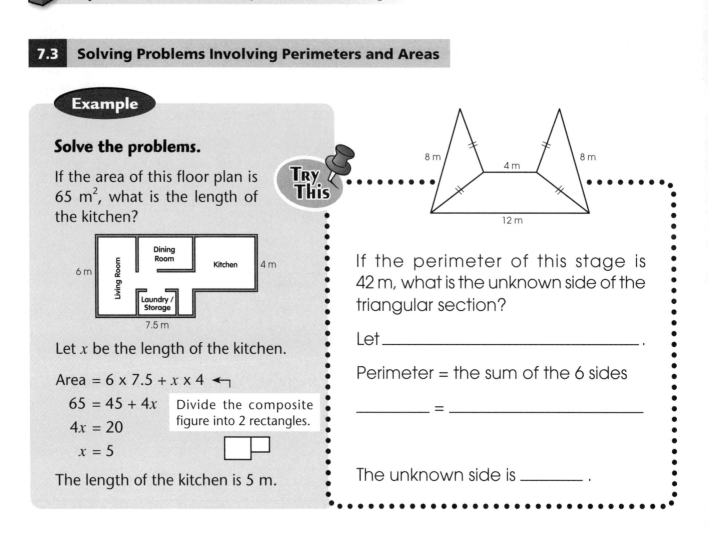

Let x be the length of the kitchen.

Area = 6 × 7.5 + x × 4

$65 = 45 + 4x$ | Divide the composite figure into 2 rectangles.

$4x = 20$

$x = 5$

The length of the kitchen is 5 m.

TRY THIS

If the perimeter of this stage is 42 m, what is the unknown side of the triangular section?

Let _____ .

Perimeter = the sum of the 6 sides

_____ = _____

The unknown side is _____ .

Solve the problems. Round the answers to the nearest hundredth. Use π = 3.14.

① Find the perimeter of the ramp.

2.3 m
2.7 m
Area = 3.62 m²
4.8 m

_____

② If the tiling costs $17.50/m², what is the cost of tiling this kitchen?

8 m
3 m
7 m
9 m

_____

③ Find the area of the track.

40 m
Perimeter = 357 m

_____

④ If the fencing costs $15/m, what is the cost of fencing for a 314-m² pool with a 2-m wide walking path?

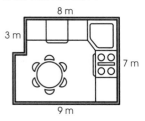

2 m

Pool

_____

ISBN: 978-1-77149-220-1

Write an equation to solve each problem.

⑤ A window consists of four 32-cm wide square panels and a semi-circle panel.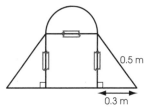

   a. If the cost of the stained glass is $26/m², what is the cost of the window made of stained glass?

   _____

   b. If the cost of trim is $12/m with a $150 labour fee, how much does it cost to trim this window?

   _____

⑥ Kevin made a toy rocket out of cardboard. The rocket contained a semi-circle, a square, and two congruent triangles.

0.5 m

0.3 m

If Kevin paints his rocket at a rate of 0.05 m²/min, how long will it take him to paint both sides of the rocket?

_____

⑦ A solar panel can convert energy from the sun into electricity at a rate of 1.4 kW/m² per hour.

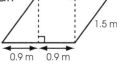

1.5 m

0.9 m   0.9 m

Find the amount of electricity that one panel can convert in an hour.

_____

⑧ Four identical circles line a square of 8 cm side length.

What is the area of the shaded part?

_____

⑨ A belt buckle consists of 2 parts. Find the perimeter and area of each part.

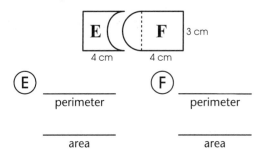

E _____   F _____
  perimeter   perimeter

_____   _____
  area   area

⑩ Find the area of the shaded and the unshaded part of a company logo.

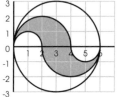

_____

Solve the problems. Show your work. Round your answers to the nearest hundredth.

⑪ Jane is decorating a rectangular mirror with an area of 10 000 cm² by putting gold chains on its border. Each gold chain is 10 cm long.

a. What dimensions should the mirror be if she wants to use the fewest gold chains? How many gold chains are needed?

Mirror*	Length (cm)	Width (cm)	Perimeter (cm)	No. of Gold Chains
A	50	200	500	50

* Each has an area of 10 000 cm².

b. If each gold chain costs $89 and the back board for the minor costs $0.59/cm², how much does Jane have to pay?

⑫ Jamie is adding a deck to the back of his house. The deck is rectangular with one side connecting to the house. If the outer perimeter of the deck is 15 m, what is the greatest amount of space he can have for the deck?

⑬ Louis wants to fence a rectangular pen that has an area of 49 m². If fencing costs $9/m, what is the least cost to fence the pen?

ISBN: 978-1-77149-220-1

Solve the problems.

⑭ A 9-m by 12-m lawn has a water valve at one corner.

    a.   If Cynthia waters the lawn with a 8-m long hose, what is the largest area of lawn she can water? _____

    b.   What is the area of lawn that cannot be watered? _____

    c.   Now she connects a sprinkler to her 8-m hose. If she places the sprinkler at the centre of her lawn, how far does it have to reach in order to water the entire lawn? _____

⑮ Kingsley wants to plant cedar shrubs around his backyard except for the side that attaches to his house measuring 16 m x 16 m. The distance between every 2 adjacent shrubs is 2 m. How many cedar shrubs does he need? _____

⑯ Willy is making rectangular boxes to package cakes. If the area of a round cake is 144π cm^2, what are the dimensions of the base of the rectangular boxes so that the cake fits right into it? _____

⑰ Stephanie wants to make a picture frame with 256 1-cm sticks and a lace trim. Find the dimensions of the frame that requires the least lace. _____

⑱ Find the perimeter of the shaded region if the sides are all trisected. _____

12 cm

15 cm

⑲

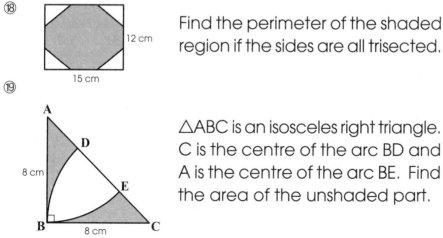

A

D

8 cm

E

B

8 cm

C

△ABC is an isosceles right triangle. C is the centre of the arc BD and A is the centre of the arc BE. Find the area of the unshaded part. _____

HINT

This is $\dfrac{1}{8}$ of a circle.

ISBN: 978-1-77149-220-1

7.4 Finding Surface Areas and Volumes of Prisms

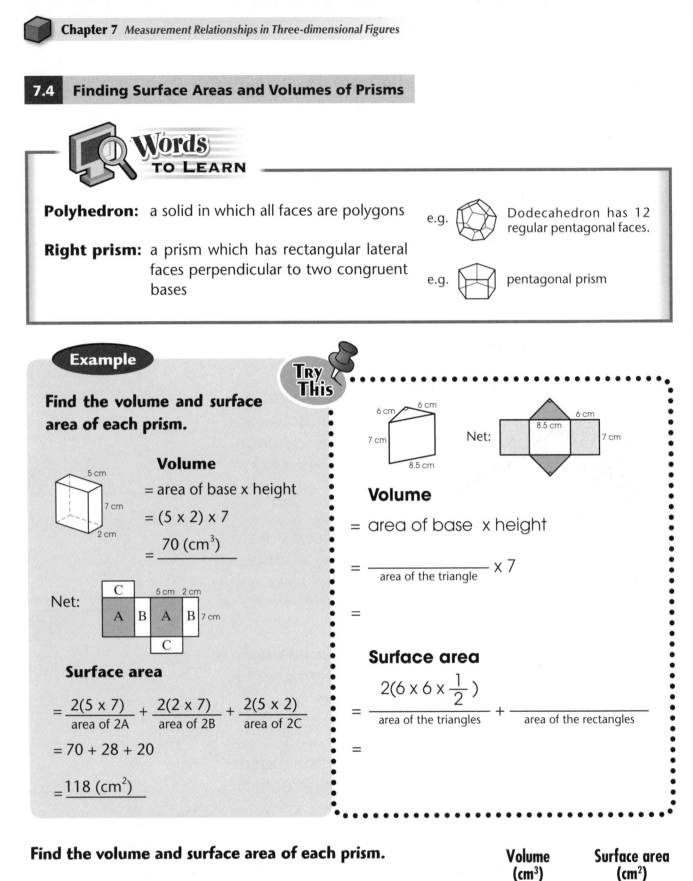

Words TO LEARN

Polyhedron: a solid in which all faces are polygons

e.g. Dodecahedron has 12 regular pentagonal faces.

Right prism: a prism which has rectangular lateral faces perpendicular to two congruent bases

e.g. pentagonal prism

Example

Find the volume and surface area of each prism.

Volume

= area of base x height

= (5 x 2) x 7

= $\underline{\quad 70 \ (cm^3)\quad}$

Net:

C

A B A B 7 cm

5 cm 2 cm

C

Surface area

= $\dfrac{2(5 \times 7)}{\text{area of 2A}}$ + $\dfrac{2(2 \times 7)}{\text{area of 2B}}$ + $\dfrac{2(5 \times 2)}{\text{area of 2C}}$

= 70 + 28 + 20

= $\underline{118 \ (cm^2)}$

Try This

Net:

6 cm 6 cm

7 cm

8.5 cm

8.5 cm 6 cm 7 cm

Volume

= area of base x height

= $\dfrac{\quad\quad\quad}{\text{area of the triangle}}$ x 7

=

Surface area

= $\dfrac{2(6 \times 6 \times \frac{1}{2})}{\text{area of the triangles}}$ + $\dfrac{\quad\quad\quad}{\text{area of the rectangles}}$

=

Find the volume and surface area of each prism.

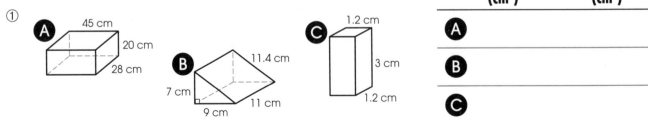

① **A** 45 cm, 20 cm, 28 cm

B 11.4 cm, 7 cm, 11 cm, 9 cm

C 1.2 cm, 3 cm, 1.2 cm

	Volume (cm³)	Surface area (cm²)
A		
B		
C		

ISBN: 978-1-77149-220-1

Find the volume and surface area of each right regular prism.

②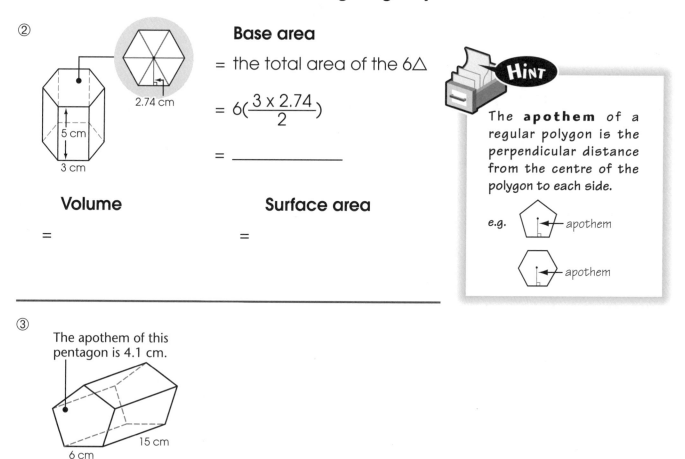

Base area

= the total area of the 6△

$= 6(\dfrac{3 \times 2.74}{2})$

= _____

Volume

=

Surface area

=

③

The apothem of this pentagon is 4.1 cm.

15 cm

6 cm

Find the volume and surface area of each figure.

④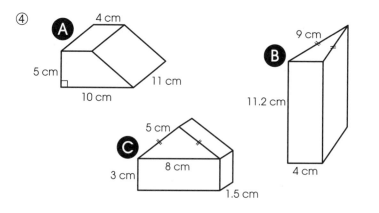

A
4 cm
5 cm
11 cm
10 cm

B
9 cm
11.2 cm
4 cm

C
5 cm
8 cm
3 cm
1.5 cm

	Volume	Surface area
Ⓐ		
Ⓑ		
Ⓒ		
Ⓓ		
Ⓔ		

Ⓓ A regular octagonal prism is 16.5 cm high and the apothem and side length of its base are 6 cm and 7.2 cm respectively.

Ⓔ A regular triangular prism is 8.8 cm high and the side length of its base is 16 cm.

Fill in the blanks. Then find the volume and surface area of each figure. Round your answers to the nearest hundredth. Use π = 3.14.

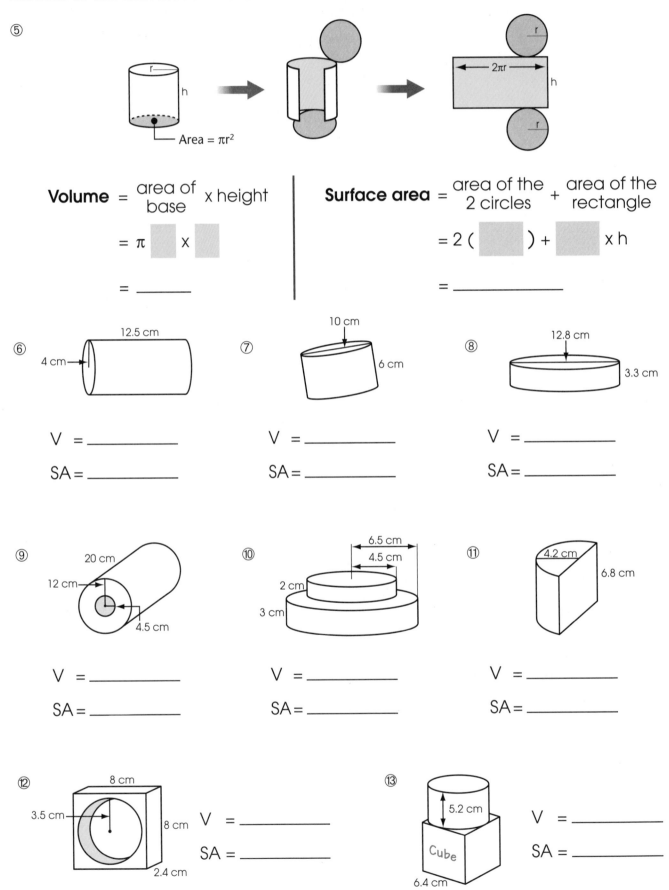

⑤

Volume = $\dfrac{\text{area of}}{\text{base}}$ x height

= π [ ] x [ ]

= _____

Surface area = $\dfrac{\text{area of the}}{\text{2 circles}}$ + $\dfrac{\text{area of the}}{\text{rectangle}}$

= 2 ([ ]) + [ ] x h

= _____

⑥ 12.5 cm 4 cm

V = _____

SA = _____

⑦ 10 cm 6 cm

V = _____

SA = _____

⑧ 12.8 cm 3.3 cm

V = _____

SA = _____

⑨ 20 cm 12 cm 4.5 cm

V = _____

SA = _____

⑩ 6.5 cm 4.5 cm 2 cm 3 cm

V = _____

SA = _____

⑪ 4.2 cm 6.8 cm

V = _____

SA = _____

⑫ 8 cm 3.5 cm 8 cm 2.4 cm

V = _____

SA = _____

⑬ 5.2 cm Cube 6.4 cm

V = _____

SA = _____

ISBN: 978-1-77149-220-1

Find the volume of each rectangular prism. Complete the table and answer the questions.

⑭

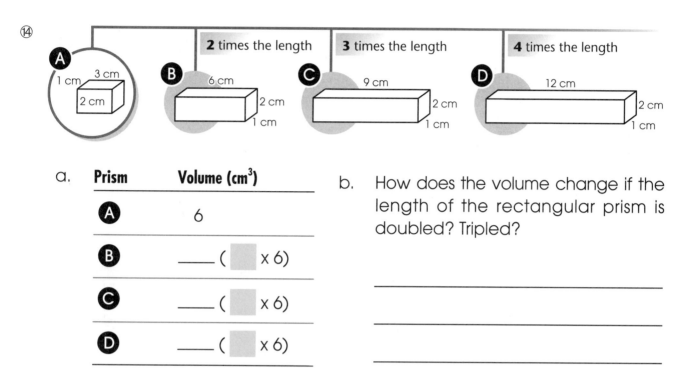

a.

Prism	Volume (cm³)
Ⓐ	6
Ⓑ	___ (⬜ x 6)
Ⓒ	___ (⬜ x 6)
Ⓓ	___ (⬜ x 6)

b. How does the volume change if the length of the rectangular prism is doubled? Tripled?

_____

_____

_____

c. The volume of a rectangular prism (Y) is 400 cm³. A prism has the same height and width as those of Y. If the length of the prism is:

- 10 times of that of Y, what is the volume of the prism?

  _____

- n times of that of Y, what is the volume of the prism?

  _____

⑮ A rectangular block of wood is cut into 3 congruent parts. Compare the volume of the original block with that of each small block.

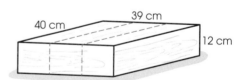

_____

⑯ A dough is in the shape of a triangular prism. Mrs. Lynn is going to cut it into 3 sections. The ratio of the length of the 3 sections is 1 : 3 : 4. If the volume of the dough is 672 cm³, what is the volume of each section?

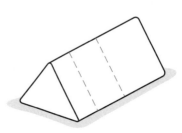

_____

Look at each group of figures. Complete the tables and fill in the blanks.

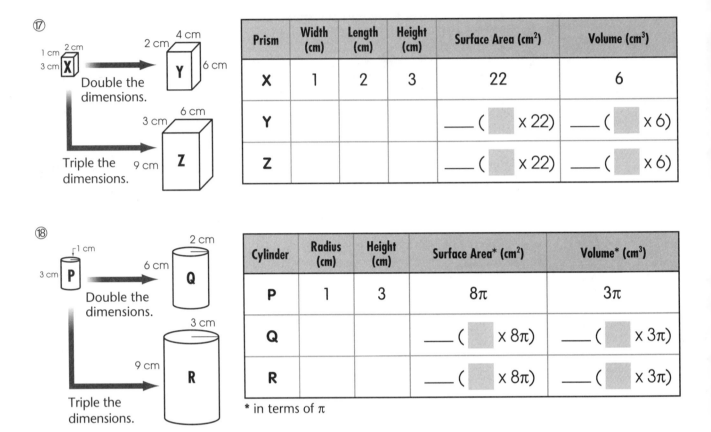

⑰

Prism	Width (cm)	Length (cm)	Height (cm)	Surface Area (cm²)	Volume (cm³)
X	1	2	3	22	6
Y				____ (▢ x 22)	____ (▢ x 6)
Z				____ (▢ x 22)	____ (▢ x 6)

⑱

Cylinder	Radius (cm)	Height (cm)	Surface Area* (cm²)	Volume* (cm³)
P	1	3	8π	3π
Q			____ (▢ x 8π)	____ (▢ x 3π)
R			____ (▢ x 8π)	____ (▢ x 3π)

* in terms of π

⑲ **Double** the dimensions of a prism or cylinder:
   • The surface area of the bigger prism or cylinder is _____ times the original one.
   • The volume of the bigger prism or cylinder is _____ times the original one.

⑳ **Triple** the dimensions of a prism or cylinder:
   • The surface area of the bigger prism or cylinder is _____ times the original one.
   • The volume of the bigger prism or cylinder is _____ times the original one.

㉑ The volume of a rectangular prism is 240 cm³. If each of its sides is doubled, the volume of the new prism is _____ .

㉒ The surface area of a cylinder is 52.5π cm². If the dimensions of a cylinder are one third of this cylinder, its surface area is _____ .

ISBN: 978-1-77149-220-1

Jack wants to build a rectangular garden shed with 96 m² of plywood. Help him complete the table to find the dimensions of the shed that gives the maximum amount of space. Then answer the questions.

HINT

For a rectangular prism,

Surface area
= $2lw + 2lh + 2wh$
= $\underline{2(lw + lh + wh)}$

Volume = $\underline{lwh}$

Garden shed A (Question 23)

$96 = 2(1 \times 4 + 1 \times h + 4 \times h)$
$96 = 2(4 + h + 4h)$
$48 = 4 + 5h$
$h = 8.8$

Substitute:
SA = 96
w = 4
l   = 1

㉓

Garden Shed*	Width (m)	Length (m)	Height (m)	Volume (m³)
A	4	1		
B	4	2		
C	4	3		
D	4	4		
E	4	5		
F	4	6		
G	4	7		

* Each shed has a surface area of 96 m².

㉔ What is the maximum amount of space of the shed with the total surface area of 96 m²? What are the dimensions? What is the shape of the shed?

_____

Each stick of butter has a volume of 729 cm³. Find the dimensions of the stick that should be manufactured to minimize the cost of packaging. Describe the shape.

㉕

Stick	Width (cm)	Length (cm)	Height (cm)	Surface Area (cm²)
A	9	5		
B	9	7		
C	9	9		
D	9	11		
E	9	13		

* Each stick has a volume of 729 cm³.

The dimensions:

The shape:

_____   _____

7.5   Finding Surface Areas and Volumes of Pyramids

Right regular pyramid:

a pyramid with a base that is a regular polygon and its apex aligned directly above the centre of the base

Height of a pyramid:

the perpendicular distance from the apex to the base

Slant height of a pyramid:

the height of each lateral triangular face

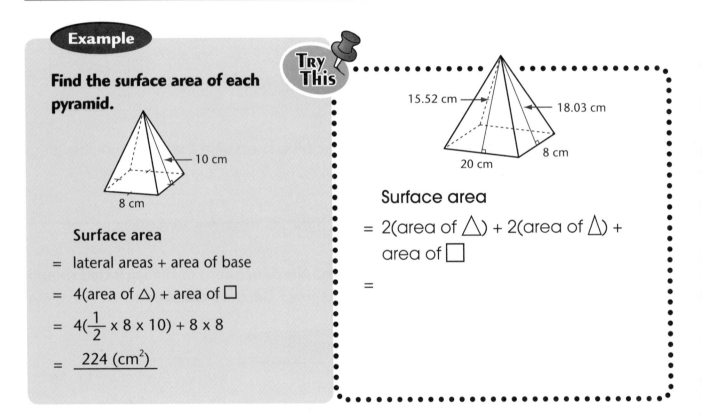

Example

Find the surface area of each pyramid.

— 10 cm

8 cm

Surface area

= lateral areas + area of base

= 4(area of △) + area of □

= 4($\frac{1}{2}$ × 8 × 10) + 8 × 8

= __224 (cm²)__

Try This

15.52 cm — → ← 18.03 cm

8 cm

20 cm

Surface area

= 2(area of △) + 2(area of △) + area of □

=

Find the surface area of each figure. Round the answers to the nearest hundredth.

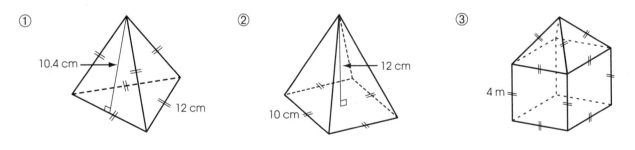

① 10.4 cm → 12 cm

② ← 12 cm   10 cm

③ 4 m

Develop a formula for finding the total surface area of a square-based pyramid. Then solve the problems by using the formula.

④

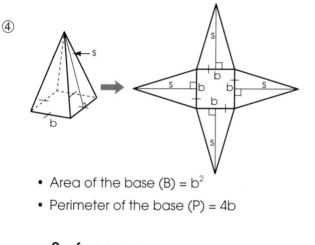

- Area of the base (B) = b^2
- Perimeter of the base (P) = 4b

Surface area

= area of 4△ + area of base

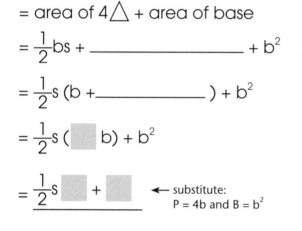

$= \frac{1}{2}bs + $ _____ $+ b^2$

$= \frac{1}{2}s (b + $ _____ $) + b^2$

$= \frac{1}{2}s ($ ▢ $b) + b^2$

$= \frac{1}{2}s$ ▢ $+$ ▢   ← substitute:
         P = 4b and B = b^2

⑤ If the slant height of a square-based pyramid is 16 cm and the side length of the base is 9.5 cm, what is its surface area?

_____

⑥ If the surface area of a square-based pyramid is 352.48 cm^2 and the side length of its base is 6.8 cm, what is its slant height?

_____

⑦ If the surface area of a square-based pyramid is 86.86 cm^2 and the area of the base is 5.76 cm^2, what is its slant height?

_____

Look at one of the lateral faces of each square-based pyramid. Find the total surface area of the square-based pyramid.

⑧

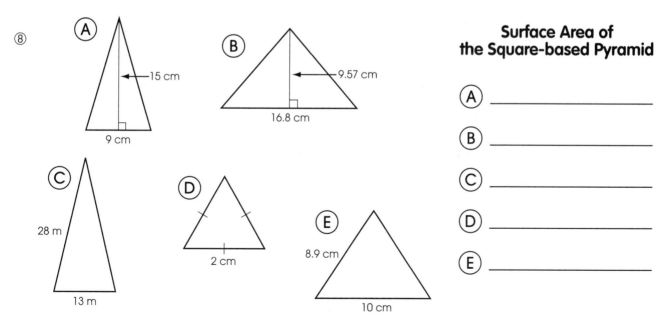

Surface Area of the Square-based Pyramid

Ⓐ _____

Ⓑ _____

Ⓒ _____

Ⓓ _____

Ⓔ _____

ISBN: 978-1-77149-220-1

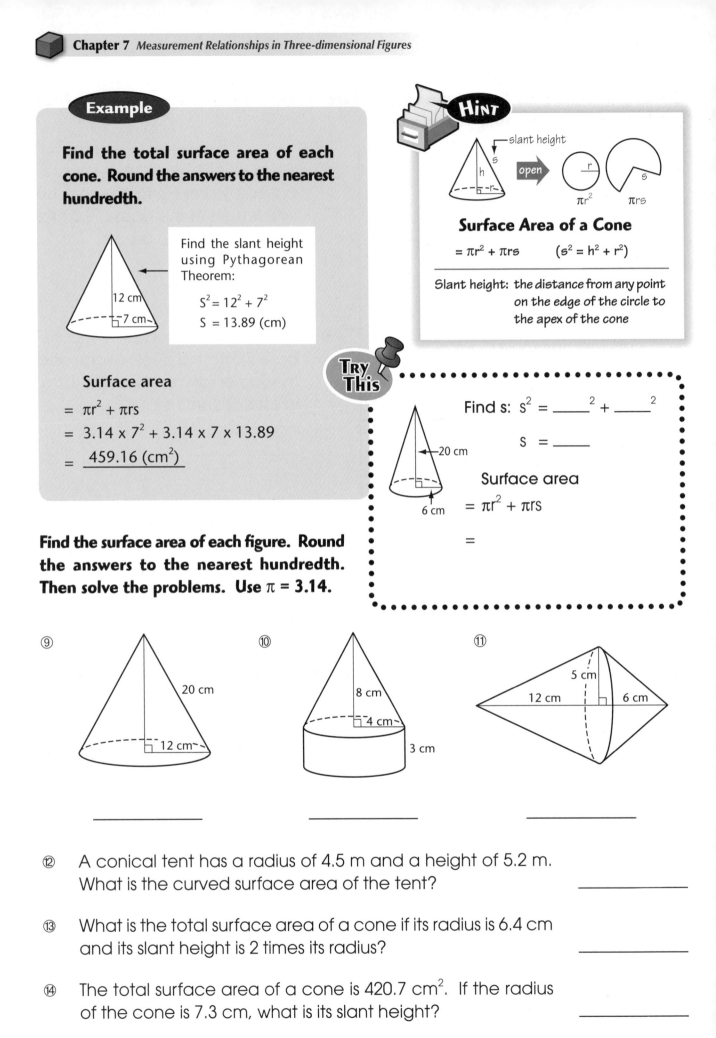

Example

Find the total surface area of each cone. Round the answers to the nearest hundredth.

Find the slant height using Pythagorean Theorem:

$$S^2 = 12^2 + 7^2$$
$$S = 13.89 \text{ (cm)}$$

12 cm

7 cm

HINT

slant height

open

πr^2　　$\pi r s$

Surface Area of a Cone

$$= \pi r^2 + \pi r s \qquad (s^2 = h^2 + r^2)$$

Slant height: the distance from any point on the edge of the circle to the apex of the cone

Surface area

$$= \pi r^2 + \pi r s$$
$$= 3.14 \times 7^2 + 3.14 \times 7 \times 13.89$$
$$= \underline{459.16 \text{ (cm}^2)}$$

TRY THIS

20 cm

6 cm

Find s: $s^2 = \underline{\quad}^2 + \underline{\quad}^2$

$$s = \underline{\quad}$$

Surface area

$$= \pi r^2 + \pi r s$$
$$=$$

Find the surface area of each figure. Round the answers to the nearest hundredth. Then solve the problems. Use π = 3.14.

⑨

20 cm

12 cm

_____

⑩

8 cm

4 cm

3 cm

_____

⑪

5 cm

12 cm

6 cm

_____

⑫ A conical tent has a radius of 4.5 m and a height of 5.2 m. What is the curved surface area of the tent? _____

⑬ What is the total surface area of a cone if its radius is 6.4 cm and its slant height is 2 times its radius? _____

⑭ The total surface area of a cone is 420.7 cm². If the radius of the cone is 7.3 cm, what is its slant height? _____

ISBN: 978-1-77149-220-1

Find the surface area or radius of each sphere or semi-sphere. Round the answers to the nearest hundredth. Use π = 3.14.

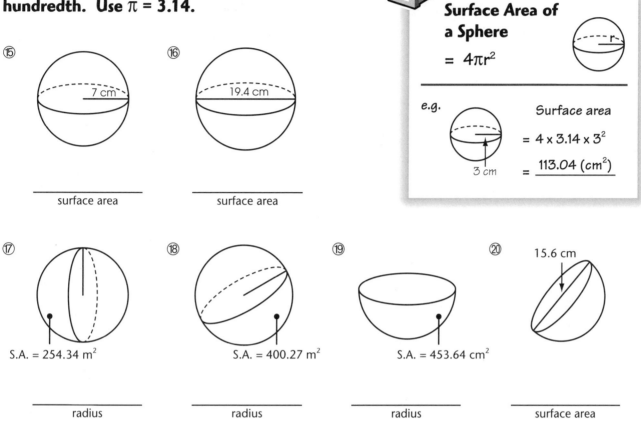

⑮ 7 cm

_____
surface area

⑯ 19.4 cm

_____
surface area

⑰ S.A. = 254.34 m²

_____
radius

⑱ S.A. = 400.27 m²

_____
radius

⑲ S.A. = 453.64 cm²

_____
radius

⑳ 15.6 cm

_____
surface area

Find the surface area of each figure. Round the answers to the nearest hundredth. Use π = 3.14.

㉑

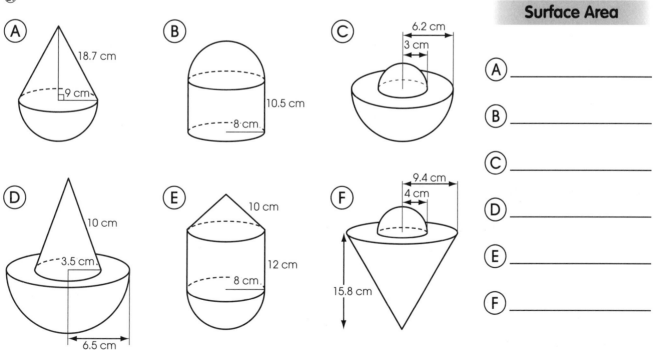

Ⓐ 18.7 cm, 9 cm

Ⓑ 10.5 cm, 8 cm

Ⓒ 6.2 cm, 3 cm

Ⓓ 10 cm, 3.5 cm, 6.5 cm

Ⓔ 10 cm, 12 cm, 8 cm

Ⓕ 9.4 cm, 4 cm, 15.8 cm

Surface Area

Ⓐ _____

Ⓑ _____

Ⓒ _____

Ⓓ _____

Ⓔ _____

Ⓕ _____

Find the volume of each figure. Round the answers to the nearest hundredth. Use π = 3.14.

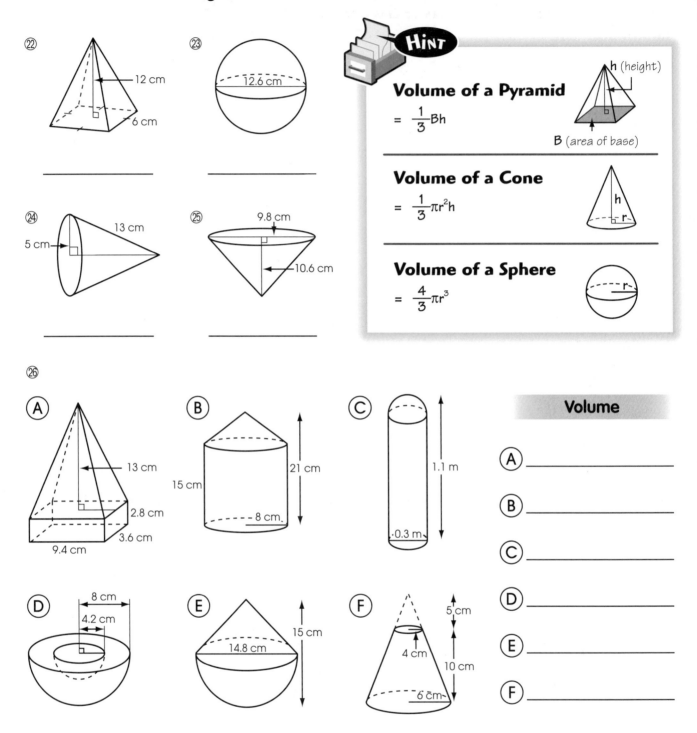

㉒ 12 cm, 6 cm

㉓ 12.6 cm

HINT

Volume of a Pyramid

$= \frac{1}{3}Bh$

h (height)

B (area of base)

Volume of a Cone

$= \frac{1}{3}\pi r^2 h$

h, r

Volume of a Sphere

$= \frac{4}{3}\pi r^3$

r

㉔ 13 cm, 5 cm

㉕ 9.8 cm, 10.6 cm

㉖

	Volume
A	_____
B	_____
C	_____
D	_____
E	_____
F	_____

Ⓐ 13 cm, 2.8 cm, 3.6 cm, 9.4 cm

Ⓑ 21 cm, 15 cm, 8 cm

Ⓒ 1.1 m, 0.3 m

Ⓓ 8 cm, 4.2 cm

Ⓔ 15 cm, 14.8 cm

Ⓕ 5 cm, 4 cm, 10 cm, 6 cm

Solve the problems.

㉗ A ball fits right inside a cube with edges of 10 cm in length. What is the volume of the ball? _____

㉘ A cone fits right inside a cylinder with a base radius of 16 cm and a height of 24 cm. What is the unoccupied volume of the cylinder? _____

ISBN: 978-1-77149-220-1

Solve the problems.

㉙ The surface areas of the sphere and the cone are the same. What is the radius of the sphere?

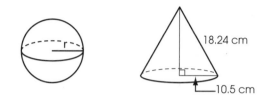

18.24 cm

10.5 cm

_____

㉚ A stick of butter is melted and refrozen into a square-based pyramid. What is the height of the pyramid?

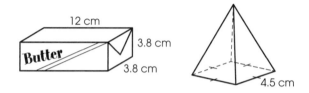

12 cm

3.8 cm

Butter

3.8 cm

4.5 cm

_____

㉛ The surface area and volume of a sphere with radius r are $4\pi r^2$ and $\frac{4}{3}\pi r^3$ respectively. If the radius of the sphere is doubled, what are the surface area and volume of the big sphere? Write the answers in terms of π.

_____

㉜ What is the volume of the largest possible pyramid that can fit into a 8-cm cube? What is its total surface area?

_____

㉝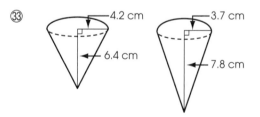

4.2 cm

6.4 cm

3.7 cm

7.8 cm

Which cone cup holds more water? By how much?

_____

㉞

The height of a vase in the shape of a square-based pyramid is 15.8 cm. If this vase can hold 1.6 L of water, what is the side length of the base?

_____

ISBN: 978-1-77149-220-1

7.6 **Solving Problems Involving Prisms, Pyramids, Cylinders, and Spheres**

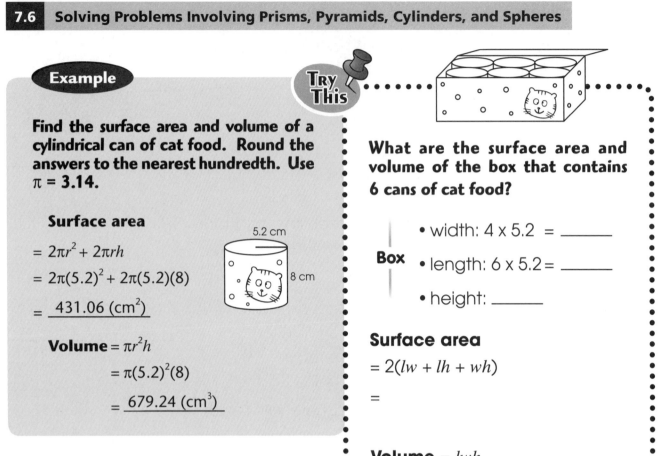

Example

Find the surface area and volume of a cylindrical can of cat food. Round the answers to the nearest hundredth. Use $\pi = 3.14$.

Surface area

$= 2\pi r^2 + 2\pi rh$

$= 2\pi(5.2)^2 + 2\pi(5.2)(8)$

$= \underline{431.06}$ (cm^2)

5.2 cm

8 cm

Volume $= \pi r^2 h$

$= \pi(5.2)^2(8)$

$= \underline{679.24}$ (cm^3)

Try This

What are the surface area and volume of the box that contains 6 cans of cat food?

Box
- width: 4 x 5.2 = _____
- length: 6 x 5.2 = _____
- height: _____

Surface area

$= 2(lw + lh + wh)$

$=$

Volume $= lwh$

$=$

Solve the problems. Round your answers to the nearest hundredth. Use $\pi = 3.14$.

① A square-based prism fits exactly into a cylinder that has a height of 16.5 cm and a diameter of 8 cm.

   a. What is the volume of the prism?

   _____

   b. How much space is unoccupied?

   _____

② Compare the figures.

3.5 cm   8 cm

14 cm

6.5 cm

14 cm

   a. Which has a greater volume?

   _____

   b. Which has a greater surface area?

   _____

ISBN: 978-1-77149-220-1

Sketch a diagram to match each question. Solve the problems. Round your answers to the nearest hundredth. Use π = 3.14.

③ A cone fits inside a cube with a side length of 8 cm. Find the maximum volume of the cone.

_____

④ A cone-shaped paper cup is 11 cm tall and has a radius of 4 cm. How many cups does it take to fill a prism that measures 10 cm x 15 cm x 30 cm?

_____

⑤ Adam used 816 cm² of cardboard to make a bottomless square-based pyramid. If the side length of the base is 16 cm, what is the height of the pyramid?

_____

⑥ The square base of a pyramid has a side length of 12.8 cm. Each triangular face has a height of 34 cm. What is its total surface area?

_____

Look at the rectangular pyramid. Answer the questions.

⑦

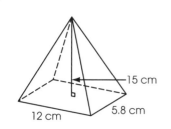

15 cm

12 cm   5.8 cm

a. What is the volume of the pyramid?

_____

b. Determine the volume of the pyramid if its length is doubled.

_____

c. Determine the volume of the pyramid if its length and width are doubled.

_____

Complete the table. Then answer the questions. Write the answers to the nearest hundredth.

⑧

Sphere	Radius	Surface Area*	Volume*
A	1 cm	4π	1.33π
B	2 cm		
C	4 cm		
D	8 cm		
E	24 cm		
F	72 cm		

* Leave the answers in terms of π.

⑨ What happens to the surface area and volume of a sphere if

a. its radius is doubled?

_____

_____

b. its radius is tripled?

_____

_____

Solve the problems. Write the answers to the nearest hundredth. Use π = 3.14.

⑩ Each billiard ball has a radius of 6 cm. Jack puts some billiard balls into a cylindrical tank with a diameter of 24 cm containing water. The water level rises 8 cm. How many billiard balls are there in the tank?

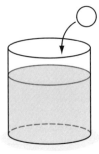

_____

⑪ If the surface area of a sphere is 163.84 cm², what is its volume?

_____

⑫ The surface area of a basketball is 576π cm². How far can a basketball travel if it makes 5 complete rolls?

_____

ISBN: 978-1-77149-220-1

Solve the problems.

⑬ An open-top cube has a volume of 512 cm³. What is its surface area?

_____

⑭ Chicken broth comes in two types of packaging. A can that is 10 cm tall with a radius 3 cm costs 75¢. A box that measures 15 cm x 5 cm x 8 cm costs $1.50. Which is a better buy?

_____

⑮ A rectangular tank measures 48 cm x 40 cm x 30 cm. Ellen fills up the tank with water and empties the water into a cylindrical tank. What is the radius of the cylindrical tank if the water level in the tank is 40 cm?

_____

⑯ A present measures 25 cm x 26 cm x 13 cm. Is a sheet of wrapping paper measuring 30 cm x 85 cm big enough to wrap this present? Explain.

_____

⑰ A publishing company ships its books in boxes of 20. Each book measures 21 cm x 29.7 cm x 2 cm. If the length of the box is 60 cm, what are the measures of the width and height so that it requires the least amount of cardboard? What is the surface area of the box?

_____

⑱ 216 dice are packed into a box. Design a box that uses the least amount of cardboard and find the surface area of the box.

Box	Length (cm)	Width (cm)	Height (cm)	Surface area (cm²)
1	4	6	9	
2				

1 cm   1 cm

1 cm

_____
surface area

ISBN: 978-1-77149-220-1

Complete MathSmart 9

Cumulative Review

In this review, the questions are classified into the four categories below.

- **K** Knowledge and Understanding
- **A** Application
- **C** Communication
- **T** Thinking

The icons beside the question numbers indicate in which categories the questions belong.

ISBN: 978-1-77149-220-1

Circle the correct answers.

① Simplify the expression.

$$3x^2 - xy + 5(x^2 - xy) - 3x(x + 2y)$$

A. $5x^2$

B. $11x^2 - 12xy$

C. $5x^2 - 12xy$

D. $5x^2 + 12xy$

② The cost of hiring an electrician, C, in dollars, for h hours, is given by the formula:

$$C = 35h + 110$$

Which of the following statements is true?

A. An electrician charges $110/h.

B. An electrician charges $110 for the service.

C. The cost of an electrician increases by 35 times for each additional hour.

D. The cost of an electrician increases by $35 for each additional hour.

③ Find the volume of the cylinder.

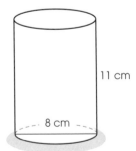

11 cm

8 cm

A. 2210.56 cm^3

B. 376.8 cm^2

C. 759.88 cm^3

D. 552.64 cm^3

ISBN: 978-1-77149-220-1

④ Find the volume of the cube.

K

    A. $64x^6y^3$

    B. $12x^6y^3$

    C. $96x^4y^2$

    D. $64x^6y$

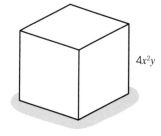

$4x^2y$

⑤ Determine which ordered pair lies on the line $y = -7x - 3$.

K

    A. $(1,10)$

    B. $(1,-10)$

    C. $(-1,-10)$

    D. $(-1,-4)$

⑥ There are 15 children in one quarter of the students in a class.

A

Let s be the number of students in the class. Which of the following equations is true?

    A. $4s = 15$

    B. $\dfrac{s}{4} = 15$

    C. $\dfrac{4}{s} = 15$

    D. $15s = 4$

⑦ What is the area of this regular hexagon?

K

    A. 41.4 cm^2

    B. 20.7 cm^2

    C. 18 cm

    D. 13.8 cm^2

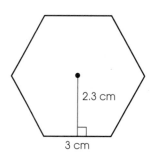

2.3 cm

3 cm

ISBN: 978-1-77149-220-1

⑧ Find the values of x and y.

K

$2 : 3 : x = 6 : y : 27$

A. $x = 9, y = 15$

B. $x = 6, y = 9$

C. $x = 9, y = 9$

D. $x = 6, y = 15$

⑨ Write the equation of the line in slope-intercept form.

K

$$3x - \frac{1}{2}y = 6$$

A. $6x - y - 12 = 0$

B. $3x = 6 + \frac{1}{2}y$

C. $x = \frac{1}{6}y + 2$

D. $y = 6x - 12$

⑩ Find the value of x.

K

$4x - 5 = 6x - 15$

A. 1

B. -1

C. -5

D. 5

⑪ Which of the following statements about the interior angles of any polygon

C   is true?

T

A. The sum of the interior angles of a pentagon is 720°.

B. The measure of each interior angle of a regular hexagon is 120°.

C. The sum of the interior angles of any polygon is 360°.

D. The measure of each interior angle of a regular polygon is 90°.

   ISBN: 978-1-77149-220-1

⑫ Find the unknown angles.

K

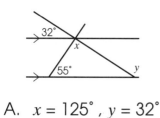

    A. $x = 125°$, $y = 32°$

    B. $x = 93°$, $y = 148°$

    C. $x = 52°$, $y = 148°$

    D. $x = 93°$, $y = 32°$

⑬ Which of the following lines has a slope of $-\dfrac{5}{6}$?

K

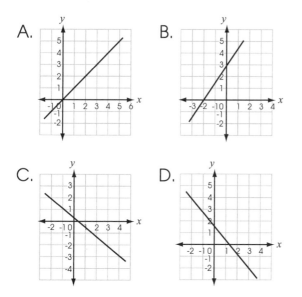

⑭ A rectangular box has a surface area of 24 cm². Which dimensions of the
box can give the maximum volume?

T

    A. 1 cm by 1 cm by 1.5 cm

    B. 2 cm by 2 cm by 2 cm

    C. 3 cm x 3 cm x 0.5 cm

    D. 3 cm by 3 cm by 3 cm

Read each sentence. Write "T" for true and "F" for false.

⑮
K

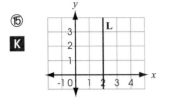

The slope of line L is 0.

_____

⑯
T

The measures of the interior angles of a quadrilateral are:

92° 128° 101° 49°

_____

⑰
K

The lines with the slopes of $\frac{1}{5}$ and -5 are perpendicular.

_____

⑱
K

1: 1 000 000

The actual dimensions of the field are 0.22 km by 0.28 km.

_____

⑲
A

Billy has $m(m^2 - n)$ and Judy has $mn(n + 1)$. The children have $m(m^2 - n^2)$ in all.

_____

Find the values of the unknowns.

⑳
K

$2 : x : y = 6 : 42 : 15$

x: _____   y: _____

㉑
K

$\frac{3}{4}x - 8 = 1$

x: _____

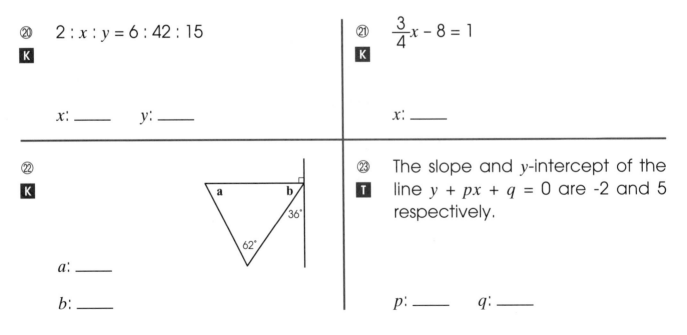

㉒
K

a: _____

b: _____

㉓
T

The slope and y-intercept of the line $y + px + q = 0$ are -2 and 5 respectively.

p: _____   q: _____

ISBN: 978-1-77149-220-1

Simplify and factor each expression. Then evaluate.

㉔ K
$$\frac{2x^2 + xy + y^2x}{x}$$

If $x = 1$ and $y = -2$, the value is _____ .

㉕ K
$$-2xy(x + y) + y(2x^2 - xy)$$

If $x = -1$ and $y = 2$, the value is _____ .

㉖ K
$$\frac{ab(a - b + a^2)}{a^2b} + \frac{b(b + ab)}{ab}$$

If $a = 1$ and $b = 2$, the value is _____ .

㉗ K
$$a^3b^2(-a - 2b) - \frac{1}{2}a^2b^2\,(-4ab + 3)$$

If $a = -1$ and $b = -2$, the value is _____ .

Find the slope, x-intercept, and y-intercept for each line. Then answer the questions.

㉘ K
L_1: $3x - 2y + 6 = 0$

L_2: $4y + 1 = 6x$

L_3: $2x - 3y + 12 = 0$

L_4: $3x + 2y = -5$

	slope	x-intercept	y-intercept
L_1			
L_2			
L_3			
L_4			

㉙ K
Which lines are parallel?

_____

㉚ K
Which lines are perpendicular?

_____

㉛ K
Graph the lines that are perpendicular. Then find the point of intersection.

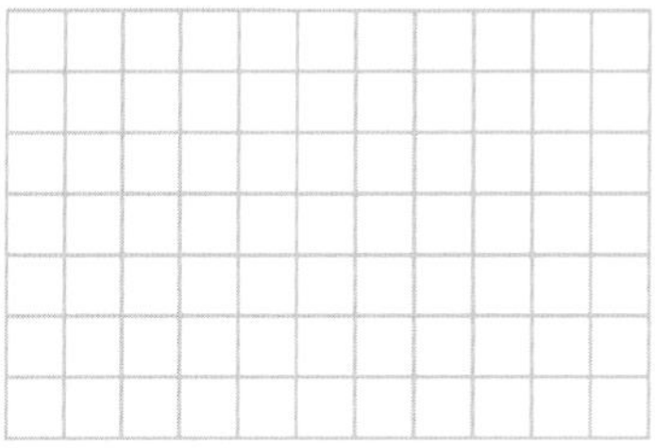

Point of intersection: _____

Find the perimeter and area of each shaded part. **Round your answers to the nearest hundredth.** **Use π = 3.14.**

③② **K** The shaded square is formed by joining the midpoints of the sides of the big square.

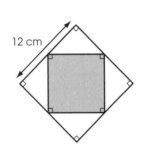

Perimeter:

Area:

③③ **T** The radius of the big circle is 10 cm.

Perimeter:

Area:

Find the surface area and volume of each figure. **Round your answers to the nearest hundredth.** **Use π = 3.14.**

③④ **T**

3 cm

8 cm

4 cm

surface area: _____ volume: _____

③⑤ **K**

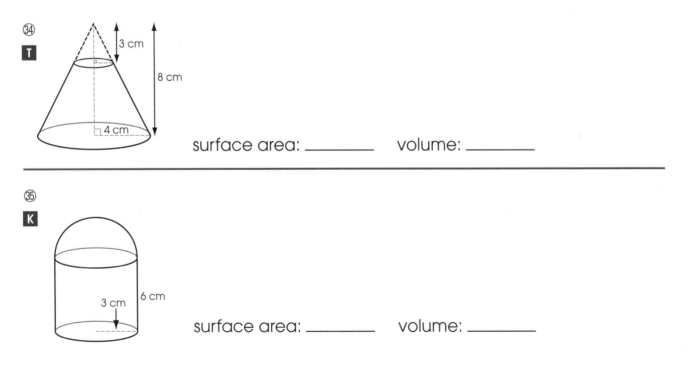

6 cm

3 cm

surface area: _____ volume: _____

ISBN: 978-1-77149-220-1

Look at the scatter plots. Then answer the questions.

③⑥
A
C

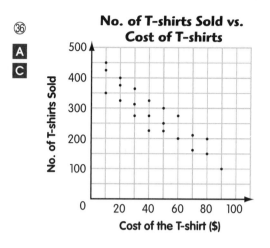

No. of T-shirts Sold vs.
Cost of T-shirts

a. Describe the relationship between the number of T-shirts sold and the cost of the T-shirts.

_____

b. Draw the line of best fit. Then write the equation of the line.

_____

c. Predict the number of T-shirts sold if the cost of the T-shirt is $70.

_____

③⑦
A
C

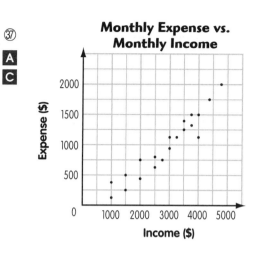

Monthly Expense vs.
Monthly Income

a. Describe the relationship between the monthly expense and the income.

_____

b. Draw the line of best fit. Then write the equation of the line.

_____

c. Predict the monthly expense if the monthly income is $3000.

_____

Paco and his sister Amy raced from their home to a park. Describe their routes in terms of speed, time, and distance.

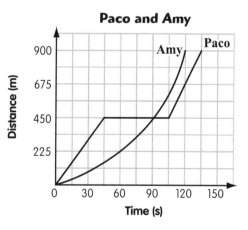

Paco and Amy

③⑧ Paco's route: _____
A
C
_____

_____

③⑨ Amy's route: _____
A
C
_____

_____

ISBN: 978-1-77149-220-1

Write an equation for each line.

④⓪ K a line passing through the point (1,4) with a slope of -4

_____

④① K a line passing through the origin and parallel to the line $\frac{1}{2}x - y + 1 = 0$

_____

④② K a line intersecting the x-axis at -3 with a slope of -2.5

_____

④③ K y varies directly with x, when $x = \frac{1}{2}$, $y = -16$

_____

④④ K y varies partial directly with x and the constant of variation is $-\frac{1}{2}$, when $x = -2$, $y = 6$

_____

Look at the table. Answer the questions.

④⑤ T What is the minimum number of students in Oakley High School?

	No. of Students
Oakley High School	$s^2 + 150$
Springland High School	$420 - 2s^2$

_____

④⑥ T What is the maximum number of students in Springland High School?

_____

④⑦ A How many students are there in Oakley High School and Springland High School?

_____

④⑧ A If s is 6, how many students are there in Springland High School?

_____

ISBN: 978-1-77149-220-1

Answer the questions.

49 A can of soup has the shape of a cylinder with a radius of 3 cm and a height of 7 cm.
A

a. What is the volume of the can?

b. What is the surface area of the label wrapped around the can?

50 A sphere fits inside a rectangular box of 6 cm by 6 cm by 7 cm. What is the greatest possible volume of the sphere? How much space is left?
A
T

51 The cost of $(2x)$ kg of nuts is $\$(8x^3 + 15x)$. How much do $(3y)$ kg of nuts cost?
A
T

52 Find the measure of each unknown angle.
T

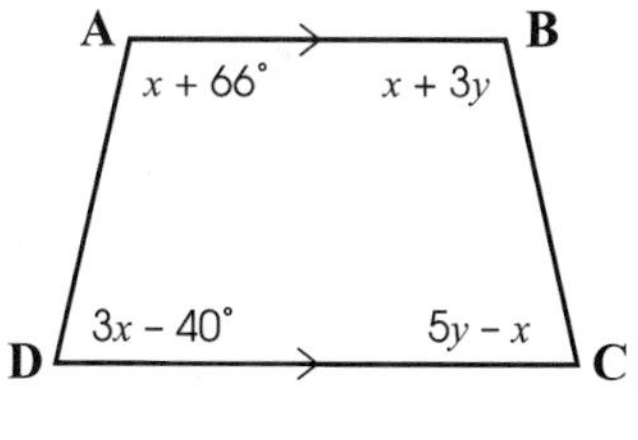

$\angle A$ = ______ $\angle B$ = ______ $\angle C$ = ______ $\angle D$ = ______

53 Determine whether or not each set of points are collinear.
T

a. (3,4) , (-1,5) , (7,3)

b. (0,-5) , (3,-1) , (-2,-2)

Answer the questions.

⑭ The slope of the line PQ is $-\frac{5}{2}$. The coordinates of the points P and Q are (-4,6)

[C]
[T] and $(-\frac{5}{2},k)$ respectively. Graph the lines and label the points on the grid.

a. What is the equation of PQ? Write in standard form and point-slope form.

_____

b. What are the coordinates of Q?

_____

c. Find the coordinates of the point where the line PQ cuts the y-axis.

_____

d. A line is perpendicular to the line PQ and passes through the point (3,3). What is the equation of the line? What is the point of intersection of the lines?

_____

⑮ a. Name the triangles that are similar. Then find the

[T] angles ∠DEB and ∠EDA.

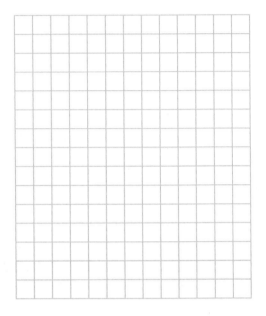

_____

b. Find the lengths of DE and CD.

_____

ISBN: 978-1-77149-220-1

The table shows the annual incomes of the people and their years of education. Plot the points on a scatter plot. Then answer the questions.

⑤⑥
A

Annual Income vs. Years of Education

Participant	Annual Income (in $10 000)	Years of Education
1	4.5	16
2	3.6	15
3	2.8	12
4	3.2	14
5	5.4	19
6	5.1	18
7	6.2	23
8	5.0	18
9	3.8	17
10	3.6	16
11	4.2	18
12	5.0	20
13	3.7	17
14	3.9	17
15	4.2	20
16	4.8	19
17	5.7	22
18	3.5	17
19	3.9	18
20	4.0	18

⑤⑦
C
Describe the correlation of the two variables.

_____

⑤⑧
K
Draw a line of best fit on the scatter plot. Then write a possible equation for the line of best fit.

_____

⑤⑨
T
If a person has more than 21 years of education, what will be his annual income?

_____

Find the areas of the shaded regions. Use π = 3.14.

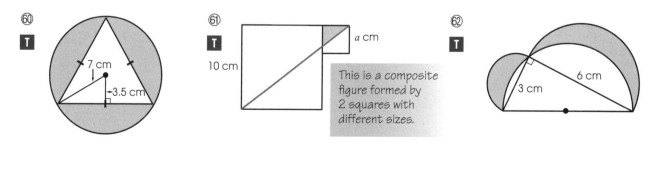

⑥⓪
T
7 cm
3.5 cm

⑥①
T
10 cm
a cm
This is a composite figure formed by 2 squares with different sizes.

⑥②
T
6 cm
3 cm

_____   _____   _____

ISBN: 978-1-77149-220-1

ISBN: 978-1-77149-220-1

Number Sense and Algebra

1. Order of Operations

↬ The rule for order of operations:

BEDMAS (**B**rackets, **E**xponents, **D**ivision, **M**ultiplication, **A**ddition, **S**ubtraction)

e.g. $(3 + 6)^2 \div 6 + 12 \times (5 - 3)$ ← Do the operations inside the brackets first.

$= 9^2 \div 6 + 12 \times 2$ ← Calculate the exponents.

$= 81 \div 6 + 12 \times 2$ ← Do the division and multiplication.

$= 13.5 + 24$ ← Do the addition.

$= \underline{37.5}$

2. Operations with Integers

↬ **Rules for Multiplication**	examples	↬ **Rules for Division**	examples
$(+) \times (+) = +$	$(+3) \times (+2) = +6$	$(+) \div (+) = +$	$(+10) \div (+2) = +5$
$(-) \times (+) = -$	$(-3) \times (+2) = -6$	$(-) \div (+) = -$	$(-10) \div (+2) = -5$
$(+) \times (-) = -$	$(+3) \times (-2) = -6$	$(+) \div (-) = -$	$(+10) \div (-2) = -5$
$(-) \times (-) = +$	$(-3) \times (-2) = +6$	$(-) \div (-) = +$	$(-10) \div (-2) = +5$

3. Square and Square Roots

↬ $\sqrt{a^2} = \sqrt{a \times a} = a$ e.g. $\sqrt{7^2} = \sqrt{7 \times 7} = 7$

↬ $\sqrt{ab} = \sqrt{a} \times \sqrt{b}$, where $a, b \geq 0$ e.g. $\sqrt{50} = \sqrt{5} \times \sqrt{10}$

↬ $\sqrt{\dfrac{c}{d}} = \dfrac{\sqrt{c}}{\sqrt{d}}$, where $c \geq 0, d > 0$ e.g. $\sqrt{\dfrac{3}{5}} = \dfrac{\sqrt{3}}{\sqrt{5}}$.

4. Distributive Property

↬ $c(a + b) = a \cdot c + b \cdot c$, e.g. $5(x + 2y) = 5x + 10y$

↬ $\dfrac{1}{d}(a + b) = \dfrac{a}{d} + \dfrac{b}{d}$, e.g. $\dfrac{1}{2}(10x + 4y) = \dfrac{10x}{2} + \dfrac{4y}{2} = 5x + 2y$

5. Factorization

↔ $a \cdot c + b \cdot c = c(a + b)$, e.g. $3mn + 4n = n(3m + 4)$ ← n is the common factor.

↔ $\dfrac{a}{d} + \dfrac{b}{d} = \dfrac{1}{d}(a + b)$, e.g. $\dfrac{x^2}{10} + \dfrac{xy}{10} = \dfrac{x}{10}(x + y)$ ← $\dfrac{x}{10}$ is the common factor.

6. Law of Exponents

For $a \neq 0$, $b \neq 0$, p is an integer, m and n are any natural numbers.

↔ $a^0 = 1$ $\Big|$ $a^1 = a$ $\Big|$ $a^{-p} = \dfrac{1}{a^p}$

e.g. $5^0 = 1$ $\Big|$ e.g. $5^1 = 5$ $\Big|$ e.g. $5^{-2} = \dfrac{1}{5^2}$

↔ $a^m \times a^n = a^{m+n}$, e.g. $5^2 \times 5^4 = 5^{2+4} = 5^6$

↔ $a^m \div a^n = a^{m-n}$, e.g. $5^3 \div 5 = 5^{3-1} = 5^2$

↔ $(a^m)^n = a^{mn}$, e.g. $(5^3)^2 = 5^{3\times2} = 5^6$

↔ $(a \times b)^m = a^m \times b^m$, e.g. $(3y)^2 = 3^2 \times y^2 = 9y^2$

↔ $\left(\dfrac{a}{b}\right)^n = \dfrac{a^n}{b^n}$, e.g. $\left(\dfrac{y}{2}\right)^3 = \dfrac{y^3}{2^3} = \dfrac{y^3}{8}$

7. Proportion

There are two ways to write a proportion.

↔ $\dfrac{a}{b} = \dfrac{c}{d}$

$a \times d = b \times c$

↔ $a : b = c : d$

$a \times d = b \times c$

8. Scientific Notation

↔ The scientific notation of a number y is in the form of:

$y = a \times 10^n$, where $1 < a < 10$ and n is an integer

e.g. 3 920 000 ← Move the decimal point 6 places to the left and multiply by 10^6.
  $= \underline{3.92 \times 10^6}$

  0.000085 ← Move the decimal point 5 places to the right and multiply by 10^{-5}.
  $= \underline{8.5 \times 10^{-5}}$

Linear Relations

1. Properties of Linear Relations

There are two ways to determine whether a relation is linear or non-linear:

 Numerically: find the first difference

e.g.

A

x	y	Δy
1	5	7 – 5 = **2**
2	7	9 – 7 = **2**
3	9	
4	11	11 – 9 = **2**

The first differences are constant.

B

x	y	Δy
1	6	7 – 6 = **1**
2	7	10 – 7 = **3**
3	10	
4	18	18 – 10 = **8**

The first differences are not constant.

A shows a linear relation and **B** shows a non-linear relation.

 Graphically: the shapes of the lines

e.g.   **C**   **D**

C shows a linear relation and **D** shows a non-linear relation.

2. Properties of Direct and Indirect Variations

 Direct Variation:

having the equation in the form of

$$y = mx$$

The graph of a direct variation crosses the y-axis at $y = 0$.

e.g. Tai Chi costs $12 per class.

$y = 12x$, y = total cost
x = no. of classes

 Indirect Variation:

having the equation in the form of

$$y = mx + b$$

The graph of an indirect variation does not cross the y-axis at $y = 0$, but at some other value, namely b.

e.g. Yoga costs $10 for registration, plus $8 per class.

$y = 8x + 10$, y = total cost
↑ x = no. of classes
initial value

ISBN: 978-1-77149-220-1

Analytic Geometry

1. The Slope of a Line

⟷ A line that rises to the right has a positive slope.

⟷ A line that falls to the right has a negative slope.

⟷ Slope (m) = $\dfrac{\text{rise}}{\text{run}}$

$\qquad = \dfrac{\text{change in } y}{\text{change in } x}$ $\left(\dfrac{y_2 - y_1}{x_2 - x_1}\right)$

$\qquad = \dfrac{\Delta y}{\Delta x}$

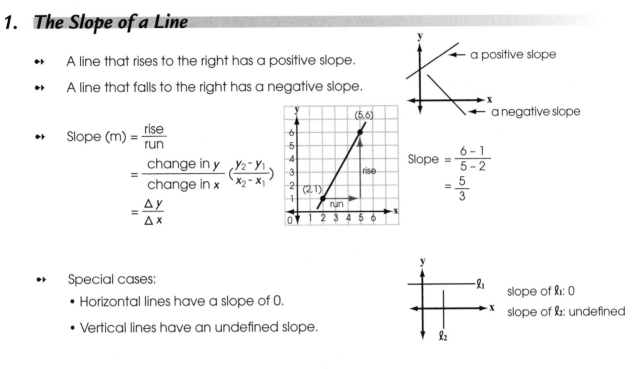

← a positive slope

← a negative slope

Slope $= \dfrac{6 - 1}{5 - 2}$

$\qquad = \dfrac{5}{3}$

⟷ Special cases:

• Horizontal lines have a slope of 0.

• Vertical lines have an undefined slope.

slope of ℓ_1: 0

slope of ℓ_2: undefined

2. Parallel Lines and Perpendicular Lines

⟷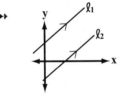

Parallel lines have the same slope.

When $\ell_1 \mathbin{/\!/} \ell_2$, $m_1 = m_2$

⟷

Perpendicular lines have slopes that are negative reciprocals of each other.

When $\ell_3 \perp \ell_4$, $m_3 = -\dfrac{1}{m_4}$

3. The Equation of a Line

Slope-intercept Form	**Standard Form**	**Point-slope Form**
$y = mx + b$	$Ax + By + C = 0$,	$y - y_1 = m(x - x_1)$,
where m = slope,	where A, B, and C are	where m = slope,
b = y-intercept	integers and A is positive	(x_1, y_1) = a point on the line

These two forms are interchangeable,

where $m = -\dfrac{A}{B}$ and $b = -\dfrac{C}{B}$.

    ISBN: 978-1-77149-220-1

Measurement and Geometry

1. Pythagorean Theorem

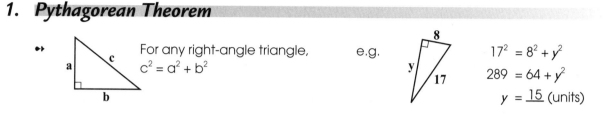

For any right-angle triangle,
$c^2 = a^2 + b^2$

e.g.

$17^2 = 8^2 + y^2$
$289 = 64 + y^2$
$y = \underline{15}$ (units)

2. Angle Properties

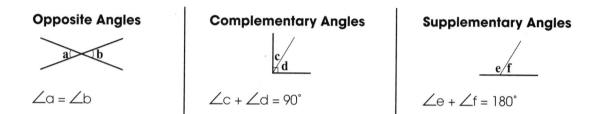

Opposite Angles

$\angle a = \angle b$

Complementary Angles

$\angle c + \angle d = 90°$

Supplementary Angles

$\angle e + \angle f = 180°$

3. Angle Properties of Parallel Lines

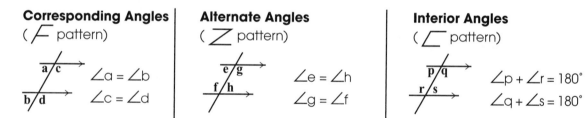

Corresponding Angles
(F pattern)

$\angle a = \angle b$
$\angle c = \angle d$

Alternate Angles
(Z pattern)

$\angle e = \angle h$
$\angle g = \angle f$

Interior Angles
(C pattern)

$\angle p + \angle r = 180°$
$\angle q + \angle s = 180°$

4. Angles Associated with Polygons

- Triangles

$a + b + c = 180°$ (sum of the interior angles in a △)
$p + q + r = 360°$ (sum of the exterior angles in a △)
$a + b = r$ (Each exterior angle is equal to the sum of the interior angles at the opposite vertices.)

- In a polygon with n sides, the sum of the interior angles is $180°(n - 2)$.

- The measure of each angle in a regular polygon is $\dfrac{180°(n - 2)}{n}$.

e.g.

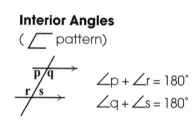

regular hexagon

sum of the interior angles
$= 180°(6 - 2)$
$= 180°(4)$
$= \underline{720°}$

measure of each angle
$= \dfrac{720°}{6}$
$= \underline{120°}$

ISBN: 978-1-77149-220-1

5. Similar Triangles

△ABC and △PQR are similar if

↔ their corresponding angles are equal.
$\angle A = \angle P, \angle B = \angle Q, \angle C = \angle R$

↔ their corresponding sides are proportional.
$\dfrac{AB}{PQ} = \dfrac{BC}{QR} = \dfrac{CA}{RP}$

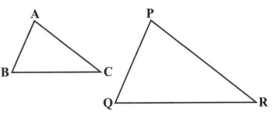

△ABC ~ △PQR

6. Measurement Units Conversion

Length	Area	Mass	Capacity and Volume
1 km = 1000 m	$1\ m^2 = 10\ 000\ cm^2$	1 kg = 1000 g	$1\ mL = 1\ cm^3$
1 m = 100 cm	$1\ km^2 = 1\ 000\ 000\ m^2$	1 g = 1000 mg	$1\ L = 1000\ mL = 1000\ cm^3$
1 dm = 10 cm			$1\ m^3 = 1\ 000\ 000\ cm^3$
1 cm = 10 mm			$1\ m^3 = 1000\ L$

7. Perimeters and Areas of Polygons

↔ Perimeter of a polygon = the sum of the length of each side

 Perimeter of a Square
$= 4s$

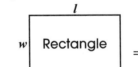 Perimeter of a Rectangle
$= 2(l + w)$

↔ Area of a Polygon

Triangle

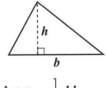

Area $= \dfrac{1}{2}bh$

Square

Area $= s^2$

Rectangle

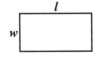

Area $= lw$

Parallelogram

Area $= bh$

Trapezoid

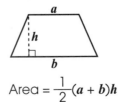

Area $= \dfrac{1}{2}(a + b)h$

ISBN: 978-1-77149-220-1

8. Perimeters and Areas of Regular Polygons

- The perimeter of a regular polygon = no. of sides x side length

  $P = nl$

  e.g.

  4 cm

  Perimeter = 6 x 4 = <u>24 (cm)</u>

- The area of a regular polygon = $\frac{1}{2}$(apothem x side length) x No. of sides

  $A = \frac{1}{2}aln$

  $= \frac{1}{2}Pa$, where $P = ln$

  e.g.

  4 cm

  3.46 cm

  Area = $\frac{1}{2}$(24)3.46

  = <u>41.52 (cm²)</u>

9. Circumferences and Areas of Circles

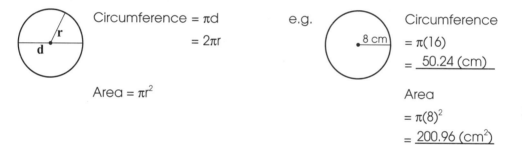

Circumference = πd

= 2πr

Area = πr²

e.g.

8 cm

Circumference

= π(16)

= <u>50.24 (cm)</u>

Area

= π(8)²

= <u>200.96 (cm²)</u>

10. Surface Areas and Volumes of Geometric Figures

- **Rectangular Prism**

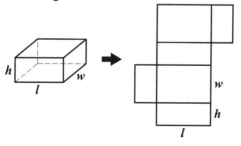

S.A. $= 2lw + 2lh + 2hw$

$= 2(lw + lh + hw)$

V $=$ base area x height

$= lwh$

- **Triangular Prism**

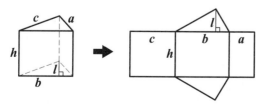

S.A. $= ah + bh + ch + 2(\frac{1}{2}bl)$

$= ah + bh + ch + bl$

V $=$ base area x height

$= \frac{1}{2}blh$

ISBN: 978-1-77149-220-1

↔ **Square-based Pyramid**

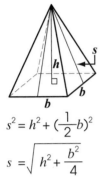

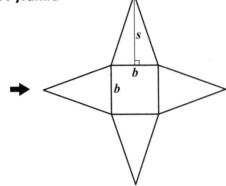

$s^2 = h^2 + (\frac{1}{2}b)^2$

$s = \sqrt{h^2 + \dfrac{b^2}{4}}$

S.A. $= 4(\frac{1}{2}bs) + b^2$
$= 2bs + b^2$

V $= \dfrac{1}{3}b^2h$

↔ **Rectangular Pyramid**

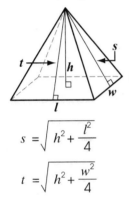

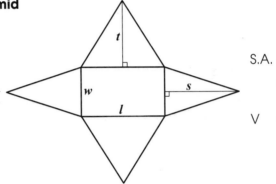

$s = \sqrt{h^2 + \dfrac{l^2}{4}}$

$t = \sqrt{h^2 + \dfrac{w^2}{4}}$

S.A. $= 2(\frac{1}{2}lt) + 2(\frac{1}{2}ws) + lw$
$= lt + ws + lw$

V $= \dfrac{1}{3}lwh$

↔ **Cylinder**

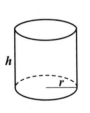

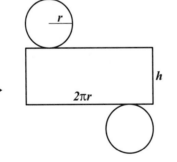

S.A. $= 2\pi r^2 + 2\pi rh$

V $= \pi r^2 h$

↔ **Sphere**

S.A. $= 4\pi r^2$

V $= \dfrac{4}{3}\pi r^3$

↔ **Cone**

$l = \sqrt{h^2 + r^2}$

S.A. $= \pi rl + \pi r^2$

V $= \dfrac{1}{3}\pi r^2 h$

ISBN: 978-1-77149-220-1

Handy Reference

You may make notes here.

ISBN: 978-1-77149-220-1

ISBN: 978-1-77149-220-1

Complete MathSmart 9

Answers

ISBN: 978-1-77149-220-1

ANSWERS

1 Basic Skills Review

1.1 Integers and Real Numbers

1. 216
2. 100 000
3. $\frac{1}{25}$
4. $\frac{1}{9}$
5. 1
6. $\frac{1}{343}$
7. $\frac{1}{16}$
8. $\frac{1}{32}$
9. 729
10. 16 or -16
11. 27 or -27
12. 13 or -13
13. 25 or -25
14. 20 or -20
15. 31 or -31
16. 49 ; 64 ; 7 ; 8 ; 7.21
17. 144 and 169 ; 12 and 13 ; 12.49
18. 81 and 100 ; 9 and 10 ; 9.90
19. 361 and 400 ; 19 and 20 ; 19.87
20. $\frac{\sqrt{361}}{\sqrt{1024}} = \frac{19}{32}$
21. $\frac{\sqrt{36}}{\sqrt{961}} = \frac{6}{31}$
22. $\frac{\sqrt{289}}{\sqrt{625}} = \frac{17}{25}$
23. $\frac{\sqrt{169}}{\sqrt{784}} = \frac{13}{28}$
24. $\sqrt{\frac{81}{10\,000}} = \frac{9}{100}$
25. $\sqrt{\frac{529}{10\,000}} = \frac{23}{100}$
26. $\sqrt{\frac{225}{100}} = \frac{15}{10} = \frac{3}{2}$

27. $= 33 - 49 \div 7$
    $= 33 - 7$
    $= 26$
28. $= 7^2 \times 8 \div 16$
    $= 49 \times 8 \div 16$
    $= 24.5$
29. $= 7 \times 9 + (-64) \times (-2)$
    $= 63 + 128$
    $= 191$
30. $= 25 \div (-5) + (-8) \times 4$
    $= -5 + (-32)$
    $= -37$
31. $= 3 \times 16 - 64 \div (-2)$
    $= 48 + 32$
    $= 80$
32. $= 3 \times (16 - 18)^2$
    $= 3 \times (-2)^2$
    $= 3 \times 4$
    $= 12$
33. $= \frac{36 - 5 \times 27}{-4 + 3 - 2}$
    $= \frac{36 - 135}{-1 - 2}$
    $= \frac{-99}{-3}$
    $= 33$
34. $= \frac{63 - (-8 \div 8)}{625 \div 5 + 3}$
    $= \frac{63 - (-1)}{125 + 3}$
    $= \frac{64}{128}$
    $= \frac{1}{2}$
35. $-\frac{5}{4}$
36. $\frac{5}{9}$
37. $-\frac{96}{5}$
38. 4
39. $-\frac{31}{12}$

Challenge

A: -9   B: 168 ; ✔   C: -12

Try This (p.6)

1. 125
2. -125
3. $\frac{1}{125}$
4. 5 or -5
5. 5

Try This (p.8)

1. 64 ; 4 ; 64 ; 20 ; 84
2. 5 ; -125 ; 5 ; -25

1.2 Ratios, Rates, Proportions, and Percents

1. apples to oranges: 2 : 3 ; 10 : 3 ; 2 : 3
   apples to all: 2 : 5 ; 10 : 13 ; 2 : 5
   oranges to all: 3 : 5 ; 3 : 13 ; 3 : 5
2. apples to oranges: 2 : 3 ; 10 : 7 ; 14 : 9
   apples to all: 2 : 5 ; 10 : 17 ; 14 : 23
   oranges to all: 3 : 5 ; 7 : 17 ; 9 : 23
3a. 1 : 3   b. 1 : 4   c. 3 : 4
4a. 2 : 1   b. 2 : 3   c. 1 : 3
5. 2.99 ; 3.18 ; the first group
6. 52.6 km/h ; 115.5 km/h ; 186.4 km/h ; the plane
7. 68 words/min ; 72 words/min ; 75 words/min ; Michael
8. 45 ; 3.75
9. $8m = 72$; $m = 9$
10. $1274 = 182y$; $y = 7$
11. $1083 = 114u$; $u = 9.5$
12. $8a = 1020$; $a = 127.5$
13. $2736 = 171k$; $k = 16$
14. 2 ; $54 = 2y$; $y = 27$; 27
15. $\frac{5}{42.5} = \frac{y}{153}$ (y = no. of combos he buys in all) ;
    $765 = 42.5y$; $y = 18$; He buys 18 combos in all.
16. 44 ; $26\,400 = 100y$; $y = 264$; 264
17. 28 ; $35m = 2800$; $m = 80$; 80
18.
M & C	St. George	General Store
$\frac{16}{100} = \frac{x}{800}$	$\frac{23}{100} = \frac{y}{800}$	$\frac{42}{100} = \frac{z}{800}$
$x = 128$	$y = 184$	$z = 336$
19. On clothing:
    $\frac{m}{100} = \frac{240}{1200}$
    $m = 20$
    On travelling:
    $\frac{n}{100} = \frac{456}{1200}$
    $n = 38$
    Jason spends 20% on clothing and 38% on travelling.

Challenge

$\frac{3}{9} = \frac{x}{270}$; $810 = 9x$; $x = 90$; There are 90 red beads.

Try This (p.10)

30 ; 18 ; 5 ; 3 ; 5 : 3

1.3 Proportional Reasoning

1a. 8:24 ; $\frac{8}{24}$ b. 2:2 ; 1

c. 4:5 ; $\frac{4}{5}$

(Suggested answers for questions 2 to 11)

2. $\frac{2}{5}$ 3. $\frac{6}{20}$ 4. $\frac{10}{18}$

5. $\frac{20}{4}$ 6. $\frac{8}{2}$ 7. $\frac{18}{8}$

8. 6:10   9. 5:9   10. 12:22

11. 5:2   12. 1:2   13. 2:3

14. 1:2   15. 3:2   16. $\frac{3}{4}$

17. $\frac{5}{2}$ 18. $\frac{2}{1}$ 19. $\frac{2}{3}$

20a. 10:9   b. 5:9
21a. 1:2   b. 5:3
c. 1:1   d. 1:8
22a. 3:4   b. 1:3
23. 3 ; 12
$\frac{3}{3}$; $\frac{48}{3}$
16

24. Solve for x:
x ; x ; 8 ; 12

Solve for y:
y ; 12 ; 20 ; y ; 12 ; 5

25. $7m = 4 \times 14$; $m = 8$
26. $16n = 160$; $n = 10$
27. $18s = 72 \times 6$; $s = 24$
28. Solve for x:
2:x = 8:28
$8x = 2 \times 28$
$x = 7$

Solve for y:
y:7 = 14:28
$28y = 7 \times 14$
$y = \frac{7}{2}$

29. Solve for b:
5:7 = 20:b
$5b = 140$
$b = 28$

Solve for a:
7:a = 28:36
$28a = 7 \times 36$
$a = 9$

30. 3:50 = 12:x
$3x = 600$
$x = 200$
He needs to pay $200.

31. 3:4 = x:28
$4x = 3 \times 28$
$x = 21$
21 cups of milk are needed.

32a. 1:100 000 ; 1
b. 5 ;
1:100 000 = 5:y ;
$y = 500 000$;
5 km
c. 1:100 000 = x:300 000 ; $x = 3$;
Texas Mall is 3 cm away from the Civic Centre on the map.
So, the actual distance between Texas Mall and Civic Centre is about 3 km
d.

Borland Town
1:100 000
Ed's Market
Texas Mall
Texas Building
←2.5 cm
Civic Centre
General Garden
Shoe Museum

33a. 100:1 ; 10
b. 4 ;
100:1 = 40:x ; $x = 0.4$;
Its actual length is 0.4 mm.
c. 100:1 = x:0.09 ; $x = 9$;
It will be 9 mm long under the microscope.

34. Conference Room: 3.1 ; 2.5
Room 1: 2.4 m x 2.2 m
Room 2: 3.9 m x 2.3 m
Storage Room: 3.3 m x 2.3 m
Clerical Section: 4.7 m x 2.5 m
Whole Office: 7.2 m x 7 m
35. 7.75 m² ; 5.28 m² ; 7.59 m² ;
11.75 m² ; 8.97 m² ; 9.06 m²
36. 6 ; 1.5 ; 1.5

37. $\frac{210}{3} = \frac{x}{1}$
$x = 70$;
Unit rate: 70 km/h

38. $\frac{15}{12} = \frac{1}{x}$
$x = 0.8$;
Unit rate: $0.80/chicken wing

39. $\frac{128}{8} = \frac{x}{1}$
$x = 16$;
Unit rate: 16 students/class

40. $\frac{8.64}{2} = \frac{x}{1}$
$x = 4.32$;
Unit rate: 4.32 L/h

41. $\frac{115.50}{14} = \frac{x}{1}$
$x = 8.25$;
Unit rate: $8.25/day

42. $\frac{897}{3} = \frac{x}{1}$
$x = 299$;
Unit rate: $299/trip
43. 90 ; 100 ; 20.7 ; 20.7
44. x ; x ; 100 ; 30 ; 30

45. $\frac{32}{100} = \frac{x}{800}$
$x = 256$;
256

46. $\frac{60}{480} = \frac{x}{100}$
$x = 12.5$;
12.5%

47. $\frac{25}{100} = \frac{x}{225.80}$
$x = 56.45$
The gift is $56.45.

48. $\frac{80}{100} = \frac{x}{39.99}$
$x = 31.99$
The sale price is $31.99.

49. $\frac{2.22}{2.96} = \frac{x}{100}$
$x = 75$;
It is 75%.

Try This (p.14)

Boys to All: 18:24 ; $\frac{18}{24}$; $\frac{3}{4}$

Girls to All: 6:24 ; $\frac{6}{24}$; $\frac{1}{4}$

ISBN: 978-1-77149-220-1

1.4 Solving Problems with Proportional Reasoning

1a. 2:1 ; 1:2 ; 4:1 b. 2:7 ; 4:7 ; 1:7
2a. 2:5 b. 3:4
  c. 2:9
3. 20 ; 157.25 ; 20 ; 17 ; 17 hours
4. $\dfrac{3}{4} = \dfrac{24}{y}$

   $3y = 96$
    $y = 32$
   32 cups of flour are needed.
5. Actual length: $\dfrac{1}{500} = \dfrac{12.5}{y}$; $y = 6250$

   Actual width: $\dfrac{1}{500} = \dfrac{8.4}{x}$; $x = 4200$

   So, the actual dimensions are 62.5 m by 42 m.
   Perimeter: 2(62.5 + 42) = 209 (m)
   Cost of fencing: $18.50 x 209 = $3866.50
6a. 14.44 ; 15.59 ; 13.9 ; 14.4
  b. B
  c. My choice is car C because it has the lowest fuel efficiency which means that it consumes the least gasoline.
7. Price reduced: $\dfrac{x}{209.99} = \dfrac{25}{100}$; $x = 52.50$

   Sale price: $209.99 – $52.50 = $157.49
   The sale price is $157.49.
8. Percent of the girls: $\dfrac{15}{34} = \dfrac{x}{100}$; $x = 44.12$

   44.12% of the students are girls.
9. Money spent: $\dfrac{x}{240} = \dfrac{60}{100}$; $x = 144$

   Money left: $240 – $144 = $96
   She will have $96 left after purchasing the computers.
10. No. of students voted: $\dfrac{x}{450} = \dfrac{36}{100}$; $x = 162$

   162 students voted in the election.
11. The plant grows: $\dfrac{x}{160} = \dfrac{20}{100}$; $x = 32$

   New height: 160 + 32 = 192 (cm)
   The plant is 192 cm now.
12. No. of members who preferred action movies last year:
   $\dfrac{x}{80} = \dfrac{40}{100}$; $x = 32$

   No. of members who prefer action movies this year:
   $\dfrac{y}{120} = \dfrac{35}{100}$; $y = 42$

   So, 10 more members prefer action movies this year.
13. 7.2 kg to 9 kg
14. 52.63 years
15. Diane
16. 13.44 m^2
17. 30 cm by 40 cm
18. 6.84 L
19.

  5.7 cm   5.7 cm
      3.9 cm

Try This (p.20)

  a. 2:3 b. 3:5

2 Algebraic Expressions

2.1 Laws of Exponents

1. 10^3 2. 4^5 3. $\dfrac{1}{5^8}$
4. 3^{10} 5. 5^5 6. 6^9
7. $\dfrac{1}{4^2}$ 8. 7^8 9. $\dfrac{1}{8^6}$
10. 8^7 11. $\dfrac{1}{6^2}$ 12. 3^3
13. 5^5 14. 9^2 15. 7^8
16. 8^2 17. $\dfrac{1}{3}$ 18. $\dfrac{1}{10^2}$
19. 2^9 20. 3^{16} 21. $\dfrac{1}{3^{10}}$
22. $\dfrac{1}{2^{12}}$ 23. 3^{10} 24. 2^{14}
25. 2^{30} 26. $\dfrac{1}{3^{12}}$
27. $\dfrac{2^6 \div 2^2}{1 \times 2^9} = \dfrac{2^4}{2^9} = \dfrac{1}{2^5} = \dfrac{1}{32}$
28. $\dfrac{5^{2+4-3}}{1+4} = \dfrac{5^3}{5} = 5^2 = 25$
29. $\dfrac{7^6 \times 7^4 \div 7}{7^6 \div 1} = \dfrac{7^{6+4-1}}{7^6} = 7^3 = 343$
30. $5^{-3} \times \dfrac{5^4}{5^6} = 5^{-3+4-6} = 5^{-5} = \dfrac{1}{3125}$
31. $3^{16} \div 3^2 \times \dfrac{3^{-6}}{9} = 3^{16-2} \times \dfrac{3^{-6}}{3^2} = 3^{14+(-6)-2} = 3^6 = 729$
32. $\dfrac{(2^9)^3 \times 2^{-9} \div 2^8}{(3^2)^2 \div 3^2 - 1} = \dfrac{2^{27+(-9)-8}}{3^{4-2}-1} = \dfrac{2^{10}}{8} = \dfrac{2^{10}}{2^3} = 2^7 = 128$
33. 2^7 ; 128 34. 2^{-5} ; $\dfrac{1}{32}$ 35. 5^7 ; 78 125
36. 3^8 ; 6561 37. 2^6 ; 64 38. 3^{-4} ; $\dfrac{1}{81}$
39. ^{2} ; ^{2} ; ^{3} ; ^{2} ; ^{2} ; 5×2^2 40. 5 ; ^{2} ; 5^2 ; 5^2
41. $\dfrac{2^3}{3}$ 42. $2^3 \times 3^3$
43. $\dfrac{7^2}{2}$ 44. $\dfrac{1}{7^2}$
45. 8.4 ; $^{-5}$ 46. 7.6 ; ^{6} 47. 8.64 x 10^{-6}
48. 1.25 x 10^7 49. 3.95 x 10^5 50. 1.7 x 10^8
51. 8.95 x 10^5 52. 2.7 x 10^7 53. 7.2 x 10^{-2}
54. 3 x 10^8 55. 1.4 x 10^7 56. 2 x 10^{-8}
57. 5 x 10^{-8} 58. 2.5 x 10^5
59a. 3.621 x 10^8 km^2 b. 1.479 x 10^8 km^2
60a. 5.72 x 10^6 L b. 2.0592 x 10^{10} L
61a. 1.5 x 10^{11} m b. 5 x 10^2 s
62a. 2.464 x 10^7 Canadians b. 3.328 x 10^7

Challenge

   $\dfrac{4}{3}\pi(6.3 \times 10^9)^3 = 3.33\pi \times 10^{11}$ (km^3)

Try This (p.24)

1. 5 ; 2 ; 7 2. 5 ; 2 ; 3 3. 5 ; 2 ; 10
4. 5

2.2 Algebraic Expressions with Exponents

(Suggested answer for each example.)

1. $3m$ and $4m$; $6m$
2. $3xy$ and $-2yx$; $5xy$
3. $2p^2$ and $4p^2$; $0.5p^2$
4. $-3a^3$ and $\frac{1}{2}a^3$; $4a^3$
5. mn^2 and $-mn^2$; $\frac{1}{2}mn^2$
6. abc and $8cba$; $6abc$
7. $6m$
8. $-5y$
9. $6k$
10. $2j$
11. $-7x^2$
12. $5w^2$
13. k
14. $6y^3$
15. x^3
16. $-0.9a^2$
17. $2 ; 7 ; 10 ; 3$
18. $-\frac{4}{5} ; \frac{1}{2} ; \frac{1}{5} ; 2\frac{1}{2}$
19. $18a + 3$
20. $3b - 1$
21. $14 - k$
22. $-7x - 6$
23. $\frac{2}{3}p + q$
24. $\frac{1}{2}c + d$
25. $5.5k - 4$
26. $1.6m - n$
27. $7x + 4y - 2$
28. $5m - n + 8$
29. $2p - 5q - 3$
30. $-1 ; 4 ; 10$
31. $(-1)^2 - 8(-1)$
    $= 9$
32. $4(-1) - 18$
    $= -22$
33. -12
34. $1\frac{1}{5}$
35. $\frac{3}{4}$
36. 1.6
37. -9
38. $\frac{1}{5}$
39. -6
40. 2
41. -2
42. $7m - 6 ; -27 ; 15$
43. $-5m + 12 ; 27 ; -3$
44. $2m + 3 ; -3 ; 9$
45. $6m - 2 ; -20 ; 16$
46. $-2m - 11 ; -5 ; -17$
47. $-3k + 14 ; 20 ; 14 ; 11 ; 5$
48. $5m - 9 ; -29 ; -19 ; -9 ; 1$
49. $2a - 4 ; -6 ; -4 ; -2 ; 2$
50. $-7x + y - 5 ; 3 ; -2 ; -19 ; -38$
51. $c + 2d ; 5 ; 5 ; 0 ; 10$
52. $8p^2 + q ; 3 ; 8 ; 33 ; 12$
53a. $2(3x + 10 + y)$
     $= 6x + 2y + 20$
b. $6(2) + 2(5) + 20$
   $= 42$
54a. $\$12.50 + \$0.50x$; $\$8.25 + \$0.75x$
b. Option A: $\$12.50 + \$0.50(5) = \$15$
   Option B: $\$8.25 + \$0.75(5) = \$12$
   She should take option A so that she can earn $3 more.

Challenge

$y + (y + 1) + (y + 2) = 111 ; 3y + 3 = 111 ; 3y = 108 ;$
$y = 36$
The 3 consecutive numbers are 36, 37, and 38.

Try This (p.28)

1. $4ab$ and $-2ab$
2. $-m$ and $3m$

2.3 Extending Algebraic Skills

1. $\frac{x}{4} + 4$
2. $x^3 + 8$
3. $2x^2$
4. subtract x from 100 and then multiplied by 5
5. the product of two different numbers plus 4
6. $3 ; 2$
7. $2 ; 5$
8. $(-b)^3 \times k^3$
9. $(-5) \times (-3)^4$
10. $(\frac{1}{5})^4 \times m^2$
11. $(-\frac{1}{3})^3 \times k^2$
12. $(\frac{1}{2})^4 \times (-n)^3$
13. $16x^2 ; 64x^3$
14. $2y^2 ; 6y^3$
15. $\frac{1}{4}m^2 ; \frac{1}{8}m^3$
16. $0.01k^2 ; 0.001k^3$
17. $2x^2 ; 8x^3$
18. $8n^2 ; 16n^3$
19. $m^3 \times n^2 ; 8 ; 108$
20. $(-p)^3 \times q^2 ; -72 ; 4$
21. y^8
22. y^7
23. a^{12}
24. a^7
25. m^6
26. m^2
27. b
28. $\frac{1}{b^6}$
29. $3 ; 6 ; 5 ; 4$
30. $mn ; n ; mn ; n$
31. 3^{x+4}
32. 2^7k^7
33. $\frac{3^{m+n}}{5^m}$
34. $\frac{p}{q^2}$
35. $2p^3q^2$
36. $\frac{1}{ab}$
37. $3^m x^{m-n}$
38. $2^b y^{-a+b}$
39. 5
40. 10
41. 4
42. -6
43. 5
44. 0
45. 4
46. 0
47. 3
48. 2
49. 6
50. 4
51. A: binomial ; 4 ; 0 ; 0 ; -9
    B: trinomial ; 0 ; -9 ; 3 ; 7
    C: binomial ; 6 ; -2 ; 0 ; 0
    D: trinomial ; 1 ; 0 ; -1 ; -3
    E: monomial ; 0 ; 0 ; 9 ; 0
    F: trinomial ; -6 ; 4 ; 0 ; -3
52. $12xy + 6y^2 - 11y + 7 ; 162$
53. $4y - 2y^2 - 9yx - 12 ; -18$
54. $3xy - 2y^2 - 7y - 2 ; -14$
55. $10yx + 5y^2 - 4y + 6 ; -42$
56. Perimeter: $2x^2 + x ; x^2 - 3x ; 2x^2 + x ; x^2 - 3x ; 6x^2 - 4x$
    $80 ; 130 ; 192 ; 112 ; 170 ; 240$
57. Perimeter: $3(20 - y^2) = 60 - 3y^2$
    $48 ; 57 ; 60 ; 57 ; 48 ; 33$
58. Perimeter: $2(y^2 - x^2) + 2(y - x) = 2y^2 - 2x^2 + 2y - 2x$
    $28 ; 56 ; 84 ; 4 ; 8 ; 12$
59. Area: $(3x^2)(3x^2) = 9x^4$
    $9 ; 729 ; 2304$
60. Area: $(2y^2)(\frac{1}{2}y) = y^3$
    $8 ; 27 ; 729$
61a. $16y^5$
b. 16 384 square units
62a. $\$(x^2 + 3x + 3)$
b. $43
63a. $\$(m^2 - m + 7)$
b. $37
c. Mrs. White
64a. $(4x^2y^2 + \frac{1}{2}y^5)$ m^2
b. 160 m^2
65a. $\$(2.88n^2 + 1.52n)$
b. $8.76

Try This (p.32)

1. $2x - 10$
2. $5x + 4$
3. $\frac{x}{2} - x^2$

2.4 Applying Algebraic Skills

1a. $(12 + w)$ m b. $(24 + 4w)$ m

2a. $2m$ dollars b. $\dfrac{2m}{3}$ dollars

3a. $(2x)$ L b. $(3 - 3x)$ L

4a. Area of the figure:

$y(x - y) + \dfrac{(x - y - y)(1.4x)}{2}$

$= 0.7x^2 - y^2 - 0.4xy$

Perimeter of the figure:

$y + (x - y) + (1.4x + y) + 2x + y$

$= 2y + 4.4x$

b. $26.2 ; 41.2$

5a. Area of the shaded part:

$(\dfrac{3}{2} y^2)^2 - (\dfrac{3}{2} y^2(y^2 - y) \div 2)$

$= \dfrac{3}{2} y^4 + \dfrac{3}{4} y^3$

Perimeter of the triangle:

$(y^2 + 1) \times 2 + \dfrac{3}{2} y^2$

$= 2y^2 + 2 + \dfrac{3}{2} y^2$

$= 3\dfrac{1}{2} y^2 + 2$

b. $432 ; 58$

6. Third side: $3x(x - 1) - 2(x^2 - 2x) = x^2 + x$

The third side is $(x^2 + x)$ cm.

So, the lengths are 48 cm, 48 cm, and 72 cm.

7. Angle b: $180° - 2(x + 35°) = 110° - 2x$

The measure of angle a is 106° and angle b is 74°.

8. After 4 weeks, Jenny will have:

$(x^2 - 2x) + 4(x - 3) = x^2 + 2x - 12$

Jenny will have $87 after 4 weeks.

9a. If the value of x is 9, the width will be (-2) cm. So, 9 is not a possible value of x. However, 3 is a possible value of x.

b. x must be greater than $\dfrac{4}{3}$ cm and smaller than 8 cm.

c. The expression for the perimeter is $(2x + 24)$ cm. When $x = 7$, the perimeter is 38 cm.

10a. No, Winnie's savings will become negative if n = -1. So, 4 is a possible value of n.

b. Any numbers that are greater than $-\dfrac{1}{2}$ are the possible value of n.

c. If $n = 5$, Winnie's savings are $38.50 and Alice's are $26. Winnie has $12.50 more than Alice.

d. If $n = 8$, Winnie's savings are $59.50 and Alice's are $65. Alice has $5.50 more than Winnie.

e. Each girl has to pay $n(n - 2)$.

11a. $(9y + x)$

b. $(4y - 2x)$

c. A box of cereal costs $6, a box of candies costs $18, and a bag of marshmallows costs $2.

12a. $(2xy)$ units b. $(10xy)$ units

c. $(2xy)$ units

13a. $(8x^2y)$ units b. $(16x^4y^2\pi)$ square units

c. $9\pi ; 64\pi ; 4\pi ; \dfrac{256}{\pi} ; 256\pi^3$

Try This (p.38)

1. $0.75P$ 2. $0.25P$

3 Polynomials and Equations

3.1 Operations with Polynomials

1. 3 ; trinomial ; -5, 6 ; 9

2. 3 ; trinomial; $\dfrac{1}{3}$, -2 ; -4

3. 2 ; binomial ; -2 ; -6

4. 1 ; monomial ; 8 ; 0

5. 3 ; trinomial ; -3, 4 ; $\dfrac{1}{3}$

6. $3m^2 ; 0.8m^2$

7. $-8yx ; xy$

8. $3b^2a ; \dfrac{1}{8}ab^2$

9. $-2w^3 ; \dfrac{w^3}{4}$

10. $2x ; 3y ; z ; 2x ; 3y ; z ; x + 2y + 5z$

11. $2m - 12n$

12. $6k - m + 5n$

13. $5a + b + c$

14. $2x^2 + \dfrac{3}{4}x + 1$

15. $\dfrac{2}{3}xy + 3y^2$

16. $4y^2 + \dfrac{2}{5}$

17. $-0.7a^2 - 0.4b + 0.2$

18. $-5m^2 + m + 12.9$

19. $(12y + 4x)$ m

20. $(10a + 2a^2 + 4)$

21. $8 - 2a$

22. $3b + 15$

23. $-4m - 12$

24. $-6 + 3p$

25. $-2x - 5$

26. $-10 + 2k$

27. $-3.2 + 0.8mn - 4m^2$

28. $-p + 2q - 10pq$

29. $-20m^2 + 16m - 8$

30. $-3y^2 - 3x^2 + 3xy$

31. $6a^2 - 4ab + 2b^2$

32. $-3p + q - 4pq$

33. $x + 0.5y - 4.5$

34. $-15 + 17.5c + 5d$

35. $-10 + 2p - 2q$

36. $-3x + 6 - 3y$

37. $-10x + 5y - 6x + 2y$
$= -16x + 7y$

38. $-4p + 4q - 3p - 3q$
$= -7p + q$

39. $\dfrac{12a}{3} + \dfrac{6b}{3} - \dfrac{5a}{5}$
$= 3a + 2b$

40. $11x - 9y + 1$

41. $8a - 8b + 2$

42. $a^2 - b^2 - 4b$

43. $2m - 5n + 5\dfrac{1}{2}$

44. $xy + 2$

45. $-3a^2b - 3ab^2 + 13$

46. $-2mn - 2m^2 - 6$

47. $2 ; 4 ; x ; y ; 6$

$17.5 + 35x + 52.5 + 6y$

$= 70 + 35x + 6y$

His earnings are $(70 + 35x + 6y).

48. Area of the shaded part:

$3(a^2 + b) - 2(3b - \dfrac{1}{2}a^2)$

$= 3a^2 + 3b - 6b + a^2$

$= 4a^2 - 3b$ (m²)

The area of the shaded part is $(4a^2 - 3b)$ m².

Challenge

The average amount of gasoline it consumes every day:

$6.84 + (y + 2y + 3y + 4y + 5y + 6y) \div 7 = 6.84 + 3y$

It consumes $(6.84 + 3y)$ L of gasoline on average every day.

Try This (p.42)

binomial ;

Term: $-9x^4, \dfrac{1}{5}$; Coefficient: -9 ; –

This binomial contains coefficient -9.

constant term: $\dfrac{1}{5}$

3.2 Expanding, Simplifying, and Factoring Polynomials

1. $-3x^2 + 3y - 3xy$
2. $6m^2 + 3m$
3. $1.4p^2 - 3.5q$
4. $1.8y^3 - 7.2y^2 + 5.4y$
5. $-\frac{1}{2}n^3 + 3n^2 + 2n$
6. $\frac{2}{3}k^2 - \frac{1}{3}k^3 + k$
7. $-8u^2v + 12u^3v$
8. $24wxy - 36w^3y$
9. $2x^2 ; -xy ; y ; x ; x^2 ;$
   $6x^3 - 3x^2y + 3xy - 2xy - 2x^2y ;$
   $6x^3 - 5x^2y + xy$
10. $4m^3 + 15mn^2 - 23m^2n$
11. $-0.1u^3 + 0.4u^2v + 0.2uv^2$
12. $a^2bc + \frac{1}{2}ab^2c + \frac{1}{2}abc^2$
13. $-\frac{1}{4}ijk - \frac{5}{12}i^2k - \frac{7}{12}jk^2$
14. $6x^2y^3 ; 3xy^2 ; 2x^2y^3 - xy^2$
15. $-2a^2 + a$
16. $3mn + 2n^2 - 4n$
17. $st - 2s^2t^2 - 3st^2$
18. $6v - 4u + 3$
19. $-8p^2q - q^2 + 2p$
20. $3x ; (2x + y) ;$

    $6x^2 + 3xy ;$

    Area: $9 ; 42 ; 90 ; 285$
21. $(2mn + n) \times \frac{1}{2}m$

    $= m^2n + \frac{1}{2}mn$

    Area: $3 ; 15 ; 42 ; 90$
22. $(s^2 + 0.5st) \times 0.6s$
    $= 0.6s^3 + 0.3s^2t$
    Area: $4.8 ; 13.5 ; 28.8 ; 48.75$
23. $\frac{y}{2} + \frac{x}{3}$

    a. $(12y) \times \$(\frac{y}{2} + \frac{x}{3})$

    $= \$(6y^2 + 4xy)$

    b. $\$(0.5 + 1)$
    $= \$1.50$
24. $(2y - 4x)$

    a. $3y \times \$(2y - 4x)$

    $= \$(6y^2 - 12xy)$

    b. $\$(2 \times 2.4 - 4 \times 0.8)$
    $= \$1.60$
25. $6mn^2 + 3m^2n^2$
    $= 3mn^2(2) + 3mn^2(m)$
    $= 3mn^2(2 + m)$

    $6mn^2 = 2 \cdot 3 \cdot m \cdot n \cdot n$
    $3m^2n^2 = 3 \cdot m \cdot m \cdot n \cdot n$
    G.C.F. $= 3mn^2$
26. $2p^2q - 10pq^3$
    $= 2pq(p) - 2pq(5q^2)$
    $= 2pq(p - 5q^2)$

    $2p^2q = 2 \cdot p \cdot p \cdot q$
    $10pq^3 = 2 \cdot 5 \cdot p \cdot q \cdot q \cdot q$
    G.C.F. $= 2pq$
27. $-15a^3b - 20a^2b^2$
    $= -5a^2b(3a) - 5a^2b(4b)$
    $= -5a^2b(3a - 4b)$

    $-15a^3b = -1 \cdot 3 \cdot 5 \cdot a \cdot a \cdot a \cdot b$
    $-20a^2b^2 = -1 \cdot 2 \cdot 2 \cdot 5 \cdot a \cdot a \cdot b \cdot b$
    G.C.F. $= -5a^2b$
28. $a(a^2 - 2a + 1)$
29. $2b(b^3 + 4b - 8)$
30. $9x^2(x^2 + 9x - 2)$
31. $mn(-n^3 + mn - n^2)$
32. $5pq(q^2 - 4p^2 + 2pq)$
33. $7x^2y^2(-1 + 2xy - 4y)$
34. $s^2t^4(6s + 5t - st)$
35. $uv^2(-10 + u^3v + 5u)$
36. $4xyz^3(1 + 5xz)$
37. $-8pq^2r(2p + 3qr)$
38. $12x^2y ; 3xy$
39. $21p^3q^3 ; q$
40. $4a^3bc^2 ; 3ab^3$
41. $18m^3n^6 ; 9m^2n$
42. $7 ; 2 ;$
    $x^2(7y + 2)$
43. $6x^2 + 2xy - 8y^2$
    $= 2(3x^2 + xy - 4y^2)$
44. $-7m^2n^2 - 7mn$
    $= -7mn(mn + 1)$
45. $16x^2 + 20xy$
    $= 4x(4x + 5y)$
46. $m(5m + mn - 23n)$
47. $a(-8a^2 - a + 6)$
48. $3x$
49. $pq(1 - 2q)$
50. $v(4v - 2u + 3u^2v - 6uv^2)$
51. Area: $3wy(w + 4y)$
    Length: $w + 4y$
52. Area: $2ab(3a + 1 + 4b)$
    Length: $\frac{1}{2}(3a + 1 + 4b)$

53a. Sonic: $(3xy + x^2 - y^2)$
    Coleman: $(xy - 2x^2 + 8y^2)$
    Lucas: $(y^2 + 5x^2 - 3xy)$
    Emma: $(x^2 - 6xy + 18y^2)$
  b. $36 ; 8$ plates/h ;
    60 plates/h ; 40 plates/h
  c. Lucas
54a. $2mn(n - 1 + 7m)$ marbles
  b. $n(n - 1 + 7m)$ marbles
  c. 168 marbles ; 160 marbles

Try This (p.46)

1. $4m^2 ; -6 ; 12m^2 - 18$
2. $-3mn ; 5m ; -6mn^2 + 10mn$

ISBN: 978-1-77149-220-1

ANSWERS

3.3 Applying Polynomials

1a. $(2x + y)$ m
 b. $2(3x + 2x + y) = 10x + 2y$
   The length of the molding is $(10x + 2y)$ m.
2a. $5
 b. $(2y^2 + y + 5)$
3a. Train's Speed $= \dfrac{3t^4 + 2t^2}{2t}$

   $= \dfrac{t^2(3t^2 + 2)}{2t}$

   $= t(\dfrac{3}{2}t^2 + 1)$ (km/h)

   Plane's Speed $= \dfrac{t^4 + \frac{1}{2}t^2}{0.5t}$

   $= \dfrac{0.5t^2(2t^2 + 1)}{0.5t}$

   $= t(2t^2 + 1)$ (km/h)

   Ship's Speed $= \dfrac{5t^4 - 50t^2}{5t}$

   $= \dfrac{5t^2(t^2 - 10)}{5t}$

   $= t(t^2 - 10)$ (km/h)

 b. t is the common factor of the three expressions. But the coefficients of t^2 in the expression for the plane is the greatest. So, the plane has the highest speed.
 c. Train: $5(\dfrac{3}{2}(5)^2 + 1) = 192.5$ (km/h)

   Plane: $5(2(5)^2 + 1) = 255$ (km/h)
   Ship: $5(5^2 - 10) = 75$ (km/h)
4a. The cost of a dining set:
   $2m(m^2 - 6) + 4m(5m + 3)$
   $= 2m^3 + 20m^2$
   $= 2m^2(m + 10)$
   So, the cost of a dining set is $2m^2(m + 10)$.
 b. Each installment:
   $\dfrac{2m^2(m + 10)}{m} = 2m(m + 10)$

   He needs to pay $2m(m + 10)$ for each installment.
 c. $192 ; $1152
   $288 ; $2304
   $750 ; $11 250
5. Height:
   $= 2\left(\dfrac{6x^2y + 6y^2}{4(x^2 + y)}\right)$

   $= \dfrac{12y(x^2 + y)}{4(x^2 + y)}$

   $= 3y$
   $3(9) = 27$; height $= 27$
6. Diagonal:
   $d^2 = (3y)^2 + (4y)^2$
   $d^2 = 9y^2 + 16y^2$
   $d = 5y$
   $5(8) = 40$; diagonal $= 40$
7. Width:
   $= \dfrac{8y(y + 1)}{2} - y(4y - 1)$

   $= 4y(y + 1) - y(4y - 1)$
   $= 4y^2 + 4y - 4y^2 + y$
   $= 5y$
   $5(10) = 50$; width $= 50$

8a. Perimeter of the square: $12p(p + q)$
   Length of the base:
   $12p(p + q) - 2(6p^2 - q) = 12pq + 2q$
 b. Length of each equal side: $(6(4)^2 - 3) = 93$
   Length of the base: $12(4)(3) + 2(3) = 150$
   Height: $93^2 = 75^2 + h^2$
      $h = 55$
   The height of the triangle is 55 units.
9a. $(4n - 1)$ b. $(4n + 1)$
 c. peaches, $2 more   d. $(16n^2)$
10a. $2x(x + 3y)$ km   b. $\dfrac{1}{4}(x + 3y)$ h

 c. $\dfrac{1}{5}(x + 3y)$ h ; $\dfrac{1}{20}(x + 3y)$ h would be saved.
11a. $2pr^2(4p + 1)$ b. $2p(4p + 1)$ tiles are needed.

Try This (p.52)
   $2m^2 - m$; $7m^2 + 4m$
   $10m^2 - 5m - 7m^2 - 4m$
   $= 3m^2 - 9m$
   Ellen has $(3m^2 - 9m)$ left.

ISBN: 978-1-77149-220-1

3.4 Solving First-degree Equations

1. $\dfrac{1}{3}$; $\dfrac{5}{3}$; 3 ; $\dfrac{13}{3}$ 2. 7 ; 13 ; 19 ; 25

3. $-\dfrac{1}{2}$; $\dfrac{3}{2}$; $\dfrac{7}{2}$; $\dfrac{11}{2}$

4a. x ; y b. 40 ; $x = 24$; 24

5. Let x be the no. of \$5 bills and y be the no. of toonies.
$5x - 2y = 14$; $5x - 2(8) = 14$; $x = 6$;
Sam has 6 \$5 bills.

6. Let x be the no. of groups of girls and y be the no. of groups of boys.
$6x + 5y = 235$; $6(25) + 5y = 235$; $y = 17$;
There are 17 groups of boys.

7. 5 8. 1 9. 11

10. 8 11. 64 12. -10

13. 5 14. -6.4 15. $\dfrac{7}{5}$

16. $4y = -20$
   $y = -5$

17. $\dfrac{1}{2}m = 7$
   $m = 14$

18. $-2k = 12$
   $k = -6$

19. $2n = 24$
   $n = 12$

20. $y = 4$ 21. $x = 2$ 22. $b = -\dfrac{1}{5}$

23. $c = -\dfrac{1}{2}$ 24. $k = -\dfrac{1}{3}$ 25. $m = -\dfrac{2}{3}$

26. Let x be the no. of chocolate chip cookies.
$6x + 8(3) = 144$; $x = 20$
She buys 20 boxes of chocolate chip cookies.

27. Let x be the weight of each big marble.
$12x - 288 = 24$; $x = 26$
Each big marble weighs 26 g.

Challenge

$2y + 8 = 84$; $y = 38$; The other 2 sides are each 38 cm long.

Try This (p.56)

1. -1 ; 3 ; 7 ; $(0,-1)$, $(1,3)$, $(2,7)$ 2. 1 ; 3 ; 5 ; $(1,1)$, $(4,3)$, $(7,5)$

3.5 Solving and Rearranging First-degree Equations

1. y ; $y + 5$; $3y$; $y + 5 + 3y = 60$

2. x ; $2x$; $2x - 3 = 9$; $2(x - 4) = 8$

3. h ; $\dfrac{1}{3}h$; $\dfrac{1}{3}h^2 \div 2 = 8$

4. 4 5. 11 6. 6

7. 11 8. 50 9. 7

10. $4y = 8$; $y = 2$ 11. $3t = 12$; $t = 4$

12. 7 13. 4

14. 6 15. -1.5

16. ✗ ; check: $3(9) - 1 = 26$;
   $3x = 15 + 1$
   $x = \dfrac{16}{3}$

17. ✗ ; check: $4(7) + 6 = 34$; -22
   $4y = -22 - 6$
   $y = -7$

18. ✗ ; check: $12 + 18 = 30$; check: $6 + 2(18) = 42$;
   $12 + 18 - 6 = 2m$;
   $m = 12$

19. Let x be the number of mugs Jackie bought.
$30 - 2.4x = 1.2$;
$x = 12$
Check: $30 - 2.4(12) = 1.2$
Jackie bought 12 mugs.

20. Let y be the measure of angle B.
$3y + y = 90°$;
$y = 22.5°$
Check: $3(22.5°) + 22.5° = 90°$
Angle B is 22.5° and Angle A is 67.5°.

21. L.C.D. = 12
12 ; 12 ; 12 ;
$8 = 9m + 24$;
$m = -\dfrac{16}{9}$

22. L.C.D. = 8
$\dfrac{1}{4}x \times 8 = \dfrac{x + 2}{8} \times 8 - 1 \times 8$
$2x = x + 2 - 8$;
$x = -6$

23. $x = 6$ 24. $x = 20$ 25. $y = -21$

26. $m = 30$ 27. $y = -\dfrac{3}{4}$ 28. $m = 32$

29. $k = 6$ 30. $x = 10$ 31. $p = \dfrac{13}{4}$

32. $y = 3$ 33. $n = -4$ 34. $x = -2$

35. $i = -1$ 36. $m = 7$ 37. $y = \dfrac{2}{3}$

38. $x = \dfrac{-5}{2}$ 39. $m = \dfrac{4}{7}$ 40. $b = \dfrac{4}{3}$

41. $a = \dfrac{5}{7}$ 42. $k = -\dfrac{5}{2}$ 43. $m = 1$

44. $x = 2$

45. $\dfrac{h}{2} = x + y$; $x = \dfrac{h}{2} - y$ 46. $px = 3 - 4y$; $x = \dfrac{3 - 4y}{p}$

47. $ax = 6g$; $x = \dfrac{6g}{a}$ 48. $x = 8q\left(\dfrac{3}{4k}\right)$; $x = \dfrac{6q}{k}$

49. $\dfrac{xb}{3} = p - 1$; $x = \dfrac{3(p - 1)}{b}$

50a. $p = 4 - qc + v$ b. 3

51a. $q = \dfrac{4 - p + v}{c}$ b. $-\dfrac{5}{2}$

52a. $c = \dfrac{4 - p + v}{q}$ b. 1

53a. $v = p + qc - 4$ b. -4

Try This (p.60)

x ; $2x$; $x + 2x + x + 2x = 64$

Try This (p.64)

18 ; $6y$; $8y$; 18 ; $8y = 24$; $y = 3$

3.6 Solving Problems with Equations

1a. $\frac{p}{2} = l + w$; $l = \frac{p}{2} - w$

b. $l = \frac{24}{2} - 4$;

   $l = 8$ (cm)

2a. $\frac{9}{5}C = F - 32°$; $F = \frac{9}{5}C + 32°$

b. $F = \frac{9}{5}(20°) + 32°$; $F = 68°$

3. 60 ; 15 ; 15

4. Let x be the distance travelled.
   $0.75x + 3 = 8.25$; $0.75x = 5.25$
   $x = 7$
   You can ride 7 kilometres with $8.25.

5. Let d be the distance travelled.
   $85 = \frac{d}{6.5}$
   $d = 85(6.5)$
   $d = 552.5$
   Uncle Tim can go 552.5 km.

6. Let y be the temperature in Nunavut and x be the number of years.
   $y = 0.12x + 4$
   $y = 0.12(25) + 4$
   $y = 7$
   The temperature in Nunavut would be 7°C in June 2025.

7. Let x be the number of cakes.
   $\frac{1}{3} = \frac{x}{72}$
   $3x = 72$
   $x = 24$
   We can make 24 cakes with 72 eggs.

8. $72 + 0.06y = 120$; $0.06y = 48$;
   $y = 800$; $800

9. $0.1x + 0.05y = 3.5$, x = no. of dimes and y = no. of nickels
   $0.1(25) + 0.05y = 3.5$
   $0.05y = 1$
   $y = 20$
   There are 20 nickels.

10. $3x + 5y = 42$, x = no. of computers and y = no. of sets of stereos
    $3(9) + 5y = 42$
    $5y = 15$
    $y = 3$
    She assembled 3 sets of stereos.

11. $0.05x + 0.12y = 550$, x = the amount invested in AIV and y = the amount invested in ENE
    $0.05(2000) + 0.12y = 550$
    $100 + 0.12y = 550$
    $y = 3750$
    She invested $3750 in ENE.

12. 18 girls

13. Reze is 20 years old, Tammy is 10 years old, and Jenny is 2 years old.

14. 15, 17, and 19

15. 30 black buttons

16. 5.375 cm

17. 6 hours

18. 78 children

Try This (p.66)

   $3V$; πr^2 ; 8π ; 2^2 ; 6

4 Linear Relations

4.1 Graphs and Relations

1. B ; C ; A

2. The charge increases in steps in relation to the number of guests. For example, for 0 to 9 guests, the charge is $300; for 10 to 19 guests, the charge is $500; and so on.

3. The number of bacteria increases rapidly as time goes by. For example, there are 1 million bacteria after 1 hour; the number of bacteria grows up to 49 million after 7 hours.

4. No. of Cups of Flour: 5 ; $7\frac{1}{2}$
   No. of Loaves: 2 ; 4 ; 6

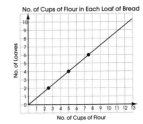

5. $12\frac{1}{2}$ cups of flour

6. $-2x$; $-x$; $1\frac{1}{2}$;

x	y	(x,y)
-4	$5\frac{1}{2}$	$(-4, 5\frac{1}{2})$
0	$1\frac{1}{2}$	$(0, 1\frac{1}{2})$
4	$-2\frac{1}{2}$	$(4, -2\frac{1}{2})$

$\frac{1}{2}$; 1

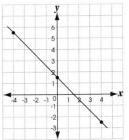

7. $y = 3x - 2$;

x	y	(x,y)
-1	-5	(-1,-5)
0	-2	(0,-2)
2	4	(2,4)

$-\frac{1}{2}$; 1

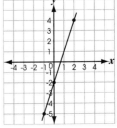

8. $y = \frac{2}{3}x - \frac{1}{3}$

x	y	(x,y)
-4	-3	(-4,-3)
0	$-\frac{1}{3}$	$(0, -\frac{1}{3})$
2	1	(2,1)

-1 ; $1\frac{2}{3}$

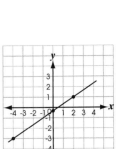

 ISBN: 978-1-77149-220-1

9. $y = \frac{1}{2}x - \frac{1}{2}$

x	y	(x,y)
-3	-2	(-3,-2)
-1	-1	(-1,-1)
5	2	(5,2)

$-1\frac{1}{2}$; 1

10. Trace the dotted lines.
Line AB: 3 ; 4 ; $\frac{3}{4}$

Line CD: 6 ; 3 ; 2

Line EF: 6 ; 5 ; $\frac{6}{5}$

CD

11. MN: 4 ; ST: 1 ; PQ: 1 ; UV: $\frac{5}{2}$; XY: $\frac{7}{4}$

ST and PQ

Challenge

$\frac{5x - 7}{x} = 3$; $x = \frac{7}{2}$

The distance is $\frac{21}{2}$ m.

Try This (p.70)

up ; steady ; top ; at a high speed at the beginning and slowed down towards the ground.

4.2 Linear and Non-linear Relations

1. rhombus
2. trapezoid
3. hexagon

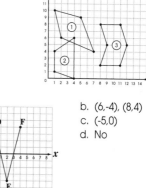

4a.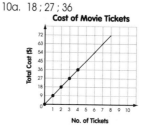

b. (6,-4), (8,4)
c. (-5,0)
d. No

5a.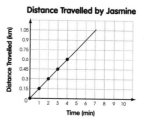

b.

Area		
A	24	square units
B	12	square units
C	6	square units

c. Triangles A and C
d. Triangle C
e. Move it 4 units down.
f. (Suggested answer) (0,1), (0,4), (3,4), (3,1)
6. linear
7. non-linear
8. linear
9. non-linear

10a. 18 ; 27 ; 36

Cost of Movie Tickets

b. It is a straight line graph. It shows a linear relation.
c. $63

11a. 0.3 ; 0.45 ; 0.6

Distance Travelled by Jasmine

b. It is a straight line graph. It shows a linear relation.
c. 0.75 km
d. 6 min

12a. 7 ; 7 ; 7 ; 7 ; 7 ; 7 ; The sum of coordinates of each ordered pair is 7.

b.

It is a straight line graph. It shows a linear relation.

c. No
d. (Suggested answer) (0,7), (3,4)
e. B

13a. 10 ; 9 ; 8 ; 7 ; 6

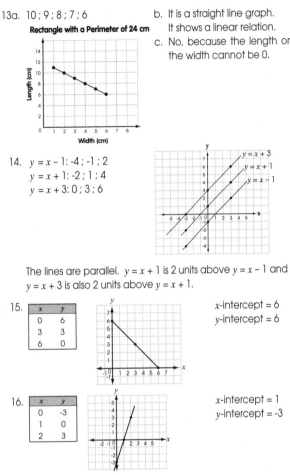

Rectangle with a Perimeter of 24 cm

b. It is a straight line graph. It shows a linear relation.

c. No, because the length or the width cannot be 0.

14. $y = x - 1$: -4 ; -1 ; 2
$y = x + 1$: -2 ; 1 ; 4
$y = x + 3$: 0 ; 3 ; 6

The lines are parallel. $y = x + 1$ is 2 units above $y = x - 1$ and $y = x + 3$ is also 2 units above $y = x + 1$.

15.

x	y
0	6
3	3
6	0

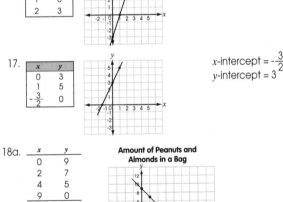

x-intercept = 6
y-intercept = 6

16.

x	y
0	-3
1	0
2	3

x-intercept = 1
y-intercept = -3

17.

x	y
0	3
1	5
$-\frac{3}{2}$	0

x-intercept = $-\frac{3}{2}$
y-intercept = 3

18a.

x	y
0	9
2	7
4	5
9	0

Amount of Peanuts and Almonds in a Bag

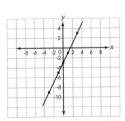

b. When the line meets the x-intercept, it means the bag contains peanuts only. When the line meets the y-intercept, it means the bag contains almonds only.

Try This (p.74)

Trace the dotted lines.
(1,4) and (9,4)

Try This (p.78)

x	y
-3	-9
-1	-5
0	-3
1	-1
3	3

It is a linear relation.

4.3 Direct and Partial Variations

1. partial ; $\frac{1}{3}$; 6

2. direct ; -4 ; 0

3. partial ; 2 ; -9

4. partial ; $\frac{1}{2}$; 4

5. y ; x ; direct

6. $y = 50x + 25$, where y = the total cost and x = no. of days
It is a partial variation.

7. $y = 331.4 + 0.6x$, where y = the speed of sound in air and
x = degree Celsius above zero
It is a partial variation.

8. $y = 16x$, where y = the total no. of floor tiles and x = no. of row
It is a direct variation.

9. 0 ; 178 ; 356
linear

10. 75 ; 125 ; 175
linear

11. 331.4 ; 337.4 ; 343.4
linear

12. 0 ; 64 ; 128
linear

13. 5 ; 5 ; 21 – 16 = 5 ; linear
14. 4 ; 26 – 15 = 11 ; 43 – 26 = 17 ; non-linear

15.

x	y	△y
1	5	
2	24	24 – 5 = 19
3	11	11 – 24 = -13
4	8	8 – 11 = -3

non-linear

16.

x	y	△y
3	18	
4	24	24 – 18 = 6
5	30	30 – 24 = 6
6	36	36 – 30 = 6

linear

17.

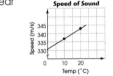

a partial variation

a direct variation

18a.

△x	x	y	△y	$\frac{△y}{△x}$
	0	90		
3	3	135	45	15
3	6	180	45	15
3	9	225	45	15

Rates of Membership

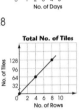

b. $y = 15x + 90$
c. $y = 15(12) + 90 = 270$; The membership fees for 1 year is $270.

19a.

△x	x	y	△y	$\frac{△y}{△x}$
	5	60		
5	10	120	60	12
5	15	180	60	12
5	20	240	60	12

Cost of Renting a Party Room

b. $y = 12x$
c. $y = 12 \times 30 = 360$; The cost is $360.

ISBN: 978-1-77149-220-1

20.

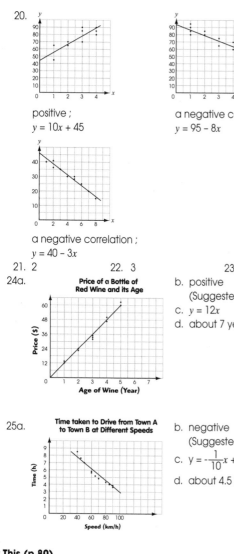

positive ;
$y = 10x + 45$

a negative correlation ;
$y = 95 - 8x$

a negative correlation ;
$y = 40 - 3x$

21. 2   22. 3   23. 4

24a.

Price of a Bottle of Red Wine and its Age

b. positive
   (Suggested answers)

c. $y = 12x$

d. about 7 years old

25a.

Time taken to Drive from Town A to Town B at Different Speeds

b. negative
   (Suggested answers)

c. $y = -\frac{1}{10}x + 12$

d. about 4.5 hours

Try This (p.80)
neither ;
a direct variation ;
a partial variation ;
a direct variation ;

4.4 Applying Linear Models

1a.

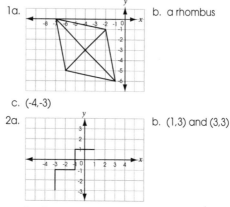

b. a rhombus

c. (-4,-3)

2a.

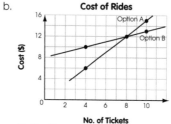

b. (1,3) and (3,3)

c. 2 units

3. (Suggested answers for the scenarios)
   ✔ A (a direct variation): Find the total cost of the chocolate bars where each bar costs $3.
   ✔ C (a partial variation): The temperature is now 5°C and it drops by 2°C per hour. Find the temperature after x hours.

4a. $y = 1.25x + 4$

b. It is a partial relation. It has a flat fee of $4.

c. $10.25 ; $19 ; $41.50

5a. $y = 1.5x$; $y = 0.5x + 8$

A				B		
	x	y			x	y
	4	6			4	10
	8	12			8	12
	10	15			10	13

b.

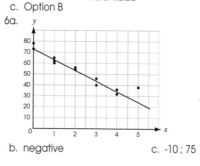

c. Option B

6a.

b. negative   c. -10 ; 75

7a.

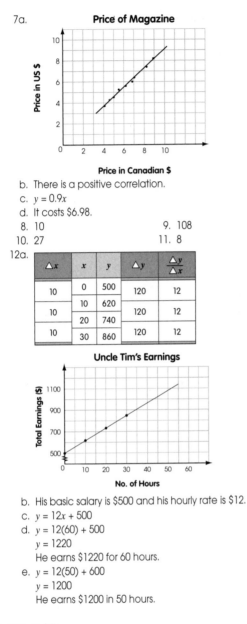

Price of Magazine

b. There is a positive correlation.

c. $y = 0.9x$

d. It costs $6.98.

8. 10

9. 108

10. 27

11. 8

12a.

$\triangle x$	x	y	$\triangle y$	$\dfrac{\triangle y}{\triangle x}$
10	0	500	120	12
10	10	620	120	12
10	20	740	120	12
10	30	860	120	12

Uncle Tim's Earnings

b. His basic salary is $500 and his hourly rate is $12.

c. $y = 12x + 500$

d. $y = 12(60) + 500$
   $y = 1220$
   He earns $1220 for 60 hours.

e. $y = 12(50) + 600$
   $y = 1200$
   He earns $1200 in 50 hours.

Try This (p.86)

1. The x-coordinates of all the points on the y-axis are 0.

2. The x-coordinates of all the points on the same vertical line are the same.

4.5 Working with Statistics

(Suggested answers for questions 1 to 3)

1. If you increase the amount of water, the height of the tree will increase too.

2. If the number of hours of watching TV increases, the scores on a Science test will decrease.

3. Cluster Sampling: Survey all Grade 4 students in a school for their favourite computer games.
   Stratified Sampling: Survey 5% to 10% of the students from Grade 2 to Grade 5 for their favourite computer games.

4. Broken line graphs ; Bar graphs ; Circle graphs

5. No Correlation

6. Strong Positive Correlation

7. Weak Negative Correlation

8. Weak Positive Correlation

9. No Correlation

10. Strong Negative Correlation

11. Age ; Average Height

12. strong positive ; they get taller

13a. **Hours of Study vs Math Score** ; strong positive

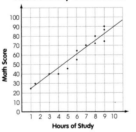

b. As the number of hours spent on studying Math increases, the test score gets higher.

c. By using extrapolation, about 11 hours of study will be needed to get 100 marks on the Math test.

14a.

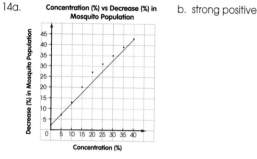

Concentration (%) vs Decrease (%) in Mosquito Population

b. strong positive

c. By interpolation, the population will decrease by about 25%.

15. A ; C ; B

16. 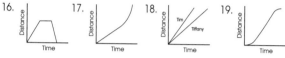 17. 18. 19.

20. The race was 100 m. Wayne won.

21. Wayne: Wayne accelerated and ran for 13 s to complete the race.
Sam: Sam ran at a steady speed and it took him 14 s to complete the race.
Ted: Ted ran at a steady speed for the first 12 s. Then he increased his speed steadily until he reached the finish line. It took him 16 s to complete the race.

22. (Suggested answers)

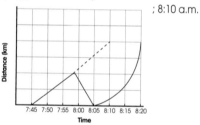

; 8:10 a.m.

Try This (p.90)

Red: its batteries, used on a specified MP3 player last at least 8 hours longer than other batteries.
Yellow: Jason performs experiments to test the lifetime of this brand and three other brands.
Green: He also collects information from consumer reports.

4.6 Reading and Interpreting Graphs

1. Hypothesis: The more popular the comics, the higher the prices will be.
Cluster sampling: Survey the students in your grade at the school.

2. Hypothesis: The fewer the number of students in a class, the better the performance of the students.
Stratified sampling: Survey and collect student reports from 5% – 10% of the classes from each of the schools in a specified area.

3a. The sales increase in warmer months and decrease in cooler months.

b. (Suggested answer)
About 500 ice cream cones will be sold in December.

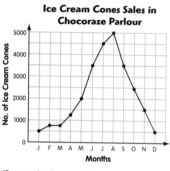

Ice Cream Cones Sales in Chocoraze Parlour

c. (Suggested answer)
$52 500

d. Yes, because it can show changes in data over time.

4a. hours of exercise and test scores

b. The number of hours of exercise you do has no relationship with the test scores.

c. The data were collected by cluster sampling.

d. No correlation

5a.

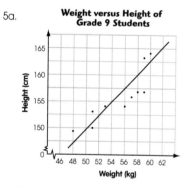

Weight versus Height of Grade 9 Students

b. They have a weak positive correlation.
(Suggested answers for part c and d.)

c. 166 cm

d. 54 kg

6a.

Weights at 1 Month Old versus Weights at 6 Years Old

Weight (kg) at Six Years Old — Weight (kg) at One Month Old

b. The heavier the child is at 1 month old, the heavier the child will be at 6 years old.

c. They have a strong positive correlation.

d. (Suggested answer) 31 kg

(Suggested answers for question 7)

7a. Population of children in the area ;
Number of tutoring schools in the area ;
Parents' willingness to send children to a tutoring school

b. She can survey the neighbourhood and get the population data from the city office.

c. What is your budget for the tutorial fee?

d. Select 5% – 10% of the students in each grade from each of the schools in the area and survey their parents.

8a. 1250 m

b. 20 min

c. (Suggested answer)
David walked to the library at a constant speed and took a rest for about 12 minutes. Then he walked to the library at a higher speed and stayed there for 20 minutes. Afterwards, he walked back home and arrived home at 11:55 a.m.

Try This (p.96)

Hypothesis: The higher the household income, the greater the household expenditure.
Primary source: Survey your parents, relatives, and neighbours.
Secondary source: Check for the related surveys conducted by Statistics Canada.

5 Analytic Geometry

5.1 Slope

1. $\overline{AB}$: positive ; $\frac{1}{4}$

$\overline{CD}$: negative ; $-\frac{2}{3}$

$\overline{EF}$: negative ; $-\frac{1}{2}$

$\overline{GH}$: positive ; 3 ; ✔

2. $y_1 ; x_1$

3. $\frac{3-1}{2-0} = 1$

4. slope $= \frac{-3-6}{6-3} = -3$

5. slope $= \frac{7-0}{1-0} = 7$

6. slope $= \frac{8-8}{12-3} = 0$

7. slope $= \frac{0-8}{2-(-5)} = -\frac{8}{7}$

8. slope $= \frac{-8-8}{-5-(-5)} =$ undefined

9. slope $= \frac{-14-(-7)}{2-(-2)} = -\frac{7}{4}$

10. slope $= \frac{-10-10}{5-(-10)} = -\frac{4}{3}$

11. slope $= \frac{-4-(-4)}{11-(-11)} = 0$

12. undefined

13. 0

14. $-\frac{7}{10}$

15. 0

16. 1

17. $-\frac{7}{3}$

18. undefined

19. $-\frac{5}{7}$

20. $\frac{2}{7}$

21. $-\frac{2}{3}$

22. $1 ; \frac{1}{2} ; \frac{5}{3} ; -3 ; -\frac{2}{3} ; -1$

23. $\overline{DE}$

24. $\overline{BC}$

25. $\overline{AB}$ and $\overline{FG}$

26. (Suggested answers)

(0,0)
(3,4)
(-5,5)
(-6,-2)

27. (Suggested answers)

(1,4)
(4,4)
(-3,1)
(-6,-3)

28.

29. They are parallel.
30. They are the same.
31. They are perpendicular.
32. Their slopes are negative reciprocal of each other.

33. $2 ; -\frac{1}{2}$; perpendicular

34. $\frac{3}{2} ; -\frac{2}{3}$; perpendicular

35. $\frac{2}{5} ; \frac{2}{5}$; parallel

36. undefined ; 0 ; perpendicular

37. 0 ; 0 ; parallel

ISBN: 978-1-77149-220-1

38. 11 ; 1 ; neither

39. ℓ_1: $-\frac{3}{5}$; 4 ; $y = -\frac{3}{5}x + 4$ ℓ_2: 2 ; -6 ; $y = 2x - 6$

   ℓ_3: 1 ; 2 ; $y = x + 2$ ℓ_4: $-\frac{2}{3}$; -4 ; $y = -\frac{2}{3}x - 4$

   ℓ_5: -1 ; 0 ; $y = -x$ ℓ_6: $\frac{1}{5}$; -4 ; $y = \frac{1}{5}x - 4$

40a. 2   b. -3
41a. 3   b. -2
42a. $-\frac{5}{4}$ b. $\frac{2}{3}$
43a. $m = \frac{3}{2}$; $b = -1$ b. $m = 4$; $b = 0$

44a. The slope is 1.50. It means each topping costs $1.50.
  b. The y-intercept is 9.50. It means a pizza with no toppings costs $9.50.
  c. $y = 1.50 \times 6 + 9.50 = 18.50$; The total cost is $18.50.
45a. slope $= \frac{-200}{10} = -20$; The water decreases at the rate of 20 L/min.
  b. y-intercept = 200 ; It means the bathtub has 200 L of water originally.
  c. $y = -20x + 200$
46a. slope $= \frac{80}{4} = 20$; 20 pages/day are read.
  b. y-intercept = 0 ; No pages are read at the beginning.
  c. $y = 20x$

Try This (p.100)
   Line A: positive ; 3 ; 1
   Line B: negative ; 4 ; 3 ; $-\frac{4}{3}$

5.2 Solving Problems Involving Rate of Change

1. Rate: $\frac{8.75 - 7.15}{2008 - 2004} = 0.4$
   The rate of change of the minimum wage is $0.40/year.
2. Rate: $\frac{930 - 1200}{2008 - 1998} = -27$
   The polar bear population decreases by 27 per year.
3. Rate: $\frac{24 - 16}{10 - 6} = 2$
   The rate of change of temperature is 2°C/h.
4. Rate: $\frac{4400 - 6500}{31 - 28} = -700$
   The parachutist drops at a rate of 700 m/min.
5. Rate: $\frac{640 - 500}{2} = 70$
   The rate of change of Sue's savings is $70/month.
6. Rate: $\frac{192 - 160}{4} = 8$
   Jason has 8 more marbles every week.
7a. $\frac{7}{3}$ b. $-\frac{4}{3}$
  c. 0   d. undefined
8. (Suggested answers for the points on the lines)

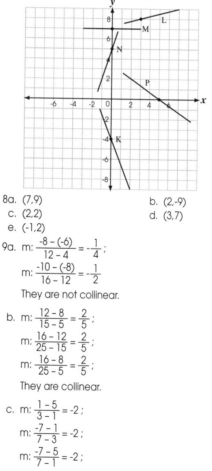

8a. (7,9)   b. (2,-9)
  c. (2,2)   d. (3,7)
  e. (-1,2)
9a. m: $\frac{-8 - (-6)}{12 - 4} = -\frac{1}{4}$;
   m: $\frac{-10 - (-8)}{16 - 12} = -\frac{1}{2}$
   They are not collinear.

 b. m: $\frac{12 - 8}{15 - 5} = \frac{2}{5}$;
   m: $\frac{16 - 12}{25 - 15} = \frac{2}{5}$;
   m: $\frac{16 - 8}{25 - 5} = \frac{2}{5}$;
   They are collinear.

 c. m: $\frac{1 - 5}{3 - 1} = -2$;
   m: $\frac{-7 - 1}{7 - 3} = -2$;
   m: $\frac{-7 - 5}{7 - 1} = -2$;
   They are collinear.

10a. 500 ; x
  b. Louis earns $0.05 for every dollar of computer sales he made.
  c. The y-intercept is $500. It means the flat rate of his base salary is $500 per week.
  d. $500 + 0.05 \times $6000 = $800
     His total salary will be $800.

11a. $y = 80 + 5x$, where y = total cost and x = no. of guests

  b. x cannot be greater than 30 or smaller than 0. The least value of y is 80.

  c. The rental cost increases by \$5 for each additional guest.

  d. The y-intercept is \$80. It means the flat rate of the rental cost is \$80.

  e. 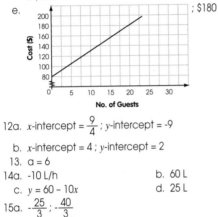 ; \$180

12a. x-intercept = $\frac{9}{4}$; y-intercept = -9

  b. x-intercept = 4 ; y-intercept = 2

13. $a = 6$

14a. -10 L/h   b. 60 L

  c. $y = 60 - 10x$ d. 25 L

15a. $-\frac{25}{3}$; $-\frac{40}{3}$

  b. The water cools down steadily at a rate of $\frac{25}{3}$ °C/min from A to B and then at a faster rate of $\frac{40}{3}$ °C/min from B to C.

  c. Yes. When the temperature of the water and the room temperature are the same, the slope of the line becomes 0.

Try This (p.106)

  $\frac{247\,000 - 274\,000}{2001 - 1996}$; -5400 ;

  5400 farms lost in Canada per year.

5.3 Equations of Lines

1. ℓ_1: $-\frac{3}{2}$; 3 ; $y = -\frac{3}{2}x + 3$

   ℓ_2: $\frac{2}{3}$; -2 ; $y = \frac{2}{3}x - 2$

   ℓ_3: $-\frac{1}{4}$; -1 ; $y = -\frac{1}{4}x - 1$

2. L_1: $y = -4x$; -4 ; 0

   L_2: $y = -\frac{1}{2}x - 2$; $-\frac{1}{2}$; -2

   L_3: $y = 2x - 1$; 2 ; -1

   L_4: $y = 3x + 2$; 3 ; 2

3.

4. 0 ; -4 ; 0.5 ; $-\frac{2}{3}$

5a. $y = -2x - 5$ b. $y = -x - 5$

6a. $y = -\frac{3}{2}x - 2$ b. $-\frac{3}{2}$; 2 ; 6 ; $y = -\frac{3}{2}x + 6$

  c. $y = -\frac{3}{2}x + 2\frac{1}{2}$ d. $y = -\frac{3}{2}x + 2$

7. $y - 7 = -2(x - (-1))$ 8. $y - (-6) = -\frac{1}{3}(x - 4)$

   $y = -2x + 5$ $y = -\frac{1}{3}x - \frac{14}{3}$

9. $y - 3 = \frac{1}{5}(x - 2)$ 10. $y - (-8) = \frac{1}{4}(x - (-5))$

   $y = \frac{1}{5}x + \frac{13}{5}$ $y = \frac{1}{4}x - \frac{27}{4}$

11. $y - 4 = -1(x - 7)$ 12. $y = -\frac{2}{3}x$

    $y = -x + 11$

13. $y = -3x + 7$ 14. $y = -\frac{2}{3}x + \frac{5}{6}$

15. $y = \frac{1}{2}x - \frac{5}{2}$ 16. B ; E ; G ; H ; J ; K ; L

17. $4x - y - 5 = 0$

18. $y \times 4 = (\frac{1}{4}x + 9)4$ 19. $y \times (-2) = (-\frac{1}{2}x - 7)(-2)$

    $4y = x + 36$ $-2y = x + 14$

    $x - 4y + 36 = 0$ $x + 2y + 14 = 0$

20. $y \times 9 = (2x - \frac{7}{9})9$ 21. $2(\frac{1}{2}x - y) = 3 \times 2$

    $9y = 18x - 7$ $x - 2y = 6$

    $18x - 9y - 7 = 0$ $x - 2y - 6 = 0$

22. $2(4 - y) = (-\frac{3}{2}x)2$ 23. $2x - 5y + 5 = 0$

    $8 - 2y = 3x$

    $3x + 2y - 8 = 0$

24. $10x - 10y - 3 = 0$ 25. $2x - y - 2 = 0$

26. $x + 4y + 64 = 0$ 27. $y = x - 1$

28. $2y = -5x + 12$ 29. $9y = 3x - 4$

    $y = -\frac{5}{2}x + 6$ $y = \frac{1}{3}x - \frac{4}{9}$

30. $4y = -2x + 5$ 31. $2y = 2x - 3$

    $y = -\frac{1}{2}x + \frac{5}{4}$ $y = x - \frac{3}{2}$

32. $y = -2x + 1$

33. 6   b. 6

  c. 2 or -2

34. $\frac{1}{3}$ b. $-\frac{5}{2}$

  c. 1 or -1   d. -1

ISBN: 978-1-77149-220-1

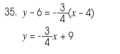

35. $y - 6 = -\dfrac{3}{4}(x - 4)$

$y = -\dfrac{3}{4}x + 9$

So, (8,3) and (-4,12) lie on the line.

36. $y = \dfrac{1}{4}x - 3$

So, (4,-2) and (-4,-4) lie on the line.

37. ℓ_1: $y - 0 = \dfrac{4}{3}(x - (-4))$

$y = \dfrac{4}{3}x + \dfrac{16}{3}$

$4x - 3y + 16 = 0$

ℓ_2: $y - 0 = -\dfrac{3}{4}(x - (-4))$

$y = -\dfrac{3}{4}x - 3$

$3x + 4y + 12 = 0$

ℓ_3: $y - (-3) = \dfrac{4}{3}(x - 0)$

$y = \dfrac{4}{3}x - 3$

$4x - 3y - 9 = 0$

ℓ_4: $y - (-4) = -\dfrac{3}{4}(x - (-7))$

$y = -\dfrac{3}{4}x - \dfrac{37}{4}$

$3x + 4y + 37 = 0$

38. Anna's savings: $y = \dfrac{1}{2}x + 2$; $m = \dfrac{1}{2}$; $b = 2$

Steve's savings: $y = -x + 8$; $m = -1$; $b = 8$

a.

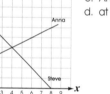

b. Steve
c. Anna
d. at the 4th month

Try This (p.110)

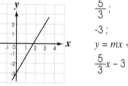

$\dfrac{5}{3}$;

-3 ;

$y = mx + b$;

$\dfrac{5}{3}x - 3$

Try This (p.112)

1. 2 ; -4 ;

$y - 2 = -4x - 20$

$y = -4x - 18$

The equation of the line is $y = -4x - 18$.

2. $-\dfrac{1}{3}$; 1

$y + 7 = -\dfrac{1}{3}x + \dfrac{1}{3}$

$y = -\dfrac{1}{3}x - \dfrac{20}{3}$

The equation of the line is $y = -\dfrac{1}{3}x - \dfrac{20}{3}$.

5.4 x- and y-Intercepts and Points of Intersection

1. x-intercept: $3x + 8(0) = 24$; $x = 8$
   y-intercept: $3(0) + 8y = 24$; $y = 3$
2. x-intercept: $2x - 9(0) = 12$; $x = 6$
   y-intercept: $2(0) - 9y = 12$; $y = -\dfrac{4}{3}$
3. x-intercept: $x - 6(0) = 15$; $x = 15$
   y-intercept: $0 - 6y = 15$; $y = -\dfrac{5}{2}$
4. x-intercept: $5(0) = 20 - 8x$; $x = \dfrac{5}{2}$
   y-intercept: $5y = 20 - 8(0)$; $y = 4$
5. L_1: x-intercept = -5 ;
   y-intercept = 2 ;
   $m = \dfrac{2}{5}$

   L_2: x-intercept = 3 ;
   y-intercept = -7 ;
   $m = \dfrac{7}{3}$

   L_3: x-intercept = -6 ;
   y-intercept = -7 ;
   $m = -\dfrac{7}{6}$

   L_4: x-intercept = 3 ;
   y-intercept = -2 ;
   $m = \dfrac{2}{3}$

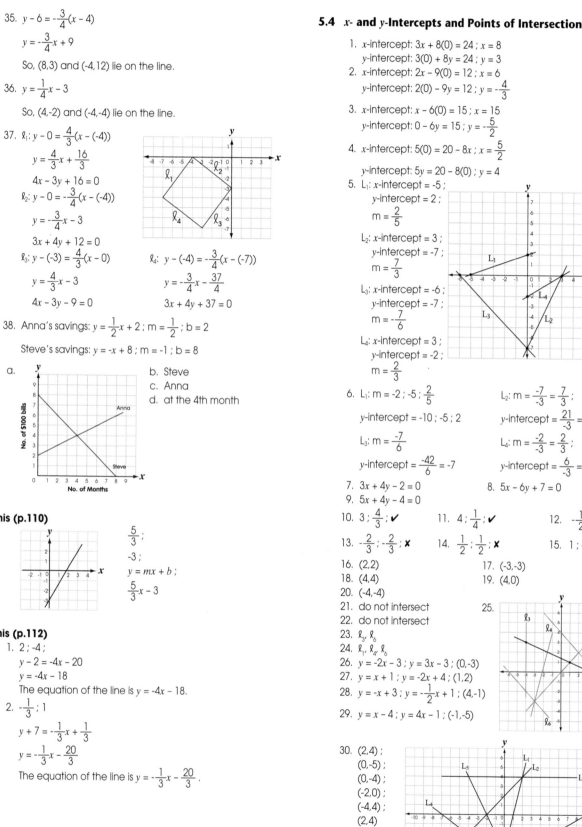

6. L_1: $m = -2$; -5 ; $\dfrac{2}{5}$
   y-intercept = -10 ; -5 ; 2

   L_2: $m = \dfrac{-7}{-3} = \dfrac{7}{3}$;
   y-intercept = $\dfrac{21}{-3} = -7$

   L_3: $m = \dfrac{-7}{6}$
   y-intercept = $\dfrac{-42}{6} = -7$

   L_4: $m = \dfrac{-2}{-3} = \dfrac{2}{3}$;
   y-intercept = $\dfrac{6}{-3} = -2$

7. $3x + 4y - 2 = 0$
8. $5x - 6y + 7 = 0$
9. $5x + 4y - 4 = 0$
10. 3 ; $\dfrac{4}{3}$; ✔
11. 4 ; $\dfrac{1}{4}$; ✔
12. $-\dfrac{1}{2}$; 1 ; ✔
13. $-\dfrac{2}{3}$; $-\dfrac{2}{3}$; ✗
14. $\dfrac{1}{2}$; $\dfrac{1}{2}$; ✗
15. 1 ; $\dfrac{1}{3}$; ✔
16. (2,2)
17. (-3,-3)
18. (4,4)
19. (4,0)
20. (-4,-4)
21. do not intersect
22. do not intersect
23. ℓ_3, ℓ_6
24. ℓ_1, ℓ_4, ℓ_6
25.

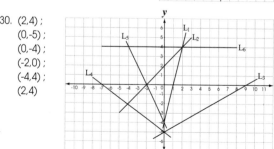

26. $y = -2x - 3$; $y = 3x - 3$; (0,-3)
27. $y = x + 1$; $y = -2x + 4$; (1,2)
28. $y = -x + 3$; $y = -\dfrac{1}{2}x + 1$; (4,-1)
29. $y = x - 4$; $y = 4x - 1$; (-1,-5)
30. (2,4) ;
    (0,-5) ;
    (0,-4) ;
    (-2,0) ;
    (-4,4) ;
    (2,4)

31. C ;
    intersect at one point

32. D ;
    same slope

33. 2 ; 3

34. 2 ; -8

35. point of intersection: (5,4)
    slope of the line: $\frac{4-0}{5-0} = \frac{4}{5}$

    $b = 0$
    $y = \frac{4}{5}x$

36. point of intersection: (-1,-3), (2,-6)

    slope of line: $\frac{(-6)-(-3)}{2-(-1)} = \frac{-3}{3} = -1$

    $b = -4$
    $y = -x - 4$

37. (3,-1), (-3,-3), (0,7)

38. Family 1: $y = \frac{2}{3}x$

    Family 2: $y = 4x + 8$

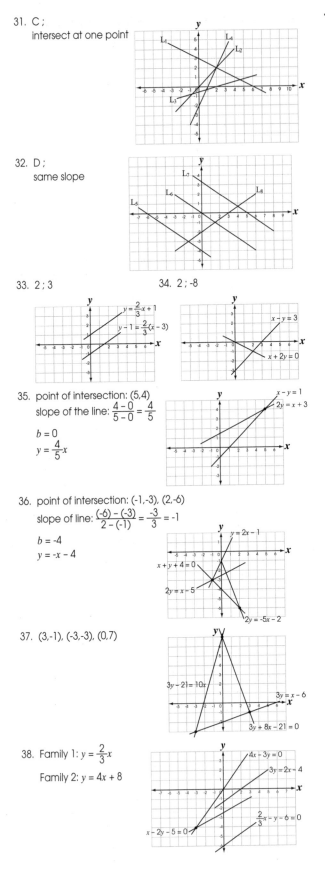

Try This (p.116)

Find the x-intercept:
$y = 0$; $4x - 5(0) - 20 = 0$; $x = 5$
Find the y-intercept:
$x = 0$; $4(0) - 5y - 20 = 0$; $y = -4$

ISBN: 978-1-77149-220-1

5.5 Solving Problems with Linear Equations

1. $k = 4$
2. $k = -3$; $p = 8$
3. $(2, 10)$
4. $k = \frac{1}{2}$; $b = -\frac{1}{2}$
5. $p = 2$; $q = -6$
6. A(6,4), B(-2,2), C(4,-3)

   $\overline{AB}$: Slope $= \frac{2}{8} = \frac{1}{4}$; y-intercept: $\frac{5}{2}$

   slope-intercept form: $y = \frac{1}{4}x + \frac{5}{2}$

   standard form: $x - 4y + 10 = 0$

   $\overline{BC}$: Slope $= -\frac{5}{6}$

   point slope form: $y - 2 = -\frac{5}{6}(x - (-2))$; $6y - 12 = -5x - 10$;

   $6y = -5x + 2$

   standard form: $5x + 6y - 2 = 0$

   slope-intercept form: $y = -\frac{5}{6}x + \frac{1}{3}$

   $\overline{AC}$: Slope $= \frac{7}{2}$

   point slope form: $y - 4 = \frac{7}{2}(x - 6)$; $2y - 8 = 7x - 42$;

   $2y = 7x - 34$

   standard form: $7x - 2y - 34 = 0$

   slope-intercept form: $y = \frac{7}{2}x - 17$

7. D(-5,2), E(3,0), F(-4,-3)

   $\overline{DE}$: Slope $= -\frac{2}{8} = -\frac{1}{4}$

   point slope form: $y - 2 = -\frac{1}{4}(x - (-5))$; $-4y + 8 = x + 5$;

   $-4y = x - 3$

   standard form: $x + 4y - 3 = 0$

   slope-intercept form: $y = -\frac{1}{4}x + \frac{3}{4}$

   $\overline{EF}$: Slope $= \frac{3}{7}$

   point slope form: $y - 0 = \frac{3}{7}(x - 3)$; $7y = 3x - 9$

   standard form: $3x - 7y - 9 = 0$

   slope-intercept form: $y = \frac{3}{7}x - \frac{9}{7}$

   $\overline{DF}$: Slope $= -5$

   point slope form: $y - 2 = -5(x - (-5))$; $y - 2 = -5x - 25$;

   $y = -5x - 23$

   standard form: $5x + y + 23 = 0$

   slope-intercept form: $y = -5x - 23$

8.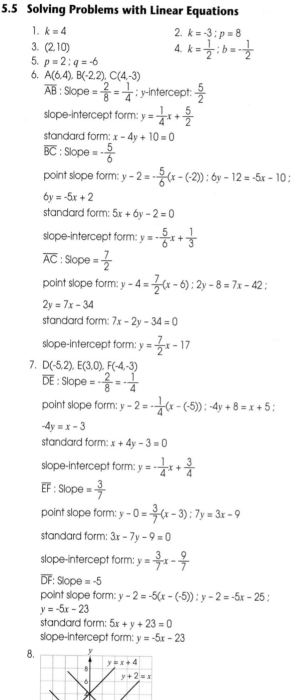

   $y = -x - 2$; (0,4), (-3,1), (0,-2), (3,1)

9a. $C_1 = 40t + 80$; $C_2 = 40t + 90$

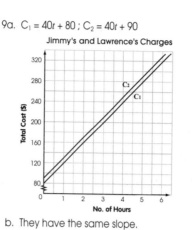

b. They have the same slope.

c. Lawrence always charges $10 more.

d. 6 hours

10a. C_1: total cost of Plan A ; C_2: total cost of Plan B

   t: no. of minutes

   $C_1 = 0.25t + 10$

   $C_2 = 0.15t + 15$

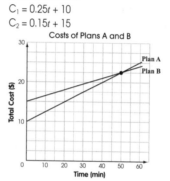

b. (50, 22.5) ; When the number of minutes used is 50, both plans cost $22.50.

c. If you use your phone for less than 50 minutes, Plan A is a better choice.

11. $y = -x$

12. $y = -2x + 2$

13. (Suggested equation)

   same slope ; $y = -\frac{2}{5}x + 9$

14a. David: $C_1 = 300 + 0.04c$

   Agnes: $C_2 = 400 + 0.03c$

   where c = total sales

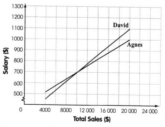

b. $10 000

c. If the amount of sales a salesman makes is over $10 000, David's salary plan is a better choice.

d. Agnes earns $150 less than David.

Try This (p.122)

   2 ; 4

   $2k - 8k - 12 = 0$

   $k = -2$

   The value of k is -2.

6　Properties of Two-dimensional Shapes

6.1　Angles of Polygons

1. 30˚ ; 63˚
2. 38˚ ; 112˚
3. 45˚ ; 50˚
4. 30˚ ; 150˚
5. 2 pairs of corresponding angles: b ; d ; b ; d
   2 pairs of alternate angles: f ; h ; f ; h
   2 pairs of interior angles: n ; q ; n ; q
6. 48˚ ;
   a = 48˚ (corresponding angles) ;
   b = 48˚ (opposite angles) ;
   d = 132˚ (alternate angles)
7. p = 180˚ – 85˚ = 95˚ (interior angles) ;
   q = 95˚ (opposite angles) ;
   s = 85˚ (alternate angles) ;
   r = 85˚ (alternate angles)
8. e = 115˚ (opposite angles) ;
   f = 115˚ (corresponding angles) ;
   g = 70˚ (opposite angles) ;
   h = 70˚ (alternate angles)
9. n = 55˚ (corresponding angles) ;
   q = 55˚ (opposite angles) ;
   m = 180˚ – 55˚ = 125˚ (supplementary angles) ;
   p = 55˚ (corresponding angles)
10. 69˚ ; 69˚
11. 60˚ ; 120˚
12. h = 63˚ ; i = 59˚ ; j = 58˚ ; k = 58˚
13. a = 55˚ ; b = 55˚ ; c = 72˚ ; d = 72˚
14. p = 49˚ ; q = 90˚ ; r = 49˚ ; s = 41˚

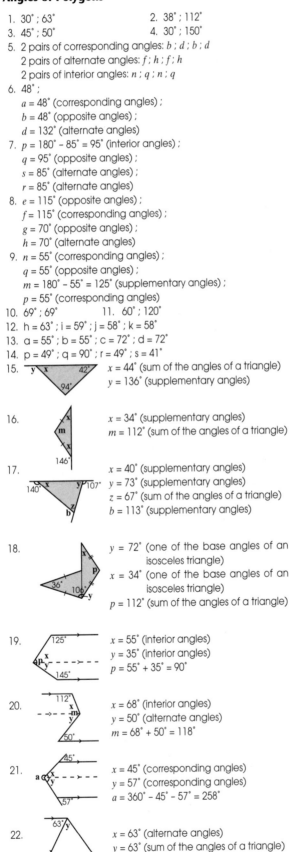

15. x = 44˚ (sum of the angles of a triangle)
    y = 136˚ (supplementary angles)

16. x = 34˚ (supplementary angles)
    m = 112˚ (sum of the angles of a triangle)

17. x = 40˚ (supplementary angles)
    y = 73˚ (supplementary angles)
    z = 67˚ (sum of the angles of a triangle)
    b = 113˚ (supplementary angles)

18. y = 72˚ (one of the base angles of an isosceles triangle)
    x = 34˚ (one of the base angles of an isosceles triangle)
    p = 112˚ (sum of the angles of a triangle)

19. x = 55˚ (interior angles)
    y = 35˚ (interior angles)
    p = 55˚ + 35˚ = 90˚

20. x = 68˚ (interior angles)
    y = 50˚ (alternate angles)
    m = 68˚ + 50˚ = 118˚

21. x = 45˚ (corresponding angles)
    y = 57˚ (corresponding angles)
    a = 360˚ – 45˚ – 57˚ = 258˚

22. x = 63˚ (alternate angles)
    y = 63˚ (sum of the angles of a triangle)

Challenge

(Case I) Triangle on the left:
180˚ = (x + 25˚) + 2(3x – 10˚)　(sum of the angles of a triangle)
180˚ = 7x + 5˚
x = 25˚
The three angles are 50˚, 65˚, and 65˚.

(Case II) Triangle on the right:
180˚ = (3x – 10˚) + 2(x + 25˚)　(sum of the angles of a triangle)
180˚ = 5x + 40˚
x = 28˚
The three angles are 74˚, 53˚, and 53˚.

Try This (p.126)

1. 75˚ ; complementary ; 15˚
2. 75˚ ; opposite
3. 42˚ ; supplementary ; 138˚
4. 75˚ ; 180˚ ; supplementary ; 105˚
5. 138˚

ISBN: 978-1-77149-220-1

6.2 Properties of Interior and Exterior Angles

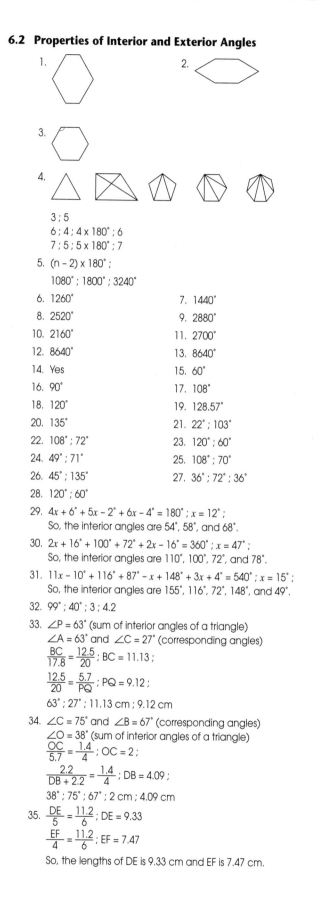

1.

2.

3.

4.

3 ; 5
6 ; 4 ; 4 x 180˚ ; 6
7 ; 5 ; 5 x 180˚ ; 7

5. $(n - 2) \times 180°$;
1080˚ ; 1800˚ ; 3240˚

6. 1260˚

7. 1440˚

8. 2520˚

9. 2880˚

10. 2160˚

11. 2700˚

12. 8640˚

13. 8640˚

14. Yes

15. 60˚

16. 90˚

17. 108˚

18. 120˚

19. 128.57˚

20. 135˚

21. 22˚ ; 103˚

22. 108˚ ; 72˚

23. 120˚ ; 60˚

24. 49˚ ; 71˚

25. 108˚ ; 70˚

26. 45˚ ; 135˚

27. 36˚ ; 72˚ ; 36˚

28. 120˚ ; 60˚

29. $4x + 6° + 5x - 2° + 6x - 4° = 180°$; $x = 12°$;
So, the interior angles are 54˚, 58˚, and 68˚.

30. $2x + 16° + 100° + 72° + 2x - 16° = 360°$; $x = 47°$;
So, the interior angles are 110˚, 100˚, 72˚, and 78˚.

31. $11x - 10° + 116° + 87° - x + 148° + 3x + 4° = 540°$; $x = 15°$;
So, the interior angles are 155˚, 116˚, 72˚, 148˚, and 49˚.

32. 99˚ ; 40˚ ; 3 ; 4.2

33. $\angle P = 63°$ (sum of interior angles of a triangle)
$\angle A = 63°$ and $\angle C = 27°$ (corresponding angles)
$\frac{BC}{17.8} = \frac{12.5}{20}$; BC = 11.13 ;
$\frac{12.5}{20} = \frac{5.7}{PQ}$; PQ = 9.12 ;
63˚ ; 27˚ ; 11.13 cm ; 9.12 cm

34. $\angle C = 75°$ and $\angle B = 67°$ (corresponding angles)
$\angle O = 38°$ (sum of interior angles of a triangle)
$\frac{OC}{5.7} = \frac{1.4}{4}$; OC = 2 ;
$\frac{2.2}{DB + 2.2} = \frac{1.4}{4}$; DB = 4.09 ;
38˚ ; 75˚ ; 67˚ ; 2 cm ; 4.09 cm

35. $\frac{DE}{5} = \frac{11.2}{6}$; DE = 9.33
$\frac{EF}{4} = \frac{11.2}{6}$; EF = 7.47
So, the lengths of DE is 9.33 cm and EF is 7.47 cm.

36.

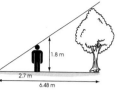

1.8 m
2.7 m
6.48 m

$\frac{\text{height}}{1.8} = \frac{6.48}{2.7}$; height of the tree = 4.32
So, the height of the tree is 4.32 m.

37. Compare the lengths of the sides of Triangle C and Triangle D:
$\frac{8}{12} = \frac{10}{15} = \frac{12}{18}$
Their corresponding sides are proportional, so Triangle C and Triangle D are similar.

38. $\frac{\text{length}}{28.6} = \frac{26}{64}$; length of the wire = 11.62 ;
So, the wire is 11.62 cm long.

Try This (p.130)
By sides: $\overline{PQ} = \overline{SR}$; $\overline{PS} = \overline{QR}$;
By angles: $p = q = s = r$;
Although all the angles are equal, the lengths of the sides are not the same. So, it is an irregular polygon.

Try This (p.133)
360˚ ;
$2x$; $x + 60°$; x ; x ; 360˚ ;
$x = 60°$;
of trapezoid ABCD are 120˚, 120˚, 60˚, and 60˚.

ISBN: 978-1-77149-220-1

ANSWERS

6.3 Angle Properties of Parallel Lines

1. $46°$; $44°$; $90°$
2. $124°$; $54°$; $56°$
3. $63°$; $63°$; $36°$
4. $36°$; $78°$; $102°$
5. $132°$; $154°$; $106°$
6. $55°$; $89°$; $23°$
7. $66°$; $126°$; $60°$
8. $64°$; $33°$; $101°$
9. $71°$; $71°$; $140°$
10. $146°$; $115°$; $77°$
11. $50°$; $78°$; $52°$; $102°$
12. $60°$; $120°$; $103°$; $103°$
13. $x = 26°$; $26°$; $65°$; $115°$

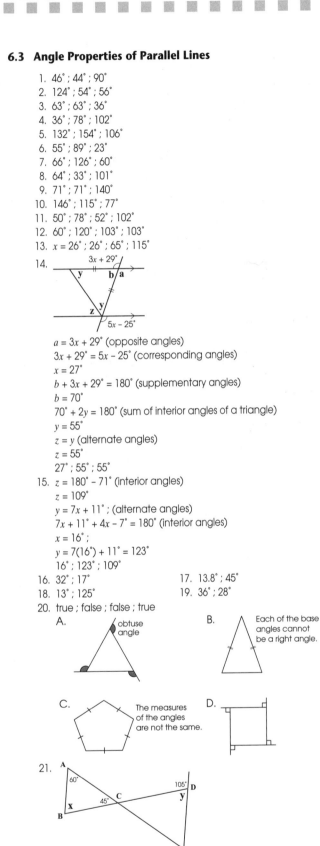

14.
$a = 3x + 29°$ (opposite angles)
$3x + 29° = 5x - 25°$ (corresponding angles)
$x = 27°$
$b + 3x + 29° = 180°$ (supplementary angles)
$b = 70°$
$70° + 2y = 180°$ (sum of interior angles of a triangle)
$y = 55°$
$z = y$ (alternate angles)
$z = 55°$
$27°$; $55°$; $55°$

15. $z = 180° - 71°$ (interior angles)
$z = 109°$
$y = 7x + 11°$; (alternate angles)
$7x + 11° + 4x - 7° = 180°$ (interior angles)
$x = 16°$;
$y = 7(16°) + 11° = 123°$
$16°$; $123°$; $109°$

16. $32°$; $17°$ 17. $13.8°$; $45°$
18. $13°$; $125°$ 19. $36°$; $28°$
20. true ; false ; false ; true

A. obtuse angle

B. Each of the base angles cannot be a right angle.

C. The measures of the angles are not the same.

D.

21.
$x + 60° + 45° = 180°$ (sum of interior angles of a triangle)
$x = 75°$
$y + 105° = 180°$ (supplementary angles)
$y = 75°$
$∵ x = y$ (alternate angles)
$∴ \overline{AB} // \overline{DE}$

22.

$x + 106° = 180°$ (supplementary angles)
$x = 74°$
$∵ x = ∠CEQ = 74°$ (corresponding angles)
$∴ \overline{AB} // \overline{CD}$

23.

Let x be the smallest angle.
$x + 2x + 3x + 4x = 360°$ (sum of interior angles)
$x = 36°$
The measures of the angles are $36°$, $72°$, $108°$, and $144°$.

24.

$2x + 90° = 180°$ (sum of interior angles of a triangle)
$x = 45°$
$x + y = 180°$ (interior angles)
$y = 135°$
The measures of the angles are $45°$, $45°$, $135°$, and $135°$.

25.

$x = 36°$ (corresponding angles)
$y + 36° = 180°$ (supplementary angles)
$y = 144°$
The measures of the angles are $36°$, $144°$, $36°$, and $144°$.

26.

$2x = 118°$
$x = 59°$
$2x + y = 180°$ (sum of interior angles of a triangle)
$y = 62°$
The measures of the angles are $59°$, $59°$, and $62°$.

Try This (p.136)
1. $112°$; $144°$ 2. $60° + 115° + 80°$; $105°$

Try This (p.138)
1. $54°$; corresponding   2. $54°$; $114°$; supplementary
3. $126°$; alternate   4. $126°$; corresponding

ISBN: 978-1-77149-220-1

6.4 Applying Geometry Knowledge

1.

$c + 49° + 72° = 180°$ (sum of the angles of a triangle)
$c = 59°$
$a = 59°$ (opposite angles)
$b = 180° - 59° - 41°$ (sum of the angles of a triangle)
$b = 80°$

2.

$y + 116° = 180°$ (supplementary angles)
$y = 64°$
$x_1 + 62° = 180°$ (interior angles)
$x_1 = 118°$
$x_2 + 64° = 180°$ (interior angles)
$x_2 = 116°$
$x = 118° + 116° = 234°$

3. $\angle EYP + 118° = 180°$ (supplementary angles)
$\angle EYP = 62°$
$\angle EPY + 106° = 180°$ (supplementary angles)
$\angle EPY = 74°$
$\angle YEP = 180° - 62° - 74°$ (sum of the angles of a triangle)
$\angle YEP = 44°$

4. $a = 54°$ (alternate angles)
$b = 43°$ (alternate angles)
$c = 180° - 43° - 54°$ (sum of the angles of a triangle)
$c = 83°$

5. $70° + 120° = 190°$
Since the sum of the interior angles formed by the transversal is not 180°, so l_1 and l_2 are not parallel.

6. $\angle AGF = 55°$ (supplementary angles)
$\angle EGB = 55°$ (opposite angles)
$\angle CHF = 55°$ (corresponding angles)

7. $x + y = 180°$

8. $\angle ABC + 132° = 180°$ (supplementary angles)
$\angle ABC = 48°$
$\angle ACB + 30° = 90°$ (complementary angles)
$\angle ACB = 60°$
$\angle BAC = 180° - 60° - 48°$ (sum of the angles of a triangle)
$\angle BAC = 72°$
$\triangle ABC$ is not an isosceles triangle because no two angles are equal in size.

9. $\angle PQO = 180° - 113°$ (supplementary angles)
$\angle PQO = 67°$
$\angle OAB = 180° - 102°$ (supplementary angles)
$\angle OAB = 78°$
$\because \angle PQO = \angle ABO, \angle OPQ = \angle OAB,$ and $\angle AOB$ – angle in common – All corresponding angles are equal.
$\therefore \triangle AOB \sim \triangle POQ$

10.

$\angle ACB = 79°$ (isosceles triangles)
$\angle CAB = 22°$ (sum of the angles of a triangle)
$\angle XAC = 180° - 22°$ (supplementary angles)
$\angle XAC = 158°$
$\angle YBC = 180° - 79°$ (supplementary angles)
$\angle YBC = 101°$
$\angle ACZ = 180° - 79°$ (supplementary angles)
$\angle ACZ = 101°$
So, the measures of the exterior angles are 158°, 101°, and 101°.

11. $\frac{1}{3}$; 44° ; 2 ; $2x$; 136° ; $x = 84°$
84°, 84°, 56°, and 136°

12. $6x + (180° - 21x) \times 2 = 180°$
$x = 5°$
The measures of the angles are 30°, 75°, and 75°.

13. $(3x - 4°) + (5x - 20°) + 4x = 360°$
$x = 32°$
The measures of the angles are 88°, 40°, and 52°.

14. $\angle ECD = \angle EAB$ (corresponding angles)
$\angle EDC = \angle EBA$ (corresponding angles)
$\angle CED$ – angle in common
So, $\triangle ECD \sim \triangle EAB$
$\frac{8.33 + 16.67}{8.33} = \frac{18.5}{CD}$; $CD = 6.16$
$\frac{25}{8.33} = \frac{9 + DB}{9}$; $DB = 18.01$
So, $CD = 6.16$ cm and $DB = 18.01$ cm.

15. 30°

16. 18 sides

17. 122.5° and 57.5°

18. 15° ($\triangle ADE$ is an isosceles triangles.)

19. $x = 50°$; $y = 130°$

20. $x = 39$; $y = 22$

21. $\frac{16.2}{3.6} = \frac{y}{(4.32 - 1.68)}$
$y = 11.88$
height of the building:
$= 11.88 + 1.68$
$= 13.56$
The building is 13.56 m tall.

Try This (p.142)

$l_1 \mathbin{//} l_2$;
$\triangle BCD$ is an isosceles triangle.

1. a ; 42° ; 69°

2. 42° ; alternate angles

3. 69° ; 42° ; supplementary angles ; 69°
$a = 69°$, $b = 42°$, and $c = 69°$

7 Measurement Relationships in Three-dimensional Figures

7.1 The Pythagorean Theorem

1. $c^2 = 9^2 + 4.2^2$; $c = 9.93$ (cm)
2. $10^2 = a^2 + 7^2$; $a = 7.14$ (cm)
3. $6.8^2 = 4^2 + b^2$; $b = 5.50$ (cm)
4. $16.5^2 = 7^2 + b^2$; $b = 14.94$ (cm)
5. A: 7 ; 5 ; $c = 8.6$; 8.6 ; 20.6
   B: $c^2 = 13^2 + 8^2$; $c = 15.26$; hypotenuse: 15.26 units ; perimeter: 36.26 units
   C: $c^2 = 6^2 + 11^2$; $c = 12.53$; hypotenuse: 12.53 units ; perimeter: 29.53 units
6. third side: $11.5^2 = a^2 + 6^2$; $a = 9.81$; perimeter: 27.31 cm
7. third side: $19^2 = a^2 + 9.8^2$; $a = 16.28$; perimeter: 45.08 cm

8. Triangle A: $c^2 = 6^2 + 2^2$; $c = 6.32$
   Triangle B: $h^2 = 6^2 + 4^2$; $h = 7.21$
   perimeter: 19.53 units

9. Triangle A: $c^2 = 5^2 + 3^2$; $c = 5.83$
   Triangle B: $h^2 = 5^2 + 7^2$; $h = 8.6$
   perimeter: 18.43 units
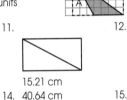

10. 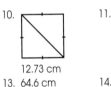 12.73 cm
11. 15.21 cm
12. 8.5 cm
13. 64.6 cm
14. 40.64 cm
15. 42 cm
16. 15 ; 20 ; 24.98
    15 + 24.98 ; 39.98
    39.98

17. Triangle A: $15^2 = y^2 + 8^2$; $y = 12.69$
    Triangle B: $12.69^2 = x^2 + 10.5^2$; $x = 7.13$
    The side in bold is 7.13 cm.

18. 50.9 cm
19. 53.31 cm
20. 33.53 cm
21. Let y be the length of the third stick.
    Possible length 1: $y^2 = 9.4^2 + 12.8^2$; $y = 15.88$
    Possible length 2: $12.8^2 = y^2 + 9.4^2$; $y = 8.69$
    The possible lengths of the third stick are 15.88 cm and 8.69 cm.
22. Let a be the distance.
    $5^2 = a^2 + 1.2^2$
    $a = 4.85$
    The distance is 4.85 m.
23. Let k be the distance.
    $5^2 = k^2 + 1.6^2$
    $k = 4.74$
    The distance is 4.74 m now.

Challenge

Let c be the width of the divider.
$c^2 = 6^2 + 6^2$; $c = 8.49$
The dimensions of the divider are 8.49 cm by 9.4 cm.

Try This (p.146)

1. 8 ; 6 ; 100 ; 10 ; 10
2. 12 ; 5 ; 144 ; 25 ; 119 ; 10.91 ; 10.91

7.2 Perimeters and Areas of Composite Figures

1. 25.2 m ; 16.71 m^2
2. 32 cm ; 36 cm^2
3. 14.4 cm ; 14.98 cm^2
4. 131.88 cm ; 329.7 cm^2
5. 16.43 m ; 11.05 m^2
6. 44.2 cm ; 46.9 cm^2
7. 57.02 cm ; 151.13 cm^2
8. 77.1 cm ; 141.13 cm^2
9. 20.41 cm ; 24.97 cm^2
10. $196 = \dfrac{\text{base} \times 19.6}{2}$; base = 20
    $\text{hypotenuse}^2 = 19.6^2 + 10^2$
    So, the base is 20 cm and the hypotenuse is 22 cm.
    Perimeter = 22 + 22 + 20 = 64 (cm)
11. 257 cm^2 ; 14.25 cm^2
12.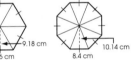

    1.2 m ; 0.8 m ; c

    $c^2 = 0.6^2 + 0.8^2$; $c = 1$;
    Amount of piping needed:
    1 + 1 + 1.2 = 3.2 (m)
    She needs 3.2 m of piping.

13. Area of hexagon:
    $= \dfrac{10.6 \times 9.18}{2} \times 6$
    $= 291.92$ (cm^2)
    Area of octagon:
    $= \dfrac{8.4 \times 10.14}{2} \times 8$
    $= 340.70$ (cm^2)
    Octagon has a greater area by 48.78 cm^2 more.

    9.18 cm ; 10.6 cm ; 10.14 cm ; 8.4 cm

14.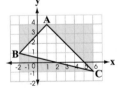

    24.5 cm

    Length of the string:
    = 2 x 24.5 x 3.14 ÷ 2 x 3
    = 230.79 (cm)
    The string is 230.79 cm long.

15. $AB^2 = 3^2 + 3^2$; $AB = 4.24$ units
    $BC^2 = 8^2 + 2^2$; $BC = 8.25$ units
    $AC^2 = 5^2 + 5^2$; $AC = 7.07$ units

    Perimeter = 4.24 + 8.25 + 7.07 = 19.56 (units)
    △ABC is a right-angled triangle.
    Area = 7.07 x 4.24 ÷ 2 = 14.99 (square units)

16.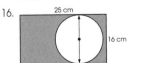

    25 cm ; 16 cm

    Area of the remaining cardboard:
    16 x 25 − $\pi 8^2$ = 199.04 (cm^2)

ISBN: 978-1-77149-220-1

17. square

18. Maximum area $= (\frac{\text{perimeter}}{4})^2$

19. Maximum area $= (\frac{96}{4})^2 = 576$ (cm²)

20. Case I:

Rectangle*	Width (m)	Length (m)	Perimeter (m)
A	1	64	130
B	2	32	68
C	4	16	40
D	8	8	32

32 m ;
8 m by 8 m

Case II:

Rectangle*	Width (m)	Length (m)	Perimeter (m)
A	1	36	74
B	2	18	40
C	3	12	30
D	4	9	26
E	6	6	24

24 m ;
6 m by 6 m

21. square

22. The dimensions are the square root of the area.

23. Minimum perimeter = 4 x $\sqrt{\text{area}}$
    Minimum perimeter of the rectangle:
    = 4 x $\sqrt{64}$ = 32 (cm)

24. A: 32.77 cm ; 51.75 cm²
    B: 34.26 cm ; 42.39 cm²
    C: 26.19 cm ; 18.81 cm²
    B ; A

25. 196 cm²

26. 40 m

27. 6 laps

28. 71.13 min

Try This (p.150)

P = 10 + 10 + 9 + 16 + 9 = 54 (cm)
A = (16 x 6 x $\frac{1}{2}$) + (16 x 9) = 192 (cm²)

Try This (p.153)

Rectangle*	Width (m)	Length (m)	Area (m²)
A	1	11	11
B	2	10	20
C	3	9	27
D	4	8	32
E	5	7	35
F	6	6	36

6 m by 6 m gives the maximum area of 36 m².
It is in the shape of a square.

7.3 Solving Problems Involving Perimeters and Areas

1. 3.62 = (2.3 + 4.8)h ÷ 2 ; h = 1.02
   Perimeter = 2.3 + 1.02 + 4.8 + 2.7 = 10.82 (m)

2. Area = 9 x 7 – 3 x 1 = 60 (m²)
   Cost = 60 m² x \$17.50/m² = \$1050

3. 357 = 40 x π + 2x ; x = 115.7
   Area = (115.7 x 40) + (20)²π = 5884 (m²)

4. $\pi r^2 = 314$; r = 10
   R = 10 + 2 = 12
   Perimeter = 24π = 75.36 (m)
   Cost = \$15/m x 75.36 m = \$1130.40

5a. Area = (0.64)² + (π(0.32)² ÷ 2) = 0.57 (m²)
    Cost = 0.57 m² x \$26/m² = \$14.83

b. Perimeter = 0.64 x 3 + (0.64π ÷ 2) = 2.92 (m)
   Cost = 2.92 m x \$12/m + \$150 = \$185.04

6. side length of the square = $\sqrt{0.5^2 - 0.3^2}$ = 0.4 (m)
   Area = $(\frac{(0.2)^2\pi}{2} + (0.4)^2 + 2(\frac{0.3 \times 0.4}{2}))$ x 2
   = 0.69 (m²)
   Time taken = 0.69 ÷ 0.05 = 13.8 (min)

7. height = $\sqrt{1.5^2 - 0.9^2}$
   = 1.2 (m)
   Area = 1.8 x 1.2 = 2.16 (m²)
   Energy converted in an hour:
   2.16 x 1.4 = 3.02 (kW)

8. Area = (8² – (2²π x 4)) ÷ 4 = 3.44 (cm²)

9. E: 15.71 cm ; 8.47 cm²
   F: 15.71 cm ; 15.53 cm²

10. Area of the shaded part:
    2²π – 1²π = 9.42 (square units)
    Area of the unshaded part:
    3²π – 9.42 = 18.84 (square units)

11a.

Mirror*	Length (cm)	Width (cm)	Perimeter (cm)	No. of Gold Chains
A	50	200	500	50
B	80	125	410	41
C	100	100	400	40

The dimensions of the mirror should be 100 cm x 100 cm.
It needs 40 gold chains.

b. Cost = 89 x 40 + 0.59 x 10 000 = 9460
   The cost is \$9460.

12. The greatest area for the deck is 25 m².

13. The dimensions with the least perimeter are 7 cm by 7 cm.
    Cost = 9 x (7 x 4) = 252
    The cost is \$252.

14a. 50.24 m²

b. 57.76 m²

c. at least 7.5 m

15. 25 cedar shrubs

16. 24 cm by 24 cm

17. 16 cm by 16 cm

18. 43.6 cm

19. 18.24 cm²

Try This (p.156)

y be the unknown side of the triangular section ;
42 ; 4 + y + 8 + 12 + 8 + y ;
42 = 32 + 2y ;
y = 5 ;
5 m

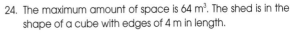

7.4 Finding Surface Areas and Volumes of Prisms

1. A: 25 200 ; 5440
   B: 346.5 ; 364.4
   C: 4.32 ; 17.28

2. 24.66 (cm^2) ;
   Volume: 24.66 x 5 = 123.3 (cm^3)
   Surface area: 2 x 24.66 + 6 x (5 x 3) = 139.32 (cm^2)

3. Base area: $\frac{6 \times 4.1}{2}$ = 61.5 (cm^2)

   Volume: 61.5 x 15 = 922.5 (cm^3)
   Surface area: 2 x 61.5 + 5 x (6 x 15) = 573 (cm^2)

4. A: 385 cm^3 ; 364.91 cm^2
   B: 196.45 cm^3 ; 281.48 cm^2
   C: 54 cm^3 ; 108 cm^2
   D: 2851.2 cm^3 ; 1296 cm^2
   E: 975.74 cm^3 ; 644.16 cm^2

5. Volume: r^2 ; h ; $\pi r^2 h$
   Surface area: πr^2 ; $2\pi r$; $2\pi r^2 + 2\pi rh$

6. 628 cm^3 ; 414.48 cm^2

7. 471 cm^3 ; 345.4 cm^2

8. 424.43 cm^3 ; 389.86 cm^2

9. 7771.5 cm^3 ; 2849.55 cm^2

10. 525.17 cm^3 ; 444.31 cm^2

11. 188.32 cm^3 ; 202.19 cm^2

12. 61.28 cm^3 ; 180.62 cm^2

13. 429.34 cm^3 ; 350.26 cm^2

14a. Prism B: 12 ; 2
    Prism C: 18 ; 3
    Prism D: 24 ; 4
  b. The volume will be 2 times the original if the length is doubled
     and 3 times the original if tripled.
  c. 4000 cm^3 ; 400n cm^3

15. The original block: 39 x 40 x 12 = 18 720 (cm^3)
    The volume of the original block is 3 times the small one.

16. Volume of A: $\frac{A}{672} = \frac{1}{8}$; A = 84 cm^3

    Volume of B: $\frac{B}{672} = \frac{3}{8}$; B = 252 cm^3

    Volume of C: $\frac{C}{672} = \frac{4}{8}$; C = 336 cm^3

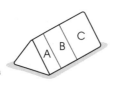

17. Prism Y: 2 ; 4 ; 6 ; 88 ; 4 ; 48 ; 8
    Prism Z: 3 ; 6 ; 9 ;198 ; 9 ; 162 ; 27

18. Cylinder Q: 2 ; 6 ; 32π ; 4 ; 24π ; 8
    Cylinder R: 3 ; 9 ; 72π ; 9 ; 81π ; 27

19. 4 ; 8

20. 9 ; 27

21. 1920 cm^3

22. 5.83π cm^2

23. Garden Shed A: 8.8 ; 35.2
    Garden Shed B: 6.67 ; 53.36
    Garden Shed C: 5.14 ; 61.68
    Garden Shed D: 4 ; 64
    Garden Shed E: 3.11 ; 62.2
    Garden Shed F: 2.4 ; 57.6
    Garden Shed G: 1.82 ; 50.96

24. The maximum amount of space is 64 m^3. The shed is in the
    shape of a cube with edges of 4 m in length.

25. Stick A: 16.2 ; 543.6
    Stick B: 11.57 ; 496.24
    Stick C: 9 ; 486
    Stick D: 7.36 ; 492.4
    Stick E: 6.23 ; 508.12
    The dimensions: 9 cm by 9 cm by 9 cm
    The shape: a cube

Try This (p.160)
Volume: 6 x 6 x $\frac{1}{2}$; 126 (cm^3)

Surface area: (7 x 8.5) + 2(6 x 7) ; 179.5 (cm^2)

ISBN: 978-1-77149-220-1

7.5 Finding Surface Areas and Volumes of Pyramids

1. 249.6 cm² 2. 360 cm²

3. 107.71 m²

4. $\frac{1}{2}$bs + $\frac{1}{2}$bs + $\frac{1}{2}$bs

   b + b + b ;

   4 ;

   P ; B

5. 394.25 cm² 6. 22.52 cm

7. 16.9 cm

8. A: 351 cm²   B: 603.79 cm²
   C: 877.24 m²   D: 10.92 cm²
   E: 247.2 cm²

9. 1205.76 cm² 10. 237.89 cm²

11. 326.72 cm² 12. 97.21 m²

13. 385.84 cm² 14. 11.05 cm

15. 615.44 cm² 16. 1181.77 cm²

17. 4.5 m 18. 5.65 m

19. 6.94 cm 20. 573.12 cm²

21. A: 1037.14 cm²   B: 1130.4 cm²
    C: 390.36 cm²   D: 469.43 cm²
    E: 1256 cm²   F: 870.19 cm²

22. 144 cm³ 23. 1046.86 cm³

24. 314 cm³ 25. 266.38 cm³

26. A: 241.39 cm³   B: 3416.32 cm³
    C: 0.07 m³   D: 916.7 cm³
    E: 1283.87 cm³   F: 481.47 cm³

27. 523.33 cm³ 28. 12 861.44 cm³

29. 8.69 cm 30. 25.67 cm

31. $16\pi r^2$; $\frac{32}{3}\pi r^3$ 32. 170.67 cm³ ; 207.04 cm²

33. the first cone cup ; 6.39 cm³ more water

34. 17.43 cm

Try This (p.166)

Surface area:

$2(\frac{1}{2} \times 20 \times 15.52) + 2(\frac{1}{2} \times 8 \times 18.03) + 20 \times 8$

= 614.64 (cm²)

Try This (p.168)

Find s: 20 ; 6 ; 20.88

Surface area:

$3.14 \times 6^2 + 3.14 \times 6 \times 20.88$

= 506.42 (cm²)

7.6 Solving Problems Involving Prisms, Pyramids, Cylinders, and Spheres

1a. Side length of the prism:
   $8^2 = 2l^2$; $l = 5.66$ (cm)
   Volume of the prism:
   5.66 x 5.66 x 16.5 = 528.59 (cm³)

b. Volume of the cylinder:
   $\pi(4)^2(16.5) = 828.96$ (cm³)
   Space unoccupied:
   828.96 – 528.59 = 300.37 (cm³)

2a. Volume of the prism: 392 cm³
   Volume of the cylinder: 1857.31 cm³
   The cylinder has a greater volume.

b. S.A. of the prism: 378 cm²
   S.A. of the cylinder: 836.81 cm²
   The cylinder has a greater surface area.

3. The maximum volume of the cone:
   $\frac{1}{3}\pi(4)^2(8)$

   = 133.97 (cm³)

4. Capacity of the paper cup:
   $\frac{1}{3}\pi(4)^2(11)$

   = 184.21 (mL)
   Capacity of the prism:
   10 x 15 x 30 = 4500 (cm³)
   No. of cups needed to fill the prism:
   4500 ÷ 184.21 = 24.43
   It takes 25 cups to fill the prism.

5. Slant height of the triangles:
   $816 = 4(16 \times a \times \frac{1}{2})$

   $32a = 816$
   $a = 25.5$
   Height of the prism:
   $a^2 = h^2 + 8^2$
   $25.5^2 = h^2 + 8^2$
   $h = 24.21$
   The height is 24.21 cm.

6. Total surface area:
   $4(12.8 \times 34 \times \frac{1}{2}) + 12.8 \times 12.8$

   = 1034.24 (cm²)
   The total surface area is
   1034.24 cm².

7a. Volume:
   $\frac{1}{3}(12 \times 5.8 \times 15) = 348$ (cm³)

b. Volume:
   $\frac{1}{3}(24 \times 5.8 \times 15) = 696$ (cm³)

c. Volume with the length and width doubled:
   $\frac{1}{3}(24 \times 11.6 \times 15) = 1392$ (cm³)

ISBN: 978-1-77149-220-1

8.

Sphere	Radius	Surface Area*	Volume*
A	1 cm	4π	1.33π
B	2 cm	16π	10.67π
C	4 cm	64π	85.33π
D	8 cm	256π	682.67π
E	24 cm	2304π	$18\,432\pi$
F	72 cm	$20\,736\pi$	$497\,664\pi$

9a. The surface area is 4 times the original and the volume is 8 times the original.

b. The surface area is 9 times the original and the volume is 27 times the original.

10. Volume of the ball:

$$\frac{4}{3} \times \pi \times 6^3$$

$= 904.32$ (cm^3)

Volume occupied:

$\pi(24 \div 2)^2(8)$

$= 3617.28$ (cm^3)

No. of balls in the tank:

$3617.28 \div 904.32 = 4$

There are 4 balls in the tank.

11. Radius of the sphere:

$4\pi r^2 = 163.84$

$r = 3.61$

Volume of the sphere:

$$\frac{4}{3}\pi (3.61)^3$$

$= 196.97$ (cm^3)

The volume is 196.97 cm^3.

12. Radius of the basketball:

$4\pi r^2 = 576\pi$

$r = 12$

Circumference of the basketball:

$2\pi(12) = 75.36$ (cm)

Distance travelled:

$5 \times 75.36 = 376.8$ (cm)

The basketball can travel 376.8 cm.

13. 320 cm^2

14. a box

15. 21.41 cm

16. No, because the area of the wrapping paper is only 2550 cm^2, but the present has a surface area of 2626 cm^2.

17. The width of the box should be 21 cm and the height should be 20 cm. The least amount of cardboard required is 5760 cm^2.

18.

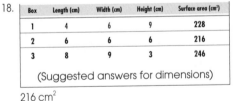

Box	Length (cm)	Width (cm)	Height (cm)	Surface area (cm²)
1	4	6	9	228
2	6	6	6	216
3	8	9	3	246

(Suggested answers for dimensions)

216 cm^2

Try This (p.172)

20.8 cm ; 31.2 cm ; 8 cm

Surface area:

$2(31.2 \times 20.8 + 31.2 \times 8 + 20.8 \times 8) = 2129.92$ (cm^2)

Volume:

$31.2 \times 20.8 \times 8 = 5191.68$ (cm^3)

Cumulative Review

1. C
2. D
3. D
4. A
5. B
6. B
7. B
8. C
9. D
10. D
11. B
12. B
13. C
14. B
15. F
16. F
17. T
18. F
19. F
20. 14 ; 5
21. 12
22. 64° ; 54°
23. 2 ; -5
24. $2x + y + y^2$; 4
25. $-3xy^2$; 12

26. $= \dfrac{a - b + a^2}{a} + \dfrac{b + ab}{a}$

$= 1 - \dfrac{b}{a} + a + \dfrac{b}{a} + b$

$= 1 + a + b$;

4

27. $= -a^4b^2 - 2a^3b^3 + 2a^3b^3 - \dfrac{3}{2}a^2b^2$

$= -a^2b^2\left(a^2 + \dfrac{3}{2}\right)$;

-10

28.

slope	x-intercept	y-intercept
$\dfrac{3}{2}$	-2	3
$\dfrac{3}{2}$	$\dfrac{1}{6}$	$-\dfrac{1}{4}$
$\dfrac{2}{3}$	-6	4
$-\dfrac{3}{2}$	$\dfrac{5}{3}$	$\dfrac{5}{2}$

29. L_1 and L_2

30. L_3 and L_4

31.

; (-3,2)

32. Side length of the shaded square:

$6^2 + 6^2 = s^2$; $s = 8.49$

Perimeter: $8.49 \times 4 = 33.96$ (cm)

Area: $8.49 \times 8.49 = 72.08$ (cm^2)

33. Perimeter: $\dfrac{2\pi(10)}{2} + \dfrac{10\pi}{2} \times 2 = 20\pi = 62.8$ (cm)

Area: $\dfrac{\pi(10)^2}{2} = 50\pi = 157$ (cm^2)

ISBN: 978-1-77149-220-1

34. Radius of the small cone:

$\frac{a}{4} = \frac{3}{8}$; $a = 1.5$

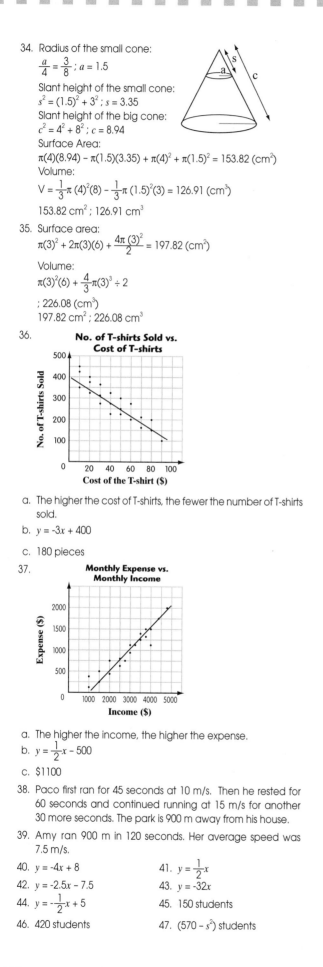

Slant height of the small cone:
$s^2 = (1.5)^2 + 3^2$; $s = 3.35$

Slant height of the big cone:
$c^2 = 4^2 + 8^2$; $c = 8.94$

Surface Area:
$\pi(4)(8.94) - \pi(1.5)(3.35) + \pi(4)^2 + \pi(1.5)^2 = 153.82$ (cm²)

Volume:
$V = \frac{1}{3}\pi(4)^2(8) - \frac{1}{3}\pi(1.5)^2(3) = 126.91$ (cm³)

153.82 cm² ; 126.91 cm³

35. Surface area:
$\pi(3)^2 + 2\pi(3)(6) + \frac{4\pi(3)^2}{2} = 197.82$ (cm²)

Volume:
$\pi(3)^2(6) + \frac{4}{3}\pi(3)^3 \div 2$

; 226.08 (cm³)
197.82 cm² ; 226.08 cm³

36.

No. of T-shirts Sold vs. Cost of T-shirts

a. The higher the cost of T-shirts, the fewer the number of T-shirts sold.

b. $y = -3x + 400$

c. 180 pieces

37.

Monthly Expense vs. Monthly Income

a. The higher the income, the higher the expense.

b. $y = \frac{1}{2}x - 500$

c. $1100

38. Paco first ran for 45 seconds at 10 m/s. Then he rested for 60 seconds and continued running at 15 m/s for another 30 more seconds. The park is 900 m away from his house.

39. Amy ran 900 m in 120 seconds. Her average speed was 7.5 m/s.

40. $y = -4x + 8$

41. $y = \frac{1}{2}x$

42. $y = -2.5x - 7.5$

43. $y = -32x$

44. $y = -\frac{1}{2}x + 5$

45. 150 students

46. 420 students

47. $(570 - s^2)$ students

48. 348 students

49a. Volume of the can:
$\pi(3)^2(7) = 197.82$ (cm³)

b. Surface area of the label:
$2\pi(3)(7) = 131.88$ (cm²)

50. The greatest possible volume:
$\frac{4}{3}\pi(3^3) = 113.04$ (cm³)

Volume of the box:
$6 \times 6 \times 7 = 252$ (cm³)

Space left:
$252 - 113.04 = 138.96$ (cm³)

51. Unit price of nuts:
$\$\frac{8x^3 + 15x}{2x} = \$(4x^2 + 7.5)$

$(3y)$ kg of nuts cost:
$\$3y(4x^2 + 7.5) = \$(12x^2y + 22.5y)$
$(3y)$ kg of nuts cost $\$(12x^2y + 22.5y)$.

52. $x + 66° + 3x - 40° = 180°$ (interior angles)
$x = 38.5°$
$x + 3y + 5y - x = 180°$ (interior angles)
$y = 22.5°$
104.5° ; 106° ; 74° ; 75.5°

53a. Slope of (3,4) and (-1,5):
$\frac{5-4}{-1-3} = -\frac{1}{4}$

Slope of (-1,5) and (7,3):
$\frac{3-5}{7-(-1)} = -\frac{1}{4}$

Slope of (3,4) and (7,3):
$\frac{3-4}{7-3} = -\frac{1}{4}$

They are collinear.

b. Slope of (0,-5) and (3,-1):
$\frac{-1-(-5)}{3-0} = \frac{4}{3}$

Slope of (3,-1) and (-2,-2):
$\frac{-2-(-1)}{-2-3} = \frac{1}{5}$

Slope of (0,-5) and (-2,-2):
$\frac{-2-(-5)}{-2-0} = -\frac{3}{2}$

They are not collinear.

54.

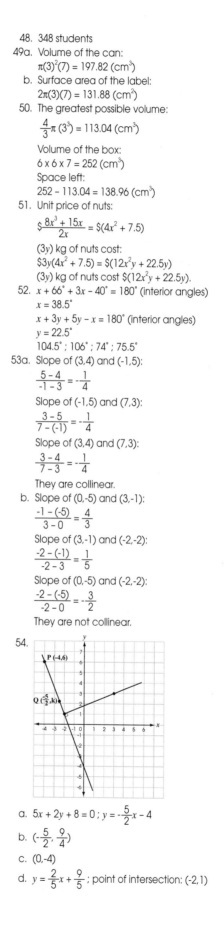

a. $5x + 2y + 8 = 0$; $y = -\frac{5}{2}x - 4$

b. $(-\frac{5}{2}, \frac{9}{4})$

c. $(0,-4)$

d. $y = \frac{2}{5}x + \frac{9}{5}$; point of intersection: (-2,1)

ISBN: 978-1-77149-220-1

55a. ∠DEC = ∠ABC (corresponding angles)
     ∠EDC = ∠BAC (corresponding angles)
     ∠DCE - angle in common
     As the corresponding angles of the triangles ABC and DEC
     are equal, so △ABC ~ △DEC.
     ∠DEB = 180° - 39° = 141° (interior angles)
     ∠EDC = 35° (sum of the angles of a triangle)
     ∠ADE = 180° - 35° = 145° (supplementary angles)

  b. $\frac{4.5 + 3.4}{3.4} = \frac{12.5}{DE}$

     DE = 5.38

     $\frac{4.8 + CD}{CD} = \frac{7.9}{3.4}$

     CD = 3.63
     So, the length of DE is 5.38 cm and CD is 3.63 cm.

56.

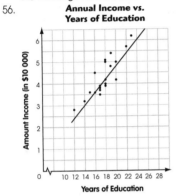

**Annual Income vs.
Years of Education**

57. They have a weak positive correlation.

58. $y = 3000x - 12\,000$

59. His annual income will be more than $50 000.

60. 90.23 cm²

61. Using proportion to find the base of the triangle:

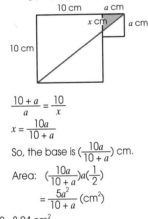

   $\frac{10 + a}{a} = \frac{10}{x}$

   $x = \frac{10a}{10 + a}$

   So, the base is $(\frac{10a}{10 + a})$ cm.

   Area: $(\frac{10a}{10 + a})a(\frac{1}{2})$

        $= \frac{5a^2}{10 + a}$ (cm²)

62. 8.94 cm²

ISBN: 978-1-77149-220-1